In print
L9.95

10⁰⁰ ck

THE REMAKING OF ISTANBUL

GOLDEN HORN

BOSPORUS

SEA OF MARMARA

EYÜP

ŞIŞLI

TEŞVIKIYE

YILDIZ PALACE

MAÇKA

PANGALTI

BEŞIKTAŞ

DOLMABAHÇE

TAKSIM

PERA

FINDIKLI

KASIMPAŞA

AZAPKAPI

TOPHANE

Mihrimah Sultan
Mosque

Mosque of Selim

GALATA

ÜSKÜDAR

UNKAPANI

Külliye of Mehmet II

Külliye of Süleyman

EMINÖNÜ

Valide Mosque

Topkapı Palace

Şehzade Mosque

Ministry of Defense
(Old Palace)

Beyazıt Mosque

Nuruosmaniye
Mosque

Hagia
Sophia

Grand Bazaar

Hippodrome

Sultan Ahmet
Mosque

0   500   1000

meters

Sally Shimazu

Istanbul and environs, circa 1900

THE REMAKING OF
ISTANBUL

Portrait of an Ottoman City in
the Nineteenth Century

ZEYNEP ÇELİK

University of California Press

Berkeley · Los Angeles · London

To Perry and Ali

University of California Press
Berkeley and Los Angeles, California

University of California Press, Ltd.
London, England

First Paperback Printing 1993

Library of Congress Cataloging-in-Publication Data

Çelik, Zeynep.
  The remaking of Istanbul : portrait of an Ottoman city in
the nineteenth century / Zeynep Çelik.
     p.   cm.
  Originally published: Seattle : University of Washington
Press, © 1986. (Publications on the Near East, University of
Washington ; no. 2).
  Includes bibliographical references and index.
  ISBN 0-520-08239-7
  1. City planning—Turkey—Istanbul—History—19th
century.   2. Istanbul (Turkey)—Buildings, structures,
etc.   I. Title.
NA9230.I8C44   1993
720'.94961'8089034—dc20   92-31825
                                                                                CIP

The paper used in this publication meets the minimum
requirements of American National Standard for Information
Sciences—Permanence of Paper for Printed Library Materials,
ANSI Z39.48–1984. ⊗

This book was made possible by generous support from:

The Aga Khan Program for Islamic Architecture at Harvard University and the Massachusetts Institute of Technology, Cambridge, Massachusetts

The Institute of Turkish Studies

The J. Paul Getty Trust

Contents

Illustrations

Unless indicated otherwise, all photographs are by the author. North is at the top of every map.

Acknowledgments

This book would not have been realized without the generous help and support of many individuals and institutions.

I am grateful to the directors and staffs of the following institutions: Başbakanlık Arşivi in Istanbul, Istanbul University Library, Topkapı Palace Museum Archive and Library, the Library of Congress, and the Doe Library of the University of California, Berkeley. The funding for the research was provided by a University of California Regents Traveling Fellowship and an American Research Institute in Turkey grant.

Spiro Kostof has been invaluable at every stage of this book—from its first draft in the dissertation stage to the final text. I thank Professor Kostof for his constructive criticism, his creative suggestions, his enthusiasm for my topic, and for being my friend. I am also indebted to Raymond Lifchez and Ira Lapidus for their conscientious reviews of my dissertation drafts. It would take pages to list the names of all my teachers and friends at the University of California, Berkeley, who supported me in so many different ways. My special thanks go to William Hickman, James Vance, Norma Evenson, Stephen Tobriner, Roger Montgomery, Ayşe Yönder, Richard Ingersoll, and D'vora Treisman.

During my research phase in Istanbul, I benefited from the help and suggestions of Suha Umur, Zarif Ongun, and Hüsamettin Aksu. The encouragement of my parents, Nevin and Edip Çelik, made my task easier. I also thank my father for introducing me to new sources.

Felicia Hecker, director of the Near Eastern Publications program at the University of Washington, has not only been an efficient and meticulous editor, but her enthusiasm and wonderful spirit have made me enjoy every step toward the publication of this book. I am also thankful to Suzanne Chun for her editorial help, to Sally Shimizu for the care with which she prepared the maps, and to Gordon Chun for his graphic advice on the maps.

Finally, I thank my husband, Perry Winston, whose contribution to this book extends from the formulation of some major themes to the selection of the visual material. I am grateful to him for his insightful guidance and for standing by me with love and understanding during this long process.

Introduction

During the nineteenth century, a concerted effort was made to transform the Ottoman capital of Istanbul into a Western-style capital, paralleling the general struggle to salvage the Ottoman Empire by reforming its traditional institutions. This book examines the transformations in the urban form of the Ottoman capital in the seventy-year period from 1838 to 1908, that is, from the Anglo-Turkish Commercial Treaty, which opened the empire to foreign capital, to the Young Turk Revolution, which marked the end of Abdülhamit II's autocratic rule. Like many non-Western cities of the nineteenth and early twentieth centuries, Istanbul was exposed to powerful cultural and physical impositions coming from Europe. Nevertheless, its response to these external influences was unique, being shaped by a complex heritage and a noncolonial status. I hope to clarify the events and ideas that surrounded the foundation of the Westernization process, which, by giving a new orientation to the development of Istanbul's physical form, planted seeds for an evolution that continues to the present day.

Istanbul, a capital of the Mediterranean basin for almost sixteen centuries (from the foundation of Constantinople in the 4th century A.D. to the end of the Ottoman Empire in the 1920s), has not been given due attention by urban and architectural historians. Compared with the rich scholarly literature on the historical urban centers of the West (one immediately thinks of Rome), there are only a handful of studies on the Byzantine/Ottoman capital. The Byzantine city to the end of Justinian's reign and the classical period of Ottoman architecture—the fifteenth and sixteenth centuries—have attracted relatively greater interest, whereas the aesthetically less climactic phases in the capital's history, such as the late Middle Ages and the eighteenth and nineteenth centuries, have been largely neglected. Nevertheless, the nineteenth century is especially important, because it opens a new era in the city's history.

Paralleling the government-sponsored transformations in the political and social spheres, post-1830s Istanbul underwent a conscious break with its Turkish-Islamic heritage. This is as dramatic a change as the conversion of Byzantine Constantinople into Ottoman Istanbul in the fifteenth century—a topic which obtained a considerable degree of scholarly attention. The "islamization" of the Byzantine city following the Ottoman conquest meant establishing new urban policies, a new type of urban administration, new institutions and organizations, as well as the promotion of new building types. The nineteenth-century modernization efforts recast the traditional urban policies based on Islamic law, replaced the urban administration, institutions, and organizations with new ones adopted from European precedents, and introduced another set of building types, this time conforming to the requirements of a modern, Westernized lifestyle.

Nineteenth-century Istanbul has a curious place in the framework of comparative urban history. In Europe, the second half of the nineteenth century was the age of the flourishing capitals. This period corresponds to the rebuilding of Paris under Napoleon III and his prefect Eugène Haussmann (1853–72), to the Viennese Ringstrasse development of the 1860s, and to the reorganization of Rome in the 1880s according to Alessandro Viviani's plan of 1882. In their drive to modernize Istanbul, the Ottoman rulers sought to emulate the European scene. A capital city with a contemporary façade would have symbolized the rejuvenation of the empire. However, in contrast to the growing wealth of the European nations, the Ottoman economy was bankrupt during this period, a fact that was reflected in the limited scale of the building activity. The ambitious goal of the Ottoman political elite to bring Istanbul up to the standards of the European capitals could produce only a piecemeal "regularization" of the urban fabric. Consequently, the city lost the integrity of its Turkish-Islamic character, but did not achieve a uniformly Western façade—even in the quarters largely inhabited by Europeans.

In this respect, the Ottoman capital differed also from colonial cities, which experienced a similar intensity of planning and construction during this period. In the colonized urban centers from Southeast Asia to Northwest Africa, Europeans took advantage of their penchant for living apart from the indigenous populations to build entire quarters based on contemporary Western urban design principles. The change in Istanbul's urban form, on the other hand, took place incrementally and resulted in a patchy and eclectic regularity.

British historian Eric Hobsbawm and his colleagues recently have shown that the past two hundred years are marked by an intensity in "inventing traditions."[1] This process of "formalization and ritualization" was observed more frequently when a rapid transformation in a society weakened the social patterns that operated within a network of old traditions.[2] Invention of new traditions came in handy, for example, for establishing and legitimizing institutions for political purposes.[3] The paraphernalia that accompanied the foundation of the new states—capital cities, flags, national anthems, military uniforms—were "invented traditions," which extended to architecture and urban design. In Europe, the allegorically decorated and symbolic public buildings and the new settings for the new public rituals (such as Vienna's Ringstrasse and Haussmann's avenues) proliferated during the second half of the nineteenth century.

For the Ottoman Empire, the time span studied in this book is characterized by rapid transformations in the search for modernization—a political goal. Importation of the recently "invented traditions" from Europe provided models of "modern" behavior.[4] Within the boundaries of this study—the study of urban form—there are three major "invented traditions" taken from the Western world. The first are the laws and legislation regarding city planning issues. The second consist of the urban design principles, which, enforced by the new laws and regulations, called for the creation of an efficient street network, monumental public squares, regular street façades, and a uniform urban fabric. The third is in the field of architecture. The new building types came with the new architectural styles, themselves recently "invented" in Europe. It is, indeed, important to keep in mind that the transformations we will be pursuing in Istanbul were recent "inventions" still in the process of being established in the Western world. The norms and the paraphernalia of the new bourgeoisie and its setting par excellence, Haussmann's Paris, served as models for many European cities just as they did for the Ottoman capital.

My approach to urban history is that of an architectural historian; thus, it differs from that of the social historian who studies the history of urban societies at large. Hobsbawm argued, as a social historian, that the contribution of urban history was in its bringing out the specific aspects of societal change and structure.[5] The analysis of the urban form was not the social historian's primary task.

John Summerson, an architectural historian, on the other hand, defined urban history as the "history of the city as an artifact" or "the history of the fabrics of cities." This did not mean focusing on architecture alone (the implication here is "monumental" architecture), but understanding the total building output: "The main issue, all the time, is tangible substance, the stuff of the city," therefore, "the physical mass of marble, bricks and mortar, steel and concrete, tarmac and rubble, metal conduits and rails." This form is the "resultant of a complex of social, psychological, and economic forces." The urban historian should constantly investigate the social, economic, and political issues in order to understand the causes and incentives of the "main issue," that is, the artifact. But, the social, economic, and political areas should not constitute the main focus.[6]

I hope to contribute to the "history of the fabrics of cities" with this book. I see urban form as a product of social, economic, and political factors and make recurrent references to them in my analyses. I have selected a transitional time bracket, characterized by substantial changes in Ottoman society, and analyzed the metamorphosis of the urban form under these changes. Thus, I conform to Hobsbawm's definition of the main goal of urban history as the explanation of "societal change and structure." However, my subject matter remains the built form.

This study begins with a historical survey of the capital's urban form, from its modest origin as an early Greek colony up to 1838, in order to provide a background that will help the reader understand the later developments. The socioeconomic issues and the reasons behind the adoption of European models as tools of modernization are covered in chapter two. Chapter three discusses the impact of Western urban design models on the transformation of the urban fabric as manifested in the replanning of many neighborhoods leveled by fires, the regularization of the main arteries, and the renovation of the waterfront—all with the goal of creating a well-communicating network. Urban transportation, again aimed at providing good communication between the geographically divided parts of the city, as well as its scattered neighborhoods, is analyzed in chapter four.

The different aspects of urban planning put into practice in the Ottoman capital between 1838 and 1908 fell short of meeting the more ambitious goal of modernizing Istanbul. The scope of these goals is expressed in three expansive urban design projects, which aimed at giving the city a radically novel urban image. These unrealized projects form the substance of chapter five. Chapter six surveys the stylistic pluralism that dominated the architectural scene and looks at some theoretical debates on the issue of style. Finally, chapter seven draws an overall image of the capital at the turn of the century and links the issues discussed throughout the book to the later developments in Istanbul's urban form.

THE REMAKING OF ISTANBUL

1.

An Architectural Survey of the City

The modern era had not yet left its mark on the Ottoman capital in the early decades of the nineteenth century. The city, unaffected by contemporary Western developments in urban design and architecture, maintained its Turkish-Islamic character. In 1838, it consisted of three main concentrations, geographically separated from each other by water: Istanbul, Galata, and Üsküdar.[1] Viewed from the sea at the point where the Golden Horn met the Bosporus, Istanbul in the west stood out as the main city, covering the largest area and dotted with many monuments that gave it its famous skyline of domes and minarets. To the north of Istanbul, across the Golden Horn, was Galata—much smaller in area and densely populated within it fortifications. Üsküdar on the eastern bank of the Bosporus did not display as high a density, but its numerous monuments expressed the importance of this suburb.

The harbor, perhaps the most vital zone of economic activity for this *ville-ventre*, which produced almost no foodstuffs, was at the entrance to the Golden Horn. The densest part of the Istanbul peninsula was its eastern half, where the major monuments were concentrated and where the streets formed a tight network. Here, between Hagia Sophia and Beyazit Square were the traces of what for centuries had been Istanbul's main thoroughfare—the Divanyolu. The great markets were located between the Divanyolu and the harbor, making this area the commercial core of the capital.[2]

Except for the commercial center, where people of different religions and ethnic groups worked side-by-side, the neighborhoods of Istanbul were ethnically organized. Muslims, the largest group, lived in the central part of the peninsula; Armenians, Greeks, and Jews were concentrated along the shores. The Marmara shore had mainly Greek and Armenian neighborhoods, while the Golden Horn was crowded with Greek and Jewish settlements. The city thinned out toward the land walls. In fact, the largest open spaces occurred immediately adjacent to the Theodosian walls. Here were orchards and vegetable gardens that duplicated the land-use pattern

*1. Istanbul, panoramic view from Galata Tower, circa 1900. At the tip
of the peninsula is the Palace of Topkapı. From left to right the skyline is
defined by Hagia Sophia, Mosque of Ahmet I, Nuruosmaniye Mosque,
Beyazıt Mosque, Beyazıt fire tower, Ministry of Defense, Külliye of
Süleyman, Şehzade Mosque, Külliye of Mehmet II, and Sultan Selim
Mosque. Galata Bridge on the left connects Karaköy to Eminönü; at
its Eminönü end is the Valide Mosque. The Unkapanı Bridge is on the
right. The largest structure on the Galata side is the Banque Ottomane.*

immediately outside the city limits. Aside from these, open spaces were
few and far between. In the center of town, At Meydanı (the Hippodrome), was the most important public square, a place for recreation and
equestrian exercises. The majority of public open spaces were contained
in the building complexes, such as the courtyards of *külliye*s (complexes
consisting of a mosque, *medrese*s or religious colleges, a bath, a hospice,
a soup kitchen, and a hospital) and mosques, which doubled as secular
spaces.

The short, crowded streets of Istanbul in the late 1830s showed an
irregular pattern; their orientation and width constantly changed and
dead ends were frequent. The widest portion of the Divanyolu was about
6.00 meters, while its average width was only 3.80 meters.[3] North of
the *külliye* of Süleyman I, another principal street, which led to the
headquarters of the *şeyhülislam*, the head of religious affairs, was only
6.00 to 7.60 meters wide. If these major arteries were so narrow, other
less important streets could not have been much wider than 2.00 or 2.30
meters! [4]

The monuments, with their regular plans and impressive scale, formed
a contrast to the dense, haphazard street network. Several complexes,
such as the Topkapı Palace, the *külliye*s, and the Grand Bazaar stood out
in the urban fabric then, as they do today.

2. Map of Istanbul, 1840, engraved by B. R. Davies

The Topkapı Palace sits in a large garden at the tip of the peninsula, on the first of the seven hills of Istanbul. The palace overlooks impressive views of Istanbul and the Golden Horn to the west, Galata and the Bosporus to the north, Üsküdar to the east, and the Sea of Marmara to the south. Organized along a series of courtyards, the palace is a conglomeration of rectangular and cubical units of various sizes, covered with many domes and extended vertically by high chimneys that enliven its skyline. On the same hill, immediately to the south of the Topkapı Palace, is that supreme creation of Byzantine architecture, the church of Hagia Sophia, and farther to the south, a seventeenth-century masterwork, the delicate *külliye* of Ahmet I.

3. Aerial view of Istanbul, circa 1920. In the foreground on the left is the Külliye *of Süleyman. The Ministry of Defense (the Old Palace) is in the large open area to the right of the* Külliye *of Süleyman. Beyazit Mosque is to the right of the Ministry of Defense. In the background are Hagia Sophia on the left and the Mosque of Ahmet I on the right. Midway between Hagia Sophia and Beyazit Mosque is the Nuruosmaniye Mosque with the Grand Bazaar next to it. The main thoroughfare leading from Hagia Sophia to Beyazit and beyond is the Divanyolu.*

The eighteenth-century Baroque mosque of Nuruosmaniye crowns the highest point of the second hill. On the northern slopes, facing the Golden Horn, are the numerous *han*s (hospices) of the commercial district. On the waterfront in Eminönü, the imposing mass of the Valide Mosque dominates the harbor.

The Grand Bazaar forms a bridge between the second and the third hills; the latter is marked by Sinan's masterpiece, the grand *külliye* of Süleyman I—an urban design scheme in itself—which towers above the harbor. The Beyazit Mosque and *medrese* (1506) are to the south of Süleyman's Mosque. The remainders of Mehmet II's palace, his first residence after the conquest, is located between the Süleyman and Beyazit complexes. By the 1830s, its garden held some governmental and military offices. The Şehzade Mehmet complex (1548) is to the west, toward the fourth hill.

The fourth hill is dominated by the *külliye* of Mehmet II. The focal point of this complex, the Mosque of Mehmet II, was substantially transformed in 1771 after the big 1766 earthquake. The complex contains a *tabhane* or printing house, a hospice, a *han*, and a hospital, along with an extensive outer courtyard system entered by eight gates and flanked on the north and the south by eight large and eight small *medrese*s.

The fifth hill is surmounted by the Mosque of Selim I, built by Süleyman I for his father in 1522. While the sixth and the seventh hills have no monumental definition, there are numerous smaller-scale mosques and churches scattered throughout these less populated areas.

Residential architecture formed the fabric between the monuments. This fabric was composed of five distinct types of houses in Istanbul: *odalar*, one-room dwellings; neighborhood houses; houses with larger gardens; *konak*s, palaces and villas; and *yalı*s, villas or seaside mansions of sultans and dignitaries.[5] The *odalar* were either detached or built in rows around a court. These were usually endowed property rented out to unmarried men who came to Istanbul in search of employment. (For this reason, they were also called *bekâr odaları*, rooms for bachelors.) Neighborhood houses were one- or two-story structures with a small courtyard or a garden shut off from the street by a wall. Houses with large gardens were often partitioned into separate quarters for men and women; they had inner and outer courts and annexes such as a belvedere, a privy, a stable, a bath, a bakehouse, and a pleasure garden. Palaces and villas (*konak*s) of government officers and rich merchants formed, with their numerous annexes, a grander version of the neighborhood houses. The villas and *yalı*s of sultans and dignitaries were built outside the land walls of Istanbul, along the Bosporus, and in Üsküdar, amid well-tended gardens and woods.

The neighborhoods (*mahalle*s) of Istanbul were organic developments that grew around religious cores (mosques, churches, and synagogues). However, social and cultural values determined the physical structure of

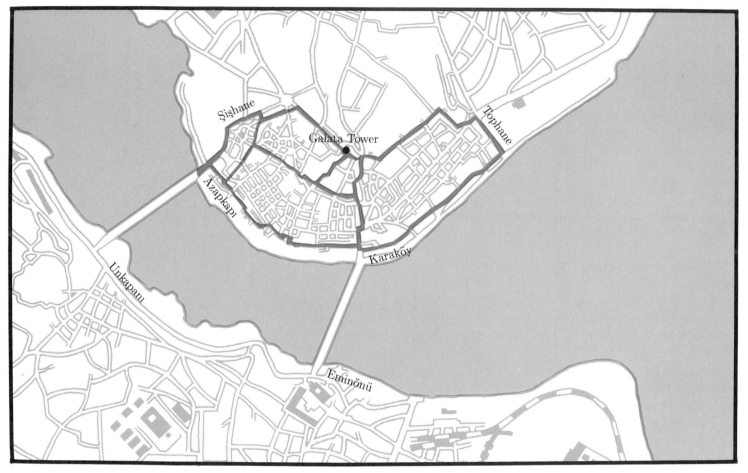

4. Walls of Galata

the neighborhoods. As there was no segregation according to income or sociopolitical status, the various house types often existed next to each other, with the exception of *bekâr odaları*, which were excluded from residential neighborhoods. The Islamic principle of privacy of women (hence, privacy of the family) was another important factor in the formation of the neighborhood structure. The search for the maximum segregation of individual houses within a dense urban setting led to the organization of residential pockets around dead-end streets, which acted as semipublic paths.[6]

The irregular street pattern evident in 1838 was a phenomenon that went back to Byzantine days. But Islamic law, which put private property rights above public property rights, assured its preservation by allowing encroachments upon the public way so long as they did not interfere with the rights of others. These projections resulted in a picturesque plasticity

in Istanbul's streetscape, made even richer by the lively colors in which
the houses were painted.

Galata's urban image was very different from that of the Istanbul
peninsula. Galata was a densely populated settlement enclosed within its
4 fifteenth-century walls. These 2.80-kilometer long and 2.00-meter thick
walls, built over five consecutive periods, defined an area of thirty-seven
5 hectares, and divided Galata into five zones. The Galata Tower marked
the highest point, while numerous smaller towers with semicircular and
square shapes lined the wall.[7]

There were several scattered settlements along the Golden Horn shore,
to the north of Galata and along the Bosporus. These settlements formed
the first stages of Galata's expansion beyond its walls, a process that
accelerated during the second half of the nineteenth century and the
early decades of the twentieth century. Of these settlements, Kasımpaşa,
along the Golden Horn, was the most densely populated neighborhood; on
the Bosporus, Tophane and Fındıklı stood out as major concentrations.
From the walled city of Galata, an artery led to the north, to Pera (lit.,
"beyond"). This artery, known as the Grande Rue de Pera, was flanked
on two sides by buildings, but its hinterland was still quite pastoral in the
mid-1800s.

In 1838, Galata was inhabited by a cosmopolitan blend of Armenians,
Greeks, Europeans, and Jews (who lived along the eastern part of the
waterfront outside the city walls). Pera was predominantly a European
quarter, mixed with a few Christian Ottoman minorities; but Kasımpaşa,
Tophane, and Fındıklı were exclusively Muslim.[8]

The tight street network of 1838 Galata, developed over many centuries, followed the topography so that what evolved was a series of concentric arcs parallel to the curved shoreline, with connectors leading ir-
regularly from the waterfront to the heights. Although there were no
principal avenues, some streets were more prominent than others. Among
these were the artery that ran along the shore from the Azapkapı Gate in
the west to the Tophane Gate in the east; the Voyvoda Caddesi, which
ran parallel to this artery; the north-south Galata Caddesi, which connected the inner parts of the suburb to the Karaköy quay; and the stepped
Yüksek Kaldırım, which provided a short, but steep access from Galata
6 Caddesi to the Galata Tower and farther up to the Grande Rue de Pera.[9]

In 1838, Galata had no monuments to rival those on the Istanbul
peninsula. Apart from the Galata Tower, the few buildings that stood out
were utilitarian structures, such as docks and artillery barracks. Farther
along the Bosporus, the summer palace of Beşiktaş, however, foretold
the future of this strip as the locus of imperial residences. The walled
section of Galata had a number of churches and monasteries, but their
scale and monumentality were of little significance. The Islamic religious
monuments, such as Sinan's Azapkapı Mosque (1577) and Kılıç Ali Paşa

5. *Galata Tower, circa 1900*

6. *View of Yüksek Kaldırım connecting
Galata to the Grande Rue, circa 1903.
Galata Tower is in the background.*

complex (1580), as well as the Baroque Nusretiye Mosque (1826), were outside the walls of Galata, along the waterfront.

THE HISTORICAL DEVELOPMENT

The chaotic urban pattern that was the Ottoman capital of the early nineteenth century was the result of the most diverse social, cultural, aesthetic, and economic influences. For almost sixteen centuries, from A.D. 330, the year Constantine founded the Eastern Roman Empire, to 1924, the year Ankara was declared the capital of the new Turkish Republic, Istanbul enjoyed a unique status as the capital city of two great civilizations: the Byzantine Empire and the Ottoman Empire. Over the centuries, the city absorbed and reflected the cultural heritage of its rulers —Eastern Orthodox Christianity followed by Islamic Ottoman civilization. Its metamorphosis from "Roma Nova" to the "sacred city of Islam" produced unparalleled configurations in its urban form. Under each empire, architects dotted the landscape with outstanding examples of monumental architecture. Its public works, urban administration, and public services, conforming to the dominant sociopolitical structures and religious beliefs, evolved into complex and sophisticated networks.

Historian Gilbert Dagron begins his *Naissance d'une capitale*, a monumental study on Contantine's city, by listing three factors that may help the reader understand the complex task of creating the new capital: first, it was an expensive city; second, it was an exceptionally large urban undertaking; and third, it was designed to be the political center of the empire and the privileged meeting place between the Hellenistic and the Roman civilizations.[10] These factors run as the main themes through the capital's long history. The large sums initially spent by Constantine were equaled by the successive Byzantine emperors (especially Justinian) and then by the Ottoman sultans. The scale of the city-building activities in Constantinople/Istanbul under both empires far surpassed that undertaken in other urban centers within the respective imperial boundaries. Constantinople was the political center of the Byzantine state, and later under Ottoman rule, it became the capital of another powerful empire. A meeting place of the Hellenistic and the Roman during its early history, the capital has continued to act as a stage for the confrontation and coexistence of different cultures ever since.

What were the elements that ran through Istanbul's long history, elements that link the ancient city to the nineteenth-century capital to the modern metropolis? What were its decisive periods of growth and construction? What defined its urban image? How has the urban image changed over the centuries? How did the city's physical structure adapt to economic, social, political, and cultural changes? What were the transformations brought by the conquest of Christianity over paganism and then Islam over Christianity? How was the capital affected by the expansion of the Ottoman Empire and later by its gradual loss of economic and political power? These are some of the important issues that must be considered in surveying Istanbul's colorful history.[11]

The Ancient City

Preliminary excavations done in the 1950s in the Eminönü district of Istanbul show that the first settlements in the Istanbul peninsula date from the late third or early second millenium B.C.[12] Unfortunately, this research has not been pursued, and data on the early settlements is very sparse. We do know, however, that the first Megarian colony, a community of tradesmen and fishermen, was established at the western end of the peninsula during the mid-seventh century B.C. There were two other Megarian colonies—one in Chalcedon (Kadıköy) on the Asiatic side of the Bosporus, to the south of Üsküdar, and one in Galata. The fortifications of the Megarian city on the Istanbul peninsula, called Byzantium in honor of one of its early rulers, encircled a rather small area corresponding to the first of the seven hills. Its harbor, crucial for a community living largely by trade, lay just beyond the walls on the Golden Horn. The Strategion in the city's center and the Thrakion, possibly in the proximity of today's Hagia Sophia Square, were the two main open spaces and were used for public and military functions. At the peninsula's highest point, where the Topkapı Palace is today, was the Acropolis, center of the colony. There stood the temples to Zeus, Apollo, Poseidon, Aphrodite, and Athena Ecbasia. Theaters and baths, a gymnasium, and a stadium constituted the major public monuments.

7

In A.D. 196, Septimius Severus of Rome destroyed Byzantium's original fortifications and built new ones that enclosed a larger area, including the first and second hills as well as the ancient harbor. Inside the Severan walls, two urban landmarks were established that were the beginning of the city's skeleton: the Forum Tetraston and the *embolos*, the main avenue that connected Tetraston to the new walls. Flanked by porticoes, this large artery became the first portion of the *mese*, the middle street. To the south, the Hippodrome was begun, but this major task, which involved construction of huge supporting walls, was not completed under Septimius Severus's reign. Also, in the southwest section of the peninsula, the baths of Zeuxippus were constructed.

The Byzantine City

In A.D. 330 when Constantine moved the seat of the Roman Empire from Rome to Byzantium, he turned his back to the old capital and created a new state.[13] Establishing a Christian empire in Byzantium was easier without the opposition from a Roman aristocracy still very much attached to paganism. Although Constantine named his new capital "Second Rome" and some later documents called it "New Rome," its name eventually became Constantinople, the city of Constantine. The name had

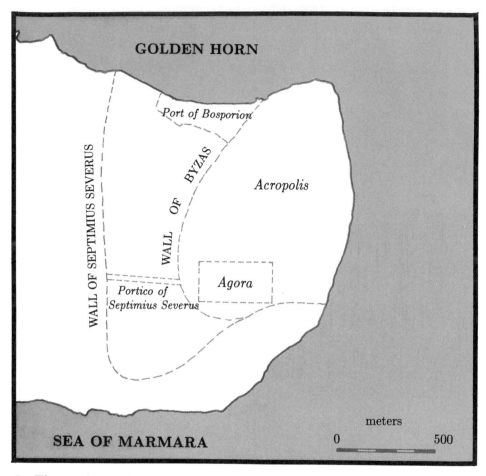

7. The ancient city

currency among even the Turks, whose documents and coins frequently referred to the capital as "Konstantiniye" until the twentieth century.

The main features of the Severan city, namely, the Hippodrome, the Forum Tetraston, the *embolos*, and the baths of Zeuxippus, determined the basic layout of Constantine's capital. But more than that, the new city became a colossal urban design project, mapped out according to a grand plan. A new set of fortifications were built that incorporated the third and the fourth hills, thereby quadrupling the size of the Greco-Roman city. Except for the terminal points of the fortifications, which correspond to today's Unkapanı on the Golden Horn and Etyemez on the Marmara shore, their exact location is unknown. Populating this large area formed an important part of the task of creating a great capital. It was believed that the presence of the court and central bureaucracy and the jobs thus created would draw large numbers of people to the capital. In order to attract notable families, Constantine built large mansions and endowed income from the estates of the fisc to the new settlers of

8

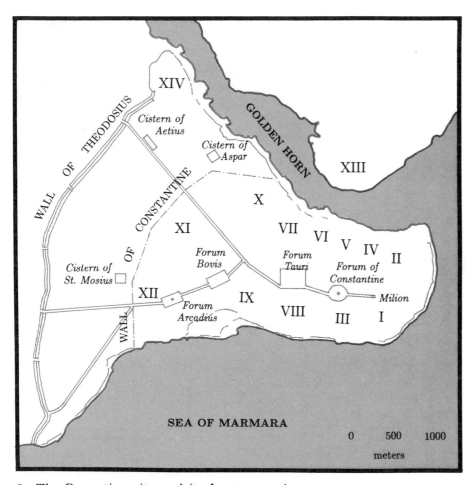

8. *The Byzantine city and its fourteen regions*

Constantinople. These efforts caused the city to grow steadily so that by 380, the population was 100,000 to 150,000, compared to the 20,000 to 30,000 inhabitants of the Severan city.

During the next centuries, new harbors were built on the Marmara shore within the boundaries of Constantine's walls. Nonetheless, the best-protected harbor was still the Bosporion at the entrance to the Golden Horn. The Golden Horn shore developed as a series of commercial quays—a pattern that would flourish during the Ottoman period. The walls along the Sea of Marmara were also begun by Constantine, but rebuilt by Arcadius (395–408) after a big earthquake.

Although furnished with architectural and urbanistic themes from the late Roman period, Constantine's capital showed a basic divergence from Rome itself. This divergence was especially striking in the stretched-out street network of Constantinople. In contrast to the "compressed" form of Rome in which the forums were clustered in groups, porticoed avenues connected the scattered forums of the new capital. The *mese*, the main

9. *View of the Hippodrome, looking south, circa 1900. The Egyptian Obelisk is in the foreground and the Colussus is in the background. The stump of the Serpent Column is just visible between these two monuments.*

porticoed avenue, was the extension of Septimius Severus's *embolos* that initially led from Tetraston to the main gate of the Severan walls. Here, Constantine built under his name an elliptical forum, which had no formal precedents among its counterparts in Rome. From Constantine's Forum, the *mese* continued toward the west and, after passing the site of today's Beyazit Square, bifurcated. Each branch led to a major gate in the city walls; however, the southern artery, the triumphal way, was the more important.

There were two other porticoed avenues: the first was at the east end of the peninsula running parallel to the shoreline facing Chalcedon (Kadıköy), the second along the Marmara shore. The buildings on both sides of the porticoed avenues were two stories high. The first story sheltered shops behind arcades, which provided refuge from the sun and the rain. The second story, reached by a stairway leading from within the arcade, included a series of linked balconies that served as a promenade lined with marble decorations and statues. Bazaars stretched along the porticoed avenues, and headquarters of various trade guilds were housed in these arcades.

Constantine duplicated the urban administration of Rome by establishing fourteen regions, each managed by a curator.[14] Under each curator were five *vico-magistri*, who administered different groups of *vici* (streets) and were responsible for the protection of the district at night. Next came the many *collegiati*, who acted as a police and fire-fighting force. The entire city was in the hands of the "prefect."[15]

Together with the Roman administration, the emperor brought the monumental building types of Rome to the new capital. Hence, a senate on Constantine's Forum, a pretorium a little farther to the east, and a milion at the beginning of the *mese*, built as a four-piered and domed structure reminiscent of the Golden Milion of Rome, became the main monuments of fourth-century Constantinople. Septimius Severus's Tetraston, renamed the Augusteon, the Forum of Augustus, was enlarged and embellished by Constantine. Constantine also completed the work of the preceding rulers. A special effort was made to finish the Hippodrome by 330 to coincide with the inaugural celebrations of the city. In fact, the construction of the new walls and the completion of the Hippodrome were primary goals in Constantine's building program. In Roman tradition, a circus was not only considered an essential part of any imperial residence, but it was also the place where the emperor met his subjects.

The pagan tradition of erecting honorary columns continued under Constantine and for two centuries thereafter. Constantine erected three columns: one for his mother, the Empress Helena, in the Augusteon; and two for himself, the first in the Augusteon and the second in the middle of his own forum. The column in Constantine's forum is the only surviving monument from Constantine's city. It was originally formed by eight porphyry drums brought from Rome and bound together by bands shaped like wreaths of laurel. These drums sat on a 5.70-meter-high stylobate, which in turn rested on four broad steps also 5.70 meters high. A bronze statue of Apollo, brought from Athens, was placed at the top of the column when Constantinople was dedicated. However, this statue was soon replaced by a bust of Constantine.

The first structures of what was to become the Great Palace were built by Constantine next to the Hippodrome. Enlarged and embellished by succeeding emperors, in Justinian's time (527–65) the Great Palace covered approximately half of the area between Hagia Sophia and what would later become the Sultan Ahmet Mosque, as well as the total area of the mosque itself. In the east, it extended as far as the walls of the present-day Topkapı Palace and in the west to the Çatladıkapı Gate. This huge area was filled with buildings in a variety of styles dating from different periods. However, only the Chalké and the Daphné belonged to Constantine's reign. The Chalké formed the entrance to the Palace; a conglomeration of buildings was erected on two sides of its monumental bronze gate. The Daphné, which took its name from a statue brought from Rome, was reached from the Chalké by a passageway consisting of a series of structures, terraces, porticoes, and possibly gardens.

Constantine, as the champion of Christianity, provided for the building of great churches. His two important edifices, the original Church of Hagia Sophia and the Church of the Holy Apostles, had short lifetimes; however, their sites became the major monumental foci for the Byzantine, as well as the Ottoman city. The first Hagia Sophia, built in 326, was an aisled basilica linked to the palace by corridors and stairs. Destroyed and rebuilt twice, it finally acquired its present form under Justinian. The Church of the Holy Apostles, sheltering Constantine's catafalque and located at the site of the fifteenth-century *külliye* of Mehmet II, was also replaced by Justinian with a building composed of domed pavilion elements on a cross plan.

The residential fabric of Constantine's city was comprised of three types of houses: the *domi*, the *tabernae*, and the *insulae*. Like their counterparts in Rome, the *domi* were large two-story, single-family mansions with pillared central halls, inhabited by wealthy and notable families. The *tabernae* were the modest residences of the common people, built along the main streets and at crossroads, often with shops on the ground floor. The *insulae*, limited to thirty meters in height, served as multistory tenement blocks.

The city continued to expand after Constantine. During the early decades of the fourth century, many mansions and middle-class dwellings

10. Fortifications of Theodosius, circa 1900

11. Fortifications along the Sea of Marmara, circa 1900

were built in the suburbs outside Constantine's walls. This spurt of building activity led to the construction of another set of walls under Theodosius II (408–50). With only one small extension in the seventh century (to
enclose the Church of St. Mary of Blachernae on the Golden Horn), these
walls would define the capital's western boundary until the mid-twentieth
century.

10   The Theodosian fortifications, formed by three parallel walls, buttressed by towers, and protected by a moat, were built at a distance of
about one kilometer west of Constantine's walls, thereby taking in the
fifth, sixth, and seventh hills. Theodosius also extended the fortifications
11 along the Marmara shore to meet the new land walls. The wall along the
Golden Horn was not built until the ninth century.

Across the Golden Horn, Galata consisted of a narrow band adjacent
to the waterfront. This zone, then called Sykae, had a porticoed avenue
parallel to the shore, which later became the principal artery of the
thirteenth century Genoese settlement. In the fifth century, Galata had
all the typical monuments of a late Roman city: church, theater, baths,

and harbor. In the late sixth century, Tiberius II (578–82) built a tower called Galatou on the quay. The tower served as an anchor for an immense chain that was strung across the Golden Horn to another tower on the sea walls of Constantinople. This chain, on the approximate site of the future Galata Bridge, protected the harbor from invading navies.

The Byzantine city, defined by the Theodosian walls, did not expand after the fifth century, but became filled with monuments and commercial and residential buildings. The zone between Constantine's walls and the Theodosian walls remained less populated than the rest of the city, with the exception of the Fourteenth Region, where the popular shrine of Blachernae and the Palace of Blachernae, or Tekfursaray, were located. This palace was built under Anastasius I (491–518) to be used by the imperial family on visits to the shrine. It was enlarged several times and finally became the main imperial residence in the mid-thirteenth century when the palace at the Hippodrome was abandoned altogether. The high density of the neighborhood around Tekfursaray must have been due to the presence of the imperial residence. The Byzantine urban pattern, characterized by dispersed settlements along the walls except for the dense region between Tekfursaray and the Golden Horn, continued into the Ottoman period.

12. Aerial view of Istanbul, circa 1910. The aqueduct of Emperor Valens runs between the Şehzade Mosque on the left and the Külliye of Mehmet II on the right in the background.

By the fifth century, the capital had acquired three principal forums along the *mese* in addition to the Augusteon and the Forum of Constantine: the Forum Tauri, the Forum Bovis, and the Forum of Arcadius. The *mese* started at the Augusteon and continued to the Forum of Constantine, where it led to the Forum Tauri, also known as the Forum of Theodosius, built by Theodosius the Great in 386. The largest of the Byzantine public squares in Constantinople, the Forum Tauri is the only public area that has survived to the present as an open space—it is now Beyazit Square. To the west of the Forum Tauri, the *mese* branched: the first branch led to the southwest and, passing through the Forum Bovis (today's Aksaray) and the Forum of Arcadius, it finally reached the Golden Gate. The second branch ended at the Gate of Adrianople.

In contrast to these wide and regular avenues, the back streets of Constantinople, the *vici*, were described by a fifth-century work, the *Notitia Urbis Constantinopolitanae*, as dark, narrow, and crooked.[16] And, just as in Ottoman times, fires often destroyed entire neighborhoods.

The population of Constantinople during the second half of the fifth century was between 200,000 and 300,000. The inner city, defined by the walls of Constantine, was so overbuilt that a zoning regulation in 450 prohibited buildings more than ten stories high. The origins of this dense pattern probably go back to Constantine's time, when the first population boom occurred.[17]

By the fifth century, the growth of the city necessitated a solution to the problem of providing water to the residents. Already in 368 an aqueduct had been constructed by Emperor Valens (364–78) to bring water to the heart of the city. Now known in Turkish as Bozdoğan Kemeri, this structure, which still stands, extends across the valley between the third and the fourth hills. At the same time, a network of underground conduits was introduced to transport water to the four corners of the peninsula. In the fifth century, many subterranean and above-ground cisterns were built to store large amounts of water for use during dry summer months. The open-air cisterns formed large rectangular holes in the urban landscape; they were converted into vegetable gardens during later Byzantine times when they lost their water storage function. The largest were the Cistern of Aetius (421), the Cistern of Aspar (459), and the Cistern of St. Mosius (ca. 500)—all located between the walls of Constantine and Theodosius.[18]

During the reign of Theodosius II (408–50), four out of the seven hills of Constantinople had gained some monumental definition. On the first hill stood the Augusteon, the Hippodrome, and the original Church of Hagia Sophia; on the second, Constantine's Forum with the column in the middle; on the third, the Forum of Theodosius; and on the fourth, the Church of the Holy Apostles. Even though these structures determined the foci for future developments, their monumentality showed different characteristics from the Ottoman complexes that would replace them be-

13. Interior view of Hagia Sophia, circa 1913

ginning in the fifteenth century. In contrast to the Ottoman monumentality, which defined an urban image punctuated by vertical elements such as domes and minarets, the early Byzantine city was not as concerned with an overall silhouette. Nevertheless, honorary columns broke through the uniformity of the skyline as early as Constantine's era. Under Justinian, the domes of Hagia Sophia and St. Eirene on the first hill and those of the Church of the Holy Apostles on the fourth hill, began to change the skyline as viewed from the Golden Horn. The Ottoman urban image was a continuation of this process started in the sixth century.

Constantinople gained some of its most famous architectural landmarks under Justinian (527–65). The Roman construction ingenuity meshed with the Hellenistic design legacy to produce a new synthesis in Justinian's buildings. Hagia Sophia (532-37) is the culmination of this synthesis (see fig. 31). A basilica covered with a great dome sitting on four pillars and buttressed by semidomes in the east and the west, it was an unprecedented structure, dominating the capital as no other building had before. In the words of Procopius, the sixth-century chronicler: *13*

It soars to a height to match the sky, and as if surging up from amongst the other buildings it stands on high and looks down upon the remainder of the city, adorning it, because it is a part of it, but glorying its beauty, because, though a part of the city and dominating it, it at the same time towers above it to such a height that the whole city is viewed from there as from a watch tower.[19]

The neighboring churches of St. Eirene (532) and SS. Sergius and Bacchus (527) were Justinian's two other important monuments. The Justinianic style, as observed in these examples, was characterized by an elevated and domed central pavilion. In addition to these tours de force, Justinian commissioned a large number of smaller churches and utilitarian, civic structures, such as cisterns, hospices, and palaces.

During the following centuries, churches of a particular style derived from the principles established under Justinian were constructed in Constantinople. The cross-in-square plan was the standard mid-Byzantine form, employed from the ninth century on. The central dome was elevated as in the Justinianic examples, but now rested upon a drum and did not spring from a pendentive ring. Hence, verticality was more accentuated than in the sixth-century churches.[20] The churches of St. Theodora (Gül Cami, 9th century), Constantine Lips (10th century), St. Savior in Chora (Kariye Cami, 11th century), known for its unequaled mosaics and frescoes (dating from the early 14th century), St. Savior Pantocrator (Zeyrek Cami, 12th century), St. Mary Pammakaristos (Fethiye Cami, 12th century), St. Mary of the Mongols (13th century), and St. Andrew in Krisei (Koca Mustafa Paşa Cami, 13th century) were among the outstanding examples of this new emphasis on verticality. These buildings were converted into mosques after the conquest and, although altered somewhat, they have survived to the present. Scattered throughout the peninsula, they formed the cores of certain neighborhoods in both Byzantine and Ottoman periods.

The development of a Byzantine architectural style was reflected on the residential scene as well. From the sixth century on, residential construction diverged from the earlier Roman prototypes. By the tenth century, the typical Byzantine house was two or three stories high with the upper stories always projecting farther than the ground floor. These projections resulted in an extensive use of bay windows—a feature that was widely repeated later in houses of the Ottoman period. The core of the house was a large hall on which all other rooms opened.[21] This plan is based on Roman types, but at the same time, projects the organizational principles of the Turkish house.

From the eleventh century on, Constantinople's foreign communities grew increasingly important as their role in Mediterranean and Black Sea commerce expanded.[22] By the tenth century, foreigners began obtaining territorial concessions in the city. The Italian colonies were the most important, and, in fact, the Amalfians obtained the first concession in 944 and settled in the area corresponding to Eminönü. In 992, the Venetians were assigned a neighborhood immediately to the west of the Amalfians. The Pisans and the Genoans settled a little farther to the west in the twelfth century. Other smaller foreign communities were the Germans, who established a neighborhood in the twelfth century in the vicinity of the Venetian quarter, some merchants from Marseilles and Narbonne, who settled in the same area, and a colony of Spanish tradesmen, who were not given a land concession.

Arabs and Jews were the largest minorities. The Muslim presence, dating from the Arab siege of 673–79, manifested itself in the three mosques built during the eighth, twelfth, and thirteenth centuries in the Muslim neighborhood located on the eastern part of the peninsula. Unlike the other minorities, Jews were not permitted to live within the city limits and were relegated to a quarter in Galata, across the Golden Horn. However, a number of Jews lived on the site of the Valide Mosque in Eminönü, outside the sea walls. Segregation of the Jewish population did not survive beyond the end of the Byzantine Empire, and in the second half of the thirteenth century, Jews were allowed to settle in Vlanga along the Sea of Marmara.

Although the Jews were the long-term residents of Galata, under Manuel I Comnenus (1143–80), Genoese merchants obtained a concession to settle in Galata in addition to their original enclave on the other side of the Golden Horn. As a result, Galata developed as a Genoese colony during the last centuries of the Byzantine Empire. In 1303, the boundaries of the colony were established, but no permit was issued for the construction of a surrounding wall. The Genoese community marked the perimeter of its territory by a deep ditch, and one year later, benefiting from the new building regulation that abolished height limits, they built tall, castlelike structures along the ditch. In 1316, the first part of the fortification was constructed and in 1349, the northern part and the Galata Tower were completed. Later in 1387 and 1397, as the colony expanded toward the northwest, the newly acquired zones were enclosed, and, finally, the eastern slope of the hill leading down to the Bosporus was surrounded by a wall.[23]

Thus, the Byzantine city was a polyglot of ethnic neighborhoods. Given this urban structure, the ethnically based quarters of Ottoman Istanbul cannot be considered a product merely of the Islamic way of life, but rather were a continuation of the earlier Byzantine policies.

The Fifteenth Century

On 30 May 1453, Mehmet II made his ceremonial entry into Constantinople and, declaring it to be his capital, inaugurated a new era of building activity aimed at making the city the economic, administrative, cultural, and religious center of his empire. A note is necessary here on the name of the city, as it is customary to call the Ottoman city Istanbul. The change from Constantinople to Istanbul was not a deliberate decision made by the Ottoman rulers. In fact, as mentioned earlier, Konstantiniye was used alternately with Istanbul in official documents until the twentieth century. "Istanbul" derives from the Greek word "stanbulin" (meaning "to the city"), used by the inhabitants of Constantinople since the tenth century. In some fifteenth-century documents, the punning name "Islambol" ("where Islam abounds") was used. However, Istanbul or Istambol prevailed in popular usage.[24]

Mehmet II's first major tasks were the repair of the Theodosian walls, which determined the western boundary of the Ottoman city, and repopulation. During the early fifteenth century, Constantinople's population was a mere 50,000, a figure that had dwindled even more just before the conquest, when many inhabitants fled the city.[25] Mehmet II permitted any fugitive who returned within a given amount of time to reoccupy his house and practice his religion. Furthermore, he settled one-fifth of his prisoners and their families along the Golden Horn, giving them houses and an exemption from taxes for a specified time. Finally, he allowed enslaved prisoners to pay their ransom and settle in the city in exchange for houses and temporary tax exemption; they were encouraged to work on building projects to earn their ransoms. The most effective method of repopulation, however, was the compulsory resettlement of Muslim, Christian, and Jewish families from different parts of the empire. To revive the economic and commercial activity in Istanbul, some well-known tradesmen were specifically urged to come to the capital.[26] Although their methods differed, Mehmet II's efforts to populate the capital recall those of its founder, Constantine.

The census figures for this period are not complete enough to arrive at definitive conclusions. However, the increase in the number of Christian

Blachernae revetement a part of that?

and Jewish houses (*hanes*) alone over the eleven years from 1478 to 1489 conveys the success of the repopulation policy. In 1478, there were 5,162 Christian and 1,647 Jewish houses in Istanbul; these numbers rose to 5,462 and 2,491 respectively in 1489.[27]

The fundamental goal in the development of Istanbul after the conquest was to create a Muslim city in which the communities could live in accordance with the philosophy of Islam. Muslim neighborhoods grew around religious complexes. To bring more of the physical city under the jurisdiction of Islamic social codes, property owners established permanent endowments of land or other immovable property by a deed of restraint. Through this act, called a *vakıf*, the owner surrendered his power over disposal of the property with the stipulation that the property be used for good purposes, namely for those compatible with Islam.[28] The first *vakıf*, established by Mehmet II himself, was Hagia Sophia, which had been converted into the Great Mosque the day the Sultan entered the city.

In a manner that recalled Constantine's division of the city into regions, Mehmet II established thirteen quarters, or *nahiyes*, on the Istanbul peninsula. The first of these was Hagia Sophia. The other twelve developed around the complexes built by sultans or paşas during the next seventy years. *Mahalles*, the subunits of *nahiyes*, grew around the smaller mosques or dervish tombs and *tekkes* (sufi convents) supported by *vakıf*s. During the fifty-year period 1546–96, the increase in the number of *vakıf*s in Istanbul from 1,594 to 3,180 clearly shows the speed of the capital's conversion into an Islamic city.[29]

The definitive change in the street fabric of the Byzantine city must have begun during Mehmet II's reign. We have noticed earlier that the back streets of Constantinople formed an irregular and very dense pattern. However, there were large main arteries that connected the great public squares. As the fifteenth-century city developed around self-contained *nahiyes* and their subunits, *mahalles*, each originating from a central node, the importance of large public open spaces and wide avenues diminished; they were gradually absorbed by the incremental growth. But, the Byzantine structure did not disintegrate immediately. In Giovanni Vavassore's plan of circa 1520, there are still broad arteries leading to each region. But these have disappeared in the plans dating from the later decades of the sixteenth century.[30]

In creating a Muslim city, Mehmet II made his largest investments in religious buildings. The process started with the conversion of Hagia Sophia into a mosque and was followed by the conversion of seventeen other churches. Mehmet II built a *türbe* (mausoleum) for Ebu Eyüp el Ensari, the Prophet Mohammed's flagbearer, in Eyüp outside the walls on the Golden Horn; this site soon became a Muslim shrine. The city was also filled with many new mosques. The *külliye* of Mehmet II (1471) on the fourth hill, on the site of the Church of the Holy Apostles, was

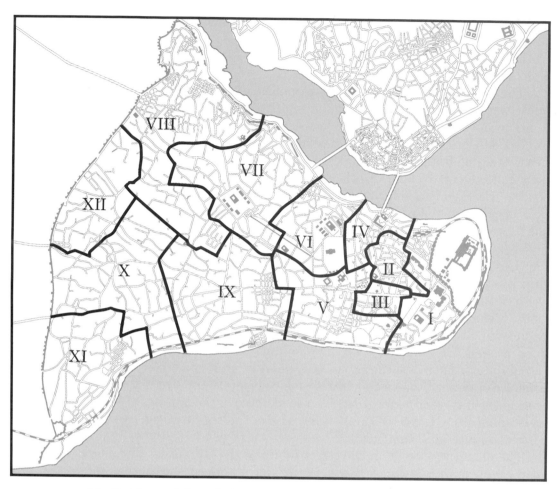

14. Nahiyes *of Istanbul, established by Mehmet II*

a symbolic gesture that firmly established the Ottoman legacy: Emperor Constantine's church was replaced by the mosque of the new conqueror, Mehmet II. Located in a relatively less populated area on the road leading to the Edirne gate, this *külliye* acted as a magnet around which Muslim neighborhoods developed. Mehmet II's complex was the first in a series of imperial *külliye*s that gave a distinct monumental character to the skyline of Ottoman Istanbul.[31]

16

During the reign of Mehmet II, 190 mosques (in addition to 17 converted churches), 24 *mektep*s or elementary schools and *medrese*s, 32 *hamam*s or baths, and 12 *han*s and markets were built in Istanbul.[32] The central part of the Grand Bazaar (*bedesten*) was completed during the early years of Mehmet II's reign. Thus, the two essential elements of the prototypical Muslim city, the central mosque and the central market

15. *G. Vavassore's plan of Istanbul, circa 1520*

were embodied in Hagia Sophia and the *bedesten*.[33] The eastern part of the Byzantine *mese* continued to serve as the main thoroughfare—now connecting these two centers of the Islamic city.

The construction of the Ottoman imperial palaces also goes back to the reign of Mehmet II. Immediately after the conquest, Mehmet II built the Eski Saray, or the Old Palace, to the south of the Forum Tauri (the site of this palace is occupied now by Istanbul University and the *külliye* of Süleyman I). However, he soon decided to move the imperial residence to a more prominent site at the eastern end of the peninsula. There, between 1459 and 1465, he built almost the entire structure of the Topkapı Palace as it stands today. The Topkapı Palace remained the official imperial residence until the construction of the Dolmabahçe Palace across the Golden Horn in 1856.

16. *Mosque of Mehmet II, circa 1895*

The Sixteenth Century

Istanbul's population grew from 16,326 houses (*hane*s) in 1477 to 80,000 by 1535. This rapid increase resulted in higher population densities in the Istanbul peninsula, as well as in the emergence of the new Muslim neighborhoods of Tophane, Fındıklı, Cihangir, and Kasımpaşa on the northern side of the Golden Horn. Although the population of Istanbul grew rapidly in the sixteenth century, the ratio of Muslims to non-Muslims remained fairly stable. In both the 1477 and 1535 censuses, Muslims constituted 58 percent, Christians 32 percent, and Jews 10 percent of the population.[34] These ratios fluctuated only marginally thereafter; for example, in the late nineteenth century, Muslims still formed 55 percent of Istanbul's population.

The expanding neighborhoods encroached upon the main Byzantine arteries so that by the late sixteenth century, the Byzantine avenues had shrunk considerably. The population density was indeed so high that many houses were built adjacent to monuments and city walls. A 1558 imperial order (*irade*), which was not enforced rigorously, called for the demolition of all houses and shops abutting city walls. The housing shortage became so acute that even some of the extensive gardens belonging to palaces and villas were taken over for construction.[35]

The sixteenth century was a time of great building activity. A synthesis of architectural forms that had evolved from the mingling of earlier Anatolian-Turkish elements with the Byzantine forms, which had already reached their perfection in the sixth century, culminated in the grand architecture of sixteenth-century Istanbul. During the long reign of Süleyman (1520–66), Istanbul was endowed with many monuments, and it was in the work of the great architect Sinan (1490-1588) that classical Ottoman architecture reached its pinnacle.[36] The chronicles attribute over 300 buildings throughout the Empire to Sinan; about 120 of these were in Istanbul alone. The monumentality of sixteenth-century Istanbul is, therefore, closely associated with Sinan and his royal patrons, Süleyman I, his wives, daughters, sons, viziers, and his heir, Selim II.

In Sinan's complexes, the site and the buildings complement and glorify each other. The silhouettes of his structures blend with their location, but at the same time elevate it. The mosque, as the spiritual and physical center, dominates the dependent structures. Its centrality is accentuated by the use of a greater dome, surrounded by a cascade of smaller domes and half-domes. Under the domes, experimenting with squares, hexagons, and octagons, Sinan created grand unified spaces in which the individuality and clarity of every component was carefully elaborated. Sinan's exploration of volumetric and spatial qualities was based on a rational expression of structural clarity. In the words of Turkish architectural historian Doğan Kuban, Sinan's central design principle was to use "the dome as the measure-giving unit and the supporting base as a mass continuum."[37]

Sinan's *külliye*s brought the ultimate Islamic and Ottoman definition to Istanbul's urban form—a process, which had begun immediately after the conquest with the construction of the *külliye* of Mehmet II. The

17. Aerial view of the Külliye *of Süleyman with the Golden Horn and Unkapanı Bridge in the background, circa 1910*

*külliye*s break up the irregular fabric of the city by their geometric and axial schemes. They are integral units organized around a central structure and have no major arteries connecting them to the surrounding environment. Hence, they repeat on a monumental scale the overriding theme of introversion in Ottoman urbanism.

17   The *külliye* of Süleyman I (1557), which crowns the third hill, occupies part of the grounds of Mehmet II's first palace. Süleymaniye is a huge socioreligious complex, consisting of a mosque with an adjacent courtyard in the center, five *medrese*s, a hospital, a medical school, a public kitchen, a caravansary, mausoleums, shops, and fountains. The impressive mass of the mosque dominates the complex visually. Here, Sinan interpreted the spatial and structural qualities of Hagia Sophia. That great Justinianic church, acknowledged as having one of the finest interior spaces in architecture, had challenged Turkish architects since the conquest. Sinan imitated the vaulting system of Hagia Sophia in the mosque of Süleyman. The building is covered by a central dome supported by two half-domes; however, the longitudinal basilical quality of the interior space in Hagia Sophia is contrasted by the centrality of Süleymaniye. This is made possible by opening the central nave to the aisles. Sinan thus created a completely perceptible interior space in Süleymaniye, replacing the "immaterialization" of Hagia Sophia by rationalization.[38]

18. Şehzade Mosque, circa 1895

The *külliye* of Süleyman I is regarded as the ultimate expression of the greatest age of the Ottoman Empire. The image of Istanbul as the center of Ottoman civilization developed during this time as well. The wealth of the empire made large investments possible and an extensive building program was undertaken. This program included many *külliye*s by Sinan. Among them are the *külliye*s of Selim I (1520) on the fourth hill, Şehzade Mehmet (1548) on the third hill, Kara Ahmet (1555) near Topkapı gate, *18* Mihrimah Sultan (1565) in Edirnekapı, and Sokullu Mehmet Paşa (1571) to the south of the Hippodrome.

Sinan's work was not restricted to the Istanbul peninsula; Üsküdar on the Asiatic side and the newly developed neighborhoods on the northern side of the Golden Horn were also dotted with his mosques and their dependencies.

The Seventeenth and Eighteenth Centuries

During the seventeenth and eighteenth centuries, Istanbul continued to develop along the same lines it had in the fifteenth and sixteenth centuries. However, the scale of the building activity was by no means comparable to that of previous centuries, due largely to the gradual decline in the economic power of the empire. The population, nevertheless, continued to escalate. Between 700,000 and 800,000 people lived in Istanbul and its suburbs in the seventeenth century.[39] This was almost twice the size of the population in 1535.[40] Not only did Istanbul's population increase, but the sixteenth-century settlements of Kasımpaşa and Tophane on the northern side of the Golden Horn, as well as Üsküdar on the Asiatic side, grew considerably.

The seventeenth century contributed two monuments to the capital: the *külliye* of Ahmet I (1616) on the site of the Byzantine Palace to the west of Hippodrome and the Valide Mosque (1597–1663) on the waterfront in Eminönü. During the second half of the seventeenth century, several smaller mosques and *medreses* were built along the Divanyolu, the old *mese*. But, the number of religious buildings erected in the seventeenth century was not comparable to that of the fifteenth and sixteenth centuries.[41]

The eighteenth century brought no significant monuments to Istanbul, but nonetheless marked an important first step toward embracing European architectural fashions. In 1720, the Ottoman Empire sent its first ambassador, Mehmet Çelebi Efendi, to Paris. In addition to his diplomatic mission, Çelebi Efendi was instructed to "visit fortresses, factories, and the works of French civilization generally and report on those which might be applicable to Turkey."[42] Upon his return from the Paris of Louis XIV, Çelebi Efendi published a report in which he described not only the technical and military establishments, but also—and with a great deal of admiration—the palaces, gardens, operas, and theaters.[43] Fascinated by the ambassador's fairytalelike accounts of the French royal setting, the Ottoman court attempted to create a new architectural repertoire with the construction of palaces and gardens in the European fashion. Many foreign architects and artists were invited to Istanbul. But, the magnificent palaces built during this time were totally destroyed in the mass revolts of the 1730s. However, the architectural language they introduced to Istanbul survived and developed into the "Ottoman Baroque," characterized by curving façades, large curved eaves, and an elaborate curvilinear surface decoration.[44]

19 Among the most striking examples of the Ottoman Baroque are the Nuruosmaniye Mosque (1775) on the second hill and the Laleli Mosque (1763) near Aksaray. Çelebi Efendi had described at length the beauty of the waterworks in French gardens, and echoes of these waterworks were found in the eighteenth-century Ottoman fountains. Until this period, Istanbul's monuments were characterized by their rectangular outlines and plain surfaces. Now the French-inspired curved walls lent a new picturesqueness to the street façades.

While the Istanbul peninsula did not experience any dramatic changes from the early seventeenth century to the 1840s, this period was a time of growth for Galata. Soon after Constantinople was conquered, Mehmet

19. *Nuruosmaniye Mosque, circa 1895*

II had incorporated Galata's administration into the Ottoman system. Under Ottoman rule, Galata survived as a cosmopolitan harbor town, but its built fabric presented characteristics different from Istanbul. According to the maps and the views of the suburb from various periods and from the descriptions of Evliya Çelebi, the seventeenth-century Ottoman chronicler, there were no gardens in the walled city and the majority of the houses were built of stone.[45]

The pattern was quite different outside the Galata walls. Up to the eighteenth century, Pera, covered with orchards and vineyards, was known as the "vignes de Pera." In the seventeenth century, a number of wealthy Europeans, including the French, English, Venetian, Dutch, and Genoese ambassadors, and other local Christians, built their ample residences and gardens there. Pera hence began to develop as an upper-class residential quarter, in contrast to the commercial Galata.[46] Nonetheless, the growth of the adjacent Greek village of Aya Dimitri (Tatavla) and the establishment of new Armenian neighborhoods in the Taksim area in the late eighteenth century began to transform this upper-class quarter into a more economically mixed one.[47]

During the eighteenth and early nineteenth centuries, Pera's physical structure evolved as a European quarter. The three major Latin churches, Ste. Marie des Drapiers, St. Antoine de Padoue, and Ste. Trinité, were built in the eighteenth century. The European community also began establishing its own public services during this period. Among these were, for example, two hospitals in Taksim, one belonging to the French and the other to the Armenians.[48] But, the real building boom in Pera occurred after 1838.

2.

The Nineteenth-Century Background

From 1838 to 1908, the Ottoman Empire underwent an intense phase of economic and sociopolitical transformation aimed at the modernization of the old system. The urban growth pattern and the planning activities undertaken in Istanbul during this time span—bracketed by the Anglo-Turkish Commercial Treaty of 1838 and the Young Turk Revolution of 1908—reflect the changes taking place on a wider scale in the empire. These two events, one economic and the other political, mark important turning points in the history of the empire.

The Anglo-Turkish Commercial Treaty of 1838 granted British tradesmen the same rights as native tradesmen by allowing the British to purchase goods anywhere in the empire.[1] Within a year, similar agreements were made with other European countries. In effect, the empire became an open market and, within a decade, its balance of trade increased fifteenfold in favor of the Europeans.

The 1908 Young Turk Revolution, at the close of our period, was, on one hand, the beginning of a new era, an era that foretold the demise of the Ottoman Empire and cleared the way for the creation of a Turkish Republic in 1923. On the other hand, it can be considered another attempt to "save" the empire, this time by replacing Abdülhamit II's autocratic rule with a constitutional form of government. The Young Turk government stayed in power until 1918—the date of the empire's defeat in World War I, and its dissolution by the victorious Allied Nations.

The Young Turks were reformers and revolutionaries who believed in radical improvements in the state and society. Paradoxically, their efforts, hindered by the external political situation that subsumed the empire in the Balkan War and World War I, resulted in the creation of a tighter mechanism of state power, repression, tyranny, and ultimately defeat. Nevertheless, their unsuccessful and incomplete ventures into a parliamentary system and radical social reforms did prepare the way for the abolition of the sultanate in 1923.[2] Their most significant contribution was in the field of public works, especially in Istanbul. The Young Turks created a new and more effective municipal organization in the capital and carried out an extensive city-building program. In the process, the police, fire brigades, public transportation services, and utilities were reorganized. As Bernard Lewis puts it, "The Young Turks may have failed to give Turkey constitutional government. They did, however, give Istanbul drains."[3]

The seventy years from 1838 to 1908 saw five sultans: Mahmut II (1808–39), Abdülmecit (1839–61), Abdülaziz (1861–76), Murat V (1876), and Abdülhamit II (1876–1909). Mahmut II was the initiator of a series of military, educational, and administrative reforms based on Western models. Abdülmecit and Abdülaziz were his true followers, enthusiasts of Westernization. The Tanzimat Charter, which made reformation according to a European model official policy, was signed in 1839, under Abdülmecit. With this charter, the relationship between the sultan and the people was defined and codified for the first time in the history of the Ottoman Empire. Concepts of equality, liberty, and human rights entered the Ottoman political discourse. However, these terms, quick and superficial adaptations from French revolutionary vocabulary, were not geared toward the masses; they accommodated instead the international commercial bourgeoisie then settling in the empire. The Tanzimat Charter thus provided the necessary institutions to foster the Western economic control made possible by the 1838 treaty.

The trend toward Westernization continued along the lines established in 1839 well into Abdülhamit II's reign. Abdülhamit II, though a reformist in the Tanzimat sense, was, at the same time, opposed to the liberal and constitutional ideas shared by the preceding sultans and statesmen. His long reign was characterized by an autocratic administration and a return to Islamic ideas on one hand, and a continuation of change and reform based on Western models on the other.[4]

In spite of some weakening under Abdülhamit II, the Tanzimat ideology was a powerful force that ran through the seven decades covered by this study. It had two main concepts that differentiated it from the classical Ottoman tradition. First, modern European society was seen as superior to the Ottoman society, and the solution for the problems of the empire was sought in the importation of Western institutions and methods. Second, old institutions, which were considered impediments to progress, needed to be eliminated so that new ones could be established.[5]

The acknowledgment of the superiority of the Western world goes back to the eighteenth century, when numerous military defeats forced the Ottoman ruling classes to look to Europe as a source for the revitalization of the empire. However, until 1839, Westernization was confined to the technological, scientific, and educational fields and was almost exclusively oriented toward the improvement of the military forces. With the Tanzimat Charter of 1839, the Western intellectual system was imported as well, resulting in more radical social changes.

The traditional Ottoman system was decentralized; responsibility for social programs, such as public health, education, and social security, was in the hands of various autonomous communities, namely, the *millet*s, or ethnic groups, guilds, and religious orders. The Tanzimat reformers put an end to this system by introducing an agenda of codification, systematization, and centralized control.[6] For example, legal reform, which opened the way for the creation of a Westernized urban administration and facilitated physical improvements in the urban fabric by means of building codes and regulations, was an offspring of the Tanzimat's greater centralization programs. Following the declaration of the Tanzimat Charter, the capital became an arena of experimentation with the installation of a European-style municipality and the application of nineteenth-century Western planning principles.

The developments between 1838 and 1908 were not only dependent on the superstructure of the Tanzimat reforms; the state of the national economy played a crucial role as well. We should briefly look at the Ottoman economy and the level of industrial development in order to understand better the power of Western influence.

During the first half of the nineteenth century, the Ottoman Empire experienced a severe challenge to its manufacturing industry. The origins of of this challenge go back to the mid-eighteenth century when the French import duty on cotton yarn and the development of machine spinning in England led to a shift in Ottoman exports from manufactured textiles to raw cotton.[7] But the role played by the 1838 Anglo-Turkish Commercial Treaty, which opened the way for the influx of European machine-made goods, was greater. The then-Austrian consul described this phenomenon: "The Treaty of 1838 is ... hostile to Ottoman industry.... Now a Belgian merchant pays 5% on goods sold in Turkey; a Turkish merchant pays 12% for exports or even for transport from one of the Ottoman states to the other."[8]

Indeed, according to the commercial treaties, local products circulating within the empire were taxed, but foreign merchandise was taxed only upon entrance and exit from Ottoman territories.[9] In the next decades, the development of the transportation networks (especially the railroads) facilitated the penetration of European goods to all corners of the empire, further threatening local manufacturing.

The recognition of this problem led to a series of ambitious attempts to create a modern Ottoman industry, and a number of state-run manufacturing facilities were built in the early 1840s. The shoreline immediately to the west of Istanbul, outside the Theodosian walls, became an industrial zone. In Zeytinburnu, a foundry was built where iron pipes, steel rails, plows, cannons, swords, knives, and similar metal objects were produced. Close by in the same district, textiles and cotton stockings were manufactured. Workers' housing in the form of two-story barracks, 200-meters long, constituted part of this industrial park.[10]

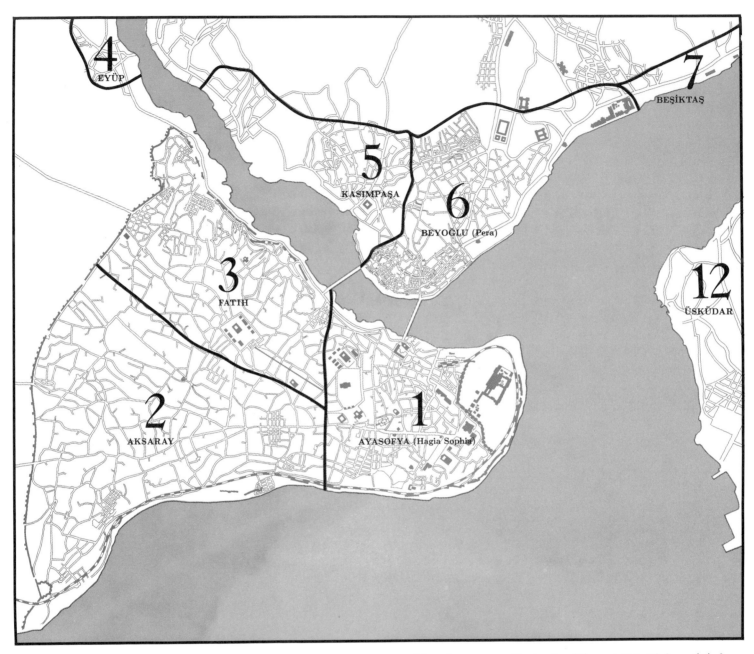

20. *Districts, 1857. Not shown are Emirgân (8) and Büyükdere (9) farther up the Bosporus on the European side; and Beykoz (10) and Beylerbeyi (11) along the Bosporus on the Asian side. Kadıköy (13) was to the southeast of Üsküdar. The Fourteenth District comprised the Princes' Islands in the Sea of Marmara.*

In Bakırköy a boatyard for the construction of small steamships was established along with factories, including a textile plant, a foundry, and a steam-driven machine shop.[11] Farther to the west, in Küçük Çekmece, a gunpowder works exhibited the desired industrial image, as one observer ironically put it, "a Turkish Manchester and Leeds, a Turkish Birmingham and Sheffield."[12]

Several other industrial sites were scattered in the suburbs of the capital and in some villages along the Bosporus, as well as other parts of the empire. The principal branches of industry during the last two decades of the nineteenth century specialized in foodstuffs (primarily sugar), glass, porcelain, tiles, metal objects, paper, chemicals, and rubber.[13] In addition to these state-operated industries, a number of concessions were issued mainly to private European companies.[14] To facilitate their operations, the companies were held exempt from certain taxes, such as the duty tax on imported machinery.[15]

All the machinery, as well as the foremen, master craftsmen, and skilled laborers were imported from Europe. The workers were English, Belgian, French, Italian, and Austrian, with a wide diversity of specializations, which included "draftsmen, erectors, filters, pattern makers, moulders, boilermakers, engine smiths, coal viewers, steam engineers, blast-furnace keepers, pudders, bar-iron rollers, and ship-builders."[16]

Ottoman industry thereby became totally dependent on European technology and expertise. As a Belgian worker expressed it at the time:

It would be very odd if we could not turn out a piece of the finest cloth occasionally, seeing that we have the best machinery of France and England, that the finest wools for the purpose are imported, via Trieste from Saxony and the best wool countries, and that we Frenchmen and Belgians work it. You could not call it Turkish cloth—it [is] only cloth made in Turkey by European machinery, out of European materials, and by good European hands.[17]

The European influence on industry also manifested itself in the form of promotional measures taken by the Ottoman government. The nineteenth-century fashion of holding international expositions in major Western cities found its way to Istanbul in 1863 when an international exposition was inaugurated at the Hippodrome in a vast (*muazzam*) construction, designed in the new manner (*tarz-ı cedid*). Local products and machinery imported from Europe were exhibited for five months, during which time many visitors, including foreigners, toured the building.[18] The construction was taken down in 1865.[19]

Thirty years later in 1893 under Abdülhamit II, a second industrial fair was planned with the goal of "promoting the development of the wealth and well-being of the country," as *The Levant Herald* put it.[20] A site covering 142,000 square meters on the northern side of the Golden Horn, in the vicinity of Şişli, was selected for the Istanbul Agricultural and

21. R. D'Aronco, project for the British pavilion at the Istanbul Agricultural and Industrial Exposition (1893)

Industrial Exposition (Dersaadet Ziraat ve Sanayi Sergi-i Umumisi).[21] Raimondo D'Aronco was appointed architect-in-chief with the agreement that some exposition buildings would be designed in a "modern style," while others would display a "national character."[22] However, the exposition never materialized.

Ottoman industrial products were exhibited in all major fairs in European cities, as well as the World Columbian Exposition of 1893 in Chicago. However, the goods sent abroad were mere showpieces. The empire's absolute dependence on Western technology and expertise prevented the development of a truly national industry strong enough to compete with the rapid technological advances in the Western world. As a result, the empire became increasingly dependent on Western products.[23] Furthermore, no effective measures could be taken to promote and protect a national industry as every decision had to conform to the commercial treaties signed with the European countries after 1838. Under these circumstances, rather than establishing the foundation for a national industry, the government's promotion policies facilitated even deeper economic penetration by the West.

The state of Ottoman industry helped to exacerbate its foreign debt problem. A rapid increase in the debt began in 1854, when the military alliances between the Ottoman Empire and France and Britain in the Crimean War gave the Ottomans an opportunity to receive large amounts of credit. The public debt was used for war expenses and deficits in the budget.[24] From then on, it became an all too common practice to take out loans from European countries.[25] By 1881, it was acknowledged that the empire was no longer capable of paying its debts, which led to the founding of the Public Debt Administration (Düyun-u Umumiye) in the same year. This organization, formed from the representatives of the loaning countries, abolished certain Ottoman taxes and gave the Europeans the right to explore and exploit Ottoman resources in return for the large sums owed by the government. Operating from its headquarters in Istanbul (designed in a neo-Turkish style by Antoine Vallaury) the Public Debt Administration penetrated the four corners of the empire with its 6,000 employees and took control of the most valuable natural resources.[26] The administration's income increased by 235 percent from 1882 to 1909.[27] From 1881 on, the Public Debt Administration managed the empire's finances to the advantage of the Western powers.

In summary, from 1838 to 1908, the Ottoman Empire staged its final but doomed struggle for survival. To recover from the economic crisis and technological underdevelopment, it attempted to enact a series of social and institutional reforms based on Western models. These reforms, not well adapted to Ottoman society and not geared toward the heart of the problem, failed to "save" the empire. They introduced, however, vital Western concepts and institutions, which, though often in conflict with the centuries-old values and traditions, were equated with progress and modernization in the minds of the Ottoman bureaucrats. In turn, cities, and especially the capital, obtained a share of the benefits resulting from these modernizing reforms.

DEMOGRAPHIC GROWTH AND
COMPOSITION OF THE POPULATION

The nineteenth-century increase in the Ottoman capital's population paralleled that of other European urban centers. Istanbul and its suburbs had about 391,000 inhabitants in 1844; in 1856, the number increased to 430,000; in 1878 to 547,437; and in 1886 to 851,527—more than doubling in four decades.[28] However by 1885, the population had stabilized; the 1906 census showed an increase of only 13,049 during the twenty-year period from 1886 to 1906.[29] This situation echoed the demographic growth of European capitals, but in Istanbul it had different origins.[30] The major European cities had either experienced a fast urbanization process brought on by the Industrial Revolution, as was the case in England; or they were the beneficiaries of government policies of centralization, which resulted in the growth of capital cities, such as Paris and Vienna. The Ottoman capital had not lived through the Industrial Revolution and was thus spared its consequences. Nor had governmental policy toward Istanbul changed, so the city continued to enjoy a privileged position as the capital of the empire.

The increase in Istanbul's population was brought about partly by the influx of Muslim refugees escaping from the political unrest in south-eastern Europe and southern Russia.[31] Moreover, there had been a rise in the number of non-Muslim foreigners entering the city. About 100,000 foreigners arrived in the Ottoman capital between 1840 and 1900, most of whom came to reap the economic benefits given to Western tradesmen and investors by the commercial treaties.[32]

The 1885 census of Ottoman subjects in the capital shows the following ethnic distribution: Muslim, 44.06 percent; Greek Orthodox, 17.48 percent; Armenian Gregorian, 17.12 percent; Jewish, 5.08 percent; Catholic, 1.17 percent; Bulgarian, 0.50 percent; Latin, 0.12 percent; and Protestant, 0.09 percent. Foreigners made up the remaining 14.74 percent.[33] The high percentage of foreigners was due in part to the adoption of foreign citizenship by non-Muslim Ottoman subjects who sought the protection embassies gave to foreigners. As the economic activities and value systems of this group were similar to those of the Europeans, their impact on the development of Istanbul reinforced the trend toward increasing Westernization.

In the Sixth District, composed of Pera, Galata, and Tophane, the population was 47 percent foreign, 32 percent non-Muslim Ottoman, and only 21 percent Muslim. The Fourth District, which included Beşiktaş and other Bosporus villages up to Rumelihisarı, was second in the number of foreign residents, with foreigners constituting approximately 10 percent of the total population, and Muslims 43 percent. In contrast to these two districts on the northern band of the Golden Horn, the percentage of foreigners living in the Istanbul peninsula was about 1.5 percent. In the First, Second, and Third districts, which comprised the whole peninsula, Muslims formed approximately 55 percent of the total population.[34]

These figures indicate the emergence of a particular settlement pattern in the second half of the nineteenth century. Foreigners lived on the northern side of the Golden Horn in the old Genoese suburb of Galata and its new extensions, while Muslims were concentrated mostly in Istanbul. Nevertheless, a considerable number of Muslims moved to the northern side of the Golden Horn during the second half of the nineteenth century. Even though we do not have population figures for districts according to income levels, it would not be unrealistic to suggest that this move was initiated by Westernized upper-class Muslims. There are two related reasons for this. First, these Turks, who had been exposed to and had tried to adopt the European ways and values, wanted to benefit from the modern amenities in the Sixth District. Second, many high government officers felt obliged to follow the sultan when the Ottoman imperial palace was transferred in 1856 from Topkapı to its new location in Dolmabahçe, and then to Yıldız farther up on the Bosporus. Upper-income Muslim neighborhoods naturally developed around these new palaces. The effects of the population growth and its distribution pattern were reflected in the physical growth of the city.

PHYSICAL GROWTH

According to an 1840 map by B. R. Davies, the population of the Ottoman capital was mainly concentrated in the Istanbul peninsula and Galata.[35] The triangle of the Istanbul peninsula, defined in the west by the Theodosian walls, was densely inhabited, with only a few scattered open spaces, used as vegetable gardens, some of which were former Byzantine cisterns. The road network in the western neighborhoods adjacent to the walls indicated a lower density than the rest of the peninsula.

Outside the walls, the Muslim neighborhood of Eyüp on the Golden Horn stood out as the largest settlement. A second Muslim neighborhood outside the walls was immediately to the west of Yedikule on the Sea of Marmara. Apart from Eyüp and Yedikule, Bakırköy (Macrikeuy) and Yeşilköy (Ayastefanos) farther to the west by the Sea of Marmara, were the only settlements of any size.

On the northern bank of the Golden Horn, the former Genoese town of Galata, still partially contained within its fifteenth-century walls, was the densest settlement, as indicated by the tight lock of its street pattern. The old city walls defined Galata's western and northern boundaries, but to the northeast, following the shoreline of the Bosporus, the Muslim suburbs of Tophane and Fındıklı were formed. These neighborhoods were much lower in density than the walled core. The density within the walled suburb of Galata was, in fact, so high that not only had the built-up area spilt over to the narrow strip outside the sea walls, but also at certain points, the sea was filled in to make room for additional structures.[36]

Pera, located on the hill to the north of the walled city of Galata, had its population concentrated along the Grande Rue de Pera, the city's main artery. Tepebaşı on the slope to the north and northwest of the Grande Rue, and Tatavla farther to the north, were the outer neighborhoods of Pera, inhabited mainly by non-Muslims. Non-Muslim cemeteries, the largest being the Grand Champs des Morts (Tepebaşı) and the Petit Champs des Morts (Taksim), were scattered throughout these settlements, creating large open spaces in the urban landscape.

The three main villages along the northern shore of the Golden Horn were Kasımpaşa, Hasköy, and Sütlüce. Kasımpaşa and Sütlüce were Muslim villages, while Hasköy had a large Jewish population.[37]

The beginnings of the future growth along the Bosporus can already be detected in Davies's map. Palaces lining the Beşiktaş shore indicate

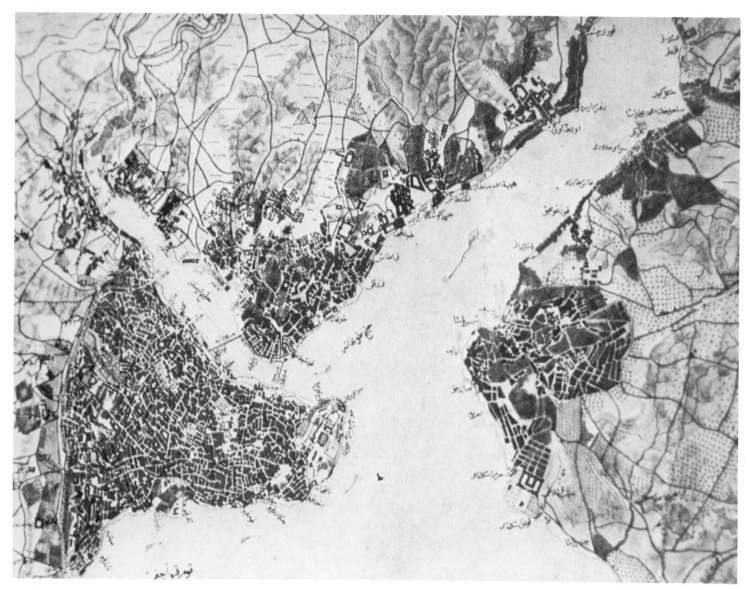

22. Map of Istanbul, 1871

the royal preference for this area. Beşiktaş itself was a large village at this date, with a mixed population of Turks, Greeks, Jews, and Armenians. It was the first of the many villages, separated only by small distances, on the European side of the Bosporus. The shoreline between these villages was lined with *yalıs*, rectilinear seaside mansions, belonging to the outstanding members of a Muslim "bourgeoisie administrative."[38]

Üsküdar, facing the entrance of the Golden Horn, was the largest settlement on the eastern bank of the Bosporus. Not as compact as Istanbul and Galata, this section of the capital, where Muslims, Armenians, Greeks, and Jews lived together, stretched over an extensive area. Kadıköy (the former Chalcedon), to the south of Üsküdar, was another relatively large village with a Muslim and Greek population.[39] The urban configuration along the Asian shore of the Bosporus followed the same pattern as that on the European side. Villages were separated by vacant areas and *yalıs* lined the waterfront.

During the second half of the nineteenth and the first decade of the twentieth century, the physical boundaries of the capital expanded dramatically.[40] On the northern side of the Golden Horn the growth came about in three main directions: from Taksim (Petit Champs) to Şişli, from Tophane toward Dolmabahçe following the shoreline, and from Dolmabahçe toward Teşvikiye and Nişantaşı on the hills above Beşiktaş. Perhaps the most striking factor is that the Istanbul side did not expand outside the old Theodosian walls. Istanbul's containment within its

23. Map of Istanbul, circa 1900

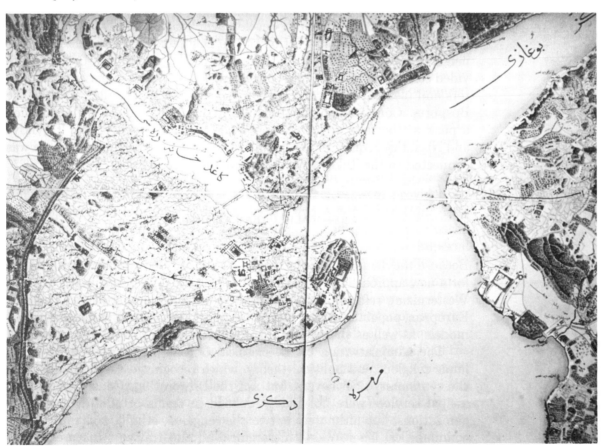

A substantial step was taken in 1855, following the Crimean War, to reorganize the urban administration. This action was provoked in part by the complaints of the French, English, and Italians, whose number had considerably increased after the war and who demanded the provision of modern amenities from the government. A *şehremaneti* was established, its title deriving from a direct translation of "préfecture de la ville," reflecting the French model it followed. The duties of the *şehremaneti* revolved around the provision of basic needs (mainly foodstuffs), regulation and collection of taxes, construction and repair of roads, cleaning and embellishment of the city, and control of markets and guilds.[47] The *şehremini* (*préfet de la ville*) executed these tasks with the help of the city council (*şehir meclisi*). The *şehremini* and the twelve members of the council, selected by the government among the "representatives of every Ottoman ethnic class and the honorable and trustworthy members of the guilds residing in Istanbul" (Istanbul'da oturan her sınıf teba-i Osmaniden ve esnafın muteber ve mutemedinden) were appointed by an imperial order.[48]

However, the council was unsuccessful in bringing the much-desired urban reform to the capital. A main reason for this failure lies in the make-up of the council itself. The representatives of the city's inhabitants and guilds were not necessarily equipped with the background and the tools to resolve the complex problems of a busy international port. Furthermore, the city lacked an independent budget. The only source of income for the new administration came from a special tax on horses and wagons; the rest of the budget was provided by the central government.[49]

In May 1855 the government formed the Commission for the Order of the City (İntizam-ı Şehir Komisyonu) to carry out a more fundamental program. The document establishing the commission argued that the capital cities of all leading countries were built to perfection, whereas Istanbul still badly needed embellishment (*tezyin*), regularization (*tanzif*), road enlargement (*tevessu*), street lighting (*tenvir-i esvak*), and improvement of building methods (*islah-ı usul-u ebniye*).[50] According to the official reports, positive results could be obtained only if these operations were carried out following certain rules and regulations. As the success of such rules had been proven in Europe, the commission should be composed of people who were familiar with European methods: "It has been decided to make use of the knowledge of Ottoman and foreign families long resident in the city and familiar with foreign ways to form a municipal commission."[51]

The commission's main contribution was the promulgation of a set of rules aimed at the regularization of the street network and the vital services connected with it. Straightening, widening, and paving the main roads in Istanbul, Pera, and Galata, along the shore from Tophane to Ortaköy, and in Üsküdar were among the first proposals.[52] The construction of sidewalks, water and sewage lines, the cleaning and lighting of the streets, and the creation of an accounting branch within the body of the municipality were other suggested priorities.[53]

In an effort to give local municipal power to different areas, the commission developed a regulation draft and proposed a municipal model that divided the city into fourteen districts.[54] A report, published in the official newspaper *Takvim-i Vekayi* in 1857, designated the Sixth District, comprising Pera, Galata, and Tophane, the experimental area for urban reform. The building activities that would focus on the regularization of streets, paving, construction of water and sewage lines, and maintenance were to be carried out here according to European methods. It was hoped that the lessons learned from the Sixth District could then be applied to the other thirteen districts.[55]

The selection of Galata as the model area was due both to the popularity this part of the city gained after the 1840s and to its largely European population. The 1857 report published in *Takvim-i Vekayi* emphasized this point:

Since to begin all things in the above-mentioned districts [meaning the thirteen districts except Galata] would be sophistry and unworthy, and since the Sixth District contains much valuable real estate and many fine buildings, and since the majority of those owning property or residing there have seen such things in other countries and understand their value, the reform program will be inaugurated in the Sixth District.[56]

The district was to be run by a director (*müdür*), appointed by the grand vizier, and a council (*meclis*) of seven members, appointed by the government. Every six months, three of the members would be changed. To be selected, an individual had to own real estate valued at a minimum of 100,000 *kuruş* within the boundaries of the Sixth District, and must have lived in the city for at least ten years. In addition to the regular members of the council, four foreign advisers were appointed by the Porte. The advisers were chosen from among those foreigners, who, besides being well-informed on municipal affairs, owned real estate valued at a minimum of 200,000 *kuruş* and had ten years prior residence in the capital.[57]

The principal difference between this council and the previous municipal commissions was the structure of the membership. For the first time, foreigners, considered reliable because of their vested interests, were actively taking part in the administration of the capital. There was a good reason for this—the scale of work to be done in the Sixth District would exceed the government budget, and potential loans from rich foreigners were seriously considered.[58]

The responsibilities of the Sixth District Administration covered market regulations, road construction and repair decisions, provision of street lighting, as well as the construction of water and sewage lines, thus coinciding with the responsibilities of the former İntizam-ı Şehir Komisyonu.[59] The first major task undertaken by the Sixth District Administration was a cadastral survey of the district, a pioneer work of its kind in the Ottoman

24. The Municipal Palace in the Sixth District

capital. Regularization of the street network together with the widening of the main arteries constituted another aspect of the extensive work completed by the Sixth District. Gas lighting and water and sewage lines were incorporated into the improved network as much as possible. After the 1870 Pera fire, *kargir* (brick or stone) construction was made obligatory by the administration. Two parks, one in Taksim, the other in Tepebaşı, were created and non-Muslim cemeteries in these locations were transported outside the city, to Şişli. The administration also undertook the construction of two hospitals and a municipal palace.[60] Previously, hospitals were established and operated as *vakıf*s in accordance with the Islamic concept of charity. This municipal project thus marks the beginning of the gradual replacement of traditional institutions with European-style ones. Fittingly, the Municipal Palace, a neoclassical "Hôtel de Ville," became the symbol of the Sixth District.

24

The wealthy groups of the Sixth District were the main beneficiaries of the new municipal reforms. Street lighting and cleaning, and garbage collection served those residing on the main streets of Pera. The poor Greeks, Armenians, and Turks living in the ravines behind Taksim, in Kasımpaşa, and on the back streets of Pangaltı, did not benefit from these services. The priority was clearly to make modern urban services available to the Europeans rather than the democratic distribution of municipal resources.[61]

The Sixth District served nonetheless as a model for all future planning and reorganization. In 1868, with a decision to implement its original plan of 1856, the Ottoman government expanded municipal administration to the whole city. A municipal regulation (Dersaadet İdare-i Belediye Nizamnamesi) was passed and the capital was once more divided into the previous fourteen districts. The goal was to embellish and regularize the city as a whole (*umumen şehrin tezyinat ve tenzifatı*) by strict control of building methods, regularization of the roads and the quays, and construction of water and sewage lines.[62] This regulation was not enforced and the Sixth District functioned autonomously until 1877, when the number of districts was increased to twenty by a new law (Dersaadet Belediye Kanunu), which deprived the Sixth District of its privileged status.

The 1868 regulation had attempted to gather the administration of the fourteen districts under the central control of the *şehremaneti*.[63] Yet it was not easy to extend urban reform to the entire city. Out of the fourteen proposed districts, only two districts besides Galata were established. One of these was the Fourteenth District, which covered the Princes' Islands; the other was Tarabya District on the Bosporus.[64] However, both of these could be considered extensions of the Sixth District, because they were the summer resorts of the Europeans residing in the city. The 1877 law that increased the number of districts to twenty by subdividing the former districts was even more unrealistic. The only reason for the 1877 decision was probably an attempt to imitate the twenty *arrondissements* of Paris.[65] One year later, the number was reduced to a more sensible ten. The municipality's sources of income had, in the meantime, been expanded by the 1877 regulation and now included taxes from building contracts, foodstuffs, commercial patents, and permits, in addition to the regular municipal tax and private donations.[66]

During the next thirty years, European municipal concepts continued to penetrate the Ottoman system. From 1878 to 1908, some further modernization was brought to the city bureaucracy; for example, the Water Company (Terkos Şirketi) and the Istanbul Gas Administration (Istanbul Gaz İdaresi), private companies formed in the mid-nineteenth century, were integrated into the municipal organization.[67]

The new institutions were not totally successful in their attempts to bring radical changes to the capital's administration. As impersonal organizations trying to function according to a new, but not yet well-defined municipal jurisdiction, they could not easily replace centuries-old practices based on the more personal control exercised by the local representatives of the *kadı*s. Their impact was hence partial and scattered. Western municipal concepts became more integrated into the city apparatus during the Young Turk rule, from which they were carried over to the Republican era. But, partial and scattered though it was, urban reform between 1838 and 1908 still brought about a dramatic transformation in Istanbul's city form and profoundly shaped its future developments.

3.

Regularization of the Urban Fabric

The institutional reforms set in motion by the declaration of the Tanzimat Charter found their extensions in the built forms—in the urban fabric on a larger scale, in architecture on a smaller scale. The result was the metamorphosis of the classical Ottoman/Islamic urban image into a more cosmopolitan one, penetrated by forms and elements adopted from Western models.

Different forces determined the scope and nature of activity on the two sides of the Golden Horn. The dense, wooden residential fabric of the Istanbul peninsula made the area vulnerable to fires. Here, the burned-out neighborhoods became arenas of experimentation where Western-inspired urban planning principles were put into practice. In Galata, however, fires played a secondary role that was limited to the older and denser neighborhoods. It was the popularity the suburb acquired after the 1840s and the subsequent physical expansion that dictated the location and scale of new urban planning practices in Galata.

The design principles were uniform and unilateral throughout the Ottoman capital with regularization of the urban fabric the goal. The new urban design philosophy came as part of the Tanzimat reform package. Mustafa Reşit Paşa, one of the authors of the Tanzimat Charter, had formulated the initial rules as early as 1836. As a result of his diplomatic missions to Paris, Vienna, and London, he had grown to admire the European cities and wanted the Ottoman capital to meet their standards. For this purpose, he advocated a "scientific" approach to planning. He argued that the regularization of the street network should pursue mathematical/geometrical rules (*kevaid-i hendese*). This meant cutting straight and wide arteries through the existing mazelike patterns. Ease of communication thus achieved would help to control the recurring fires that plagued the city. Foreign engineers and architects who knew and practiced the architectural science (*fenn-i mimari*) of modern construction were to be hired. Moreover, Turkish students were to be sent to Europe to study architecture so as to eliminate the need for foreign specialists in the future.[1] Mustafa Reşit Paşa further argued that the conversion of the built fabric from wood to *kargir* (stone or brick) would enhance fire prevention. As was typical of nineteenth-century Ottoman bureaucrats, he justified his own ideas by passing them through a Western filter. He quoted articles published in European newspapers that blamed the wood construction of Istanbul for large-scale and destructive fires.

Immediately after the declaration of the Tanzimat Charter, Mustafa Reşit Paşa's plan to appeal to foreign expertise was implemented by the government. A German engineer, Helmut Von Moltke, was hired in 1839 to improve Istanbul's street network. Von Moltke first drafted a plan of the city, then proposed a renovation scheme.[2] Like Mustafa Reşit Paşa, Von Moltke emphasized the importance of mathematical rules (*kevaid-i hendese*) for the creation of straight and wide arteries. He delineated seven main arteries and divided the street network into three categories according to width.[3] The classification of streets soon became a major theme in post-Tanzimat regulations. Von Moltke also duplicated Mustafa Reşit Paşa's proposal by promoting *kargir* construction, which, being fire resistant, would serve the public good (*menfaat-ı umumiye*). At the same time, *kargir* buildings would present an image that glorified the imperial honor (*şan-ı seniye*) of the capital, which the shapeless timber (*resimsiz ahşap*) construction had damaged seriously!

Although Von Moltke's plan was not implemented, his policies and those of Mustafa Reşit Paşa formed the essence of the new building codes. Legal reform itself was part of the Tanzimat's modernization agenda. From the 1840s on, laws and regulations adopted from European models began replacing the traditional Ottoman system based on Islamic law.

In the Islamic legal system, the only valid law was the God-given *şeriat*. Since no separation existed between religion and law, the Muslim state was not endowed with legislative powers. This Islamic tradition had evolved into a unique system in the hands of the Ottomans, who, borrowing some concepts from Byzantine administration, developed their own array of legal rules (*kanun*s). Judges (*kadı*s) managed all affairs of law and justice. Nonetheless, legislation was not codified and often local leaders relied on unwritten sources (such as customs and traditions) to settle juridical cases.

A contemporary European observer explained the necessity for the Europeanization of the Ottoman system in the following words:

So long as the Turks remained isolated as a household of strangers encamped in the midst of surrounding nations, this peculiar identification of religion and law might have continued to subsist and to answer all purposes; but from the hour that Turkey, resolving to discard the isolating and exclusive spirit of past ages, invites the approaches of European civilization, it becomes evident that ancient codes can no longer suffice. It became necessary to frame new regulations when new riches, luxuries, and all the attendant train of Western civilization introduced new crimes and subjects of contention.[4]

The first regulation governing urban planning and construction activities was prepared in 1848. Between 1848 and 1882, six major regulations were passed: the 1848 Building Regulation (Ebniye Nizamnamesi), the 1858 Regulation on Streets (Sokaklara dair Nizamname), the 1863 Street and Building Regulation (Turuk ve Ebniye Nizamnamesi), the 1875 Regulation on Construction Methods in Istanbul (Istanbul ve Belde-i Selasede Yapılacak Ebniyenin Suret-i İnşaiyesine dair Nizamname), the 1877 Istanbul Municipal Law (Dersaadet Belediye Kanunu), and the 1882 Building Law (Ebniye Kanunu).[5] These laws and regulations concentrated on similar issues.

To improve overall communication and establish citywide uniformity in the network, the streets were classified according to width. The 1848 Building Regulation proposed three types of streets: main avenues (*büyük caddeler*), which would be a minimum of 7.60 meters wide; ordinary avenues (*adi caddeler*), 6.00 meters wide; and other streets (*sair sokaklar*), 4.50 meters wide.[6] In 1863, two more categories were established; this time the widest arteries were envisioned as 11.50 meters, whereas the width of the fifth category (other streets) still remained 4.50 meters.[7] The 1882 Building Law, however, retained the five-category classification and the 11.50-meter width for the main streets, but increased the width of the fifth category from 4.50 meters to 7.60 meters.[8] All regulations stressed the need to eliminate dead ends.

The 1848 and 1863 regulations, which were concerned only with efficiency in communication, did not take into account the quality of the streets in terms of density and light. Thus, building heights were determined by construction methods alone, with brick and stone buildings being higher than timber structures.[9] This problem was addressed in the 1882 regulation, which correlated the building heights to street widths.[10]

The attempt to classify the street network was accompanied by a new rule aimed at insuring that all redevelopment conformed to approved plans.[11] For example, if an individual or a company desired to build on a vacant area, a proposal had to be submitted to the government to be evaluated for its "public good."[12] The neighborhoods destroyed by fires had to be reorganized according to a plan as well. The 1882 Building Law stated that any area that sustained the loss of a minimum of ten buildings would be considered a field (*tarla*), replanned, and replotted.[13] This practice was called the new method (*usul-u cedide*). Earlier, the 1863 law had determined that all new developments should consist of square (*murabba*) or rectangular (*müstatil*) blocks.[14] Mustafa Reşit Paşa's suggestion for geometry in city planning was thus revived and written into the legislation. This new emphasis on regularity of the urban fabric became the hallmark of modernization efforts from the 1860s on.

The proposed changes in the urban fabric called for the redefinition of expropriation rules, which was always justified by an appeal to the public good, paralleled post-1840 ordinances in Europe.[15] The 1863 regulation foresaw an equal portion of expropriation from both sides during street enlargements; the owners were not given the right to appeal, but were forced to donate the portion of their property necessary for the operation.[16] In the reorganized neighborhoods, the owners would be assigned new lots in accordance with the value of their previous properties.[17] However, the 1882 Building Law limited the amount that could be expropriated to a maximum of one-fourth of the pre-fire lot size.[18]

Construction methods were carefully detailed in order to reduce the possibility of fires. In 1848, a building declaration (*ebniye beyannamesi*) described the techniques of *kargir* construction, its advantages, and its two types, *tam kargir* and *nim kargir*. *Kargir* construction was defined in general as having stone supporting walls on the lower levels and brick walls on the upper stories. The difference between *tam kargir* and *nim kargir* lay in the materials used in beams and roof structures. In *tam kargir*, these had to be of iron or copper (it was argued that if copper were used, the building would last 2,000 years), whereas in *nim kargir* construction, wood was sufficient. In any case, the minimum lifetime of a *kargir* building was two hundred years, or double the lifetime of a timber building.[19] In 1864, the government decreed that henceforth all construction in the capital was to be in stone and brick. However, exceptions were made, and those without the necessary resources for *kargir* construction were allowed to build in timber. But, when timber was used, a dividing wall had to be erected between wood buildings to prevent the spread of flames.[20]

The 1875 regulation divided the capital into primary and secondary zones. In the primary zones, timber construction was forbidden, while in the secondary zones, it was occasionally allowed provided that *kargir* fire walls were built.[21] The rationale here was to enforce fire resistant *kargir* construction in the denser and more prestigious parts of the city. The primary zones included the eastern half of the Istanbul peninsula, defined in the west by the Unkapanı-Aksaray axis, Şişli, and the Grande Rue area in Pera, as well as the shoreline from Azapkapı to Ortaköy.[22] As we shall see, these were the areas of the capital where major investments would be made in the second half of the nineteenth and the first decade of the twentieth centuries. The ultimate goal envisioned by post-Tanzimat regulations was a city with straight and uniformly wide streets defining rectangular or square blocks composed of stone or brick buildings.

PLANNING AFTER FIRES

Istanbul's residential fabric in wood has constituted an ongoing danger for the city throughout its history. The threat of fire increased as the population grew and the built form became denser. For the first 180 years of Ottoman rule, court historians record no conflagrations in the city.[23] However, the 1633 Cibali fire marked the beginning of a long series of destructive fires. Between 1633 and 1839, 109 extensive fires took place in Istanbul and Galata. This number reached 229 between 1853 and 1906 when the nineteenth-century city lived with the constant threat of fire.[24] Edmondo De Amicis, a late nineteenth-century Italian traveler, described the helpless agony of the residents of Istanbul in the face of disaster:

... the word 'fire' means for the inhabitants of Constantinople 'every misfortune', and the cry *Yangin Var* is charged with a dread meaning, terrible, fateful, carrying with it dismay—a cry at which the entire city is moved to its very depths, and pours forth as at the announcement of a scourge from God.[25]

Before the 1840s, the continuous rebuilding necessitated by fires was carried out according to previously established patterns. The areas destroyed were rebuilt according to what had existed before the fires.[26] After 1840, the overriding concern to find radical solutions for fire prevention, paired with the fervor for modernization, resulted in a new appreciation of urban design. Every burned-down area became a stage for formal urban change.

The newly planned quarters did not always present the same characteristics. Different formal schemes emerged depending upon the scale of the fire, the topography of the area burned, and its location within the city. When the burned neighborhood was large and prestigious, its reorganization turned into a large urban design project, often including the unburned areas in its vicinity. A focal point, such as a monument or a commercial quay, led to the emergence of a wider main street in the midst of the newly planned neighborhood. When modest neighborhoods with no outstanding monumental features were burned, their fabrics could be transformed into a grid more freely. Finally, if the destroyed area was small in scale, its reorganization resulted only in a few straight and wide streets.

Major fires therefore played the greatest role in the transformation of the urban fabric. The 1856 Aksaray fire and the 1865 Hocapaşa fire were especially important in the reshaping of the Istanbul peninsula. On the northern side of the Golden Horn, the 1870 Pera fire did not result in radical changes in the urban patterns. However, it played a significant role in the capital's urban design history, because the unimplemented post-fire plans clearly show the desired prototypical urban image.

The 1856 Aksaray Fire: The First Grid

The 1856 Aksaray fire destroyed more than 650 buildings and was a major turning point in the history of Istanbul's urban form.[27] Following this fire, for the first time in the Ottoman capital, a systematic survey of the burned site was made, and an alternative urban design scheme was drawn up and implemented.[28] Pursuing Mustafa Reşit Paşa's policy of employing foreign expertise to modernize Istanbul, the government appointed an Italian engineer, Luigi Storari, to carry out the task.[29]

25. Plan of Aksaray, circa 1850

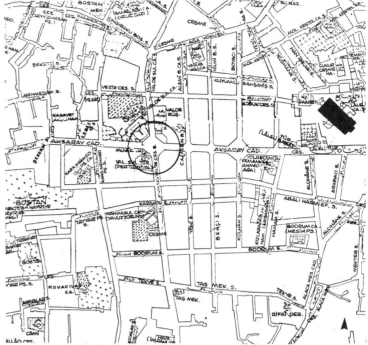

26. Plan of Aksaray, circa 1870

An imperial order specified the character of the desired plan: it was to conform to the new pattern (*heyet-i cedide*), hence it was to be regular with straight and wide streets.[30] In compliance with the order, Storari regularized the organic street network of the quarter. A main crossroads, clearly visible in the pre-fire fabric of Aksaray, corresponded to the intersection of the north-south road leading from Unkapanı on the Golden Horn to Yenikapı on the Sea of Marmara, and the east-west Aksaray Caddesi, a continuation of the Divanyolu.[31] Storari elaborated on the significance of these two arteries by widening and straightening them, and by cutting off the corners defining the crossroads, further accentuated their importance. Such an emphasis was a new concept for Istanbul. Though by no means a public square in the Western sense of the word, the new intersection was perceived as such, and, for example, was described by the *Journal de Constantinople* as a "belle place."[32]

Aksaray Caddesi was the prominent artery of this quarter, and to emphasize its importance, Storari repeated the crossroads pattern three more times along the thoroughfare. All other streets were neatly aligned. The resulting plan was not a perfect grid; it did not incorporate equal blocks with streets cutting each other at perfect right angles. Although Storari's streets were devoid of encroachments, and the numerous dead ends of the pre-fire Aksaray had disappeared, the new block sizes were still similar to the pre-fire blocks, and the residential scale was not affected. However, the seclusion of many residential blocks was diminished by the demolition of the culs-de-sac.

Echoing Von Moltke's proposal, Storari instituted a street classification according to width. His main artery, the east-west Aksaray Caddesi, was 9.50 meters wide, the others were 7.60 meters and 6.00 meters.[33]

The new neighborhood was viewed as a strong manifestation of European planning principles and was often compared to the contemporary reconstruction of Paris.[34] In fact, later critics of the Westernizing trends in urban planning blamed the Aksaray scheme for beginning a process that disregarded local heritage. For example, around the turn of the century, an architect, Mazhar Bey, comdemned the "hypocritical (*riyakar*) and unnationalistic (*milliyetsiz*) spirit of Tanzimat" for the imitation of the straight and wide arteries of Paris in Aksaray.[35] Mazhar Bey did not propose an alternative, and his criticism was too late to stop what had become an established urban design pattern.

The 1865 Hocapaşa Fire and the İ.T.K.

On 18 September 1865, Istanbul endured the most destructive fire in its history. The fire started in Hocapaşa to the west of Eminönü and soon the east wind spread the flames in several directions. A vast area, defined by the Sea of Marmara in the south, the Golden Horn in the north, the Beyazit *külliye* in the west, and the Hagia Sophia-Sultan Ahmet Mosque axis in the east, was burned to the ground in a period of thirty-two hours.[36]

27

The extent of the Hocapaşa fire (also known as *harik-i kebir*, the big fire) forced the government to search for a solution to the centuries-old problem of devastating conflagrations. This did not entail the proposal of revolutionary alternatives, but merely a persistent application of the basic guidelines established by Mustafa Reşit Paşa in 1836. A report prepared by the Judicial Court (Meclis-i Ahkam-ı Adliye) summarized the situation around two crucial points already defined in the 1830s: construction materials and the state of the street fabric. The first point was presented as the initial cause of fires: timber burned easily and quickly, so the built fabric should be converted to *kargir*—a familiar argument. Second, the condition of the streets was said to facilitate the spread of flames. Streets were described as being "crooked, narrow holes with abrupt ascents and descents," which made it almost impossible to rescue the inhabitants, let alone allow the passage of fire-fighting equipment. The street network also formed a serious obstacle to police control: "to try to provide police service in Istanbul [was] equivalent to trying to control a big forest."[37]

For these problems a double solution was proposed: regularization (straightening and widening) of the street system and conversion of timber

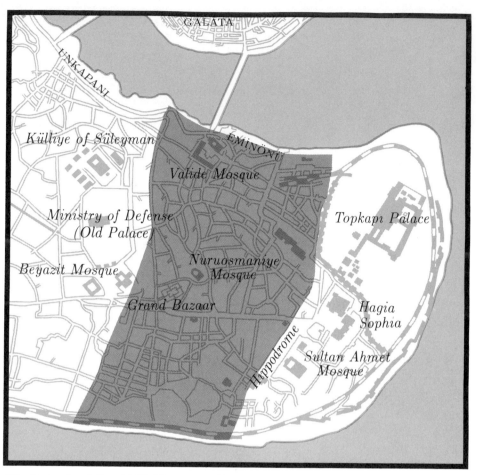

27. Extent of the 1865 Hocapaşa fire

buildings into *kargir*. It was further argued that by enlarging the streets, transportation of materials would be facilitated and construction costs reduced.[38]

A new regularization procedure was followed that anticipated the 1882 *tarla* rule, which enforced the replotting of areas where ten or more buildings had been destroyed by fires. This would mean some loss to individual owners over their pre-fire lots. Yet, the increase in land values brought about by the advantages of regular plans would balance the spatial diminution. A central authority was established to deal with the inevitable conflicts that arose from the application of the *tarla* rule on this scale. A commission, the İslahat-ı Turuk Komisyonu (İ.T.K., Commission for Road Improvement), was inaugurated to oversee an extensive program of urban planning and construction, which was pursued with efficiency and enthusiasm until 1869.[39]

The duties and the responsibilities of the İ.T.K. were clarified in a regulation, published in *Takvim-i Vekayi* as well as in the foreign language

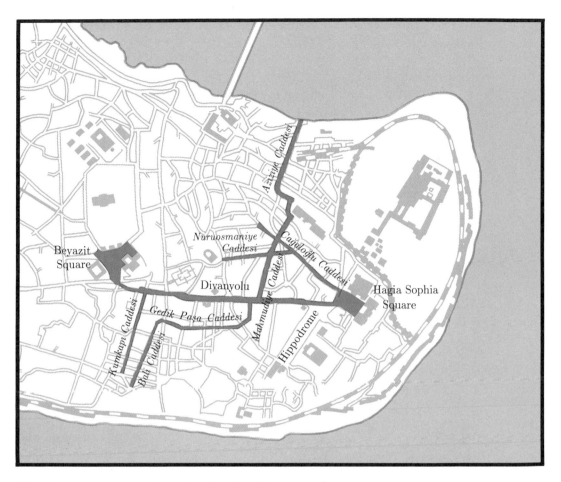

28. Main streets regularized after the Hocapaşa fire

newspapers of Istanbul.[40] The regulation defined the responsibility of the commission to be the planning of the area burned from Hocapaşa to the Divanyolu to Kumkapı and Beyazit and of other (unburned) locations needing regularization.[41] Thus, even though priority was given to the large area destroyed by the fire, the İ.T.K. was also empowered to bring modern planning to the entire city.

The nine-man commission that formulated the general policies was not formed of technocrats, but of high government officers.[42] Following the commission's guidelines, government engineers, called building officers (*ebniye memurları*), prepared a master plan in which new streets in the Hocapaşa area were classified into three categories.[43] The Divanyolu, as a main artery, would be 19.00 meters wide. Secondary arteries were projected to be 15.20 meters. These were Aziziye Caddesi, connecting the Sirkeci quay to Babıali; Mahmudiye Caddesi, extending from Babıali to the Divanyolu; the north-south Kumkapı Caddesi, providing access from the Divanyolu to Kadırga; and, Nuruosmaniye Caddesi, connecting

the Nuruosmaniye Mosque to Mahmudiye Caddesi. A third network, to be
built simultaneously with the main streets, would consist of other streets
of 11.50 meters, 9.00 meters, 7.60 meters, and 6.00 meters, depending
upon their location and relative significance.[44]

The extent of the work completed by the İ.T.K. was unparalleled in
the history of the empire since the sixteenth century and was reported
systematically to the government.[45] We shall follow the rebuilding of
Hocapaşa by reviewing three reports, dating from 1866, 1868, and 1869.

The 1866 Report. In less than one year, the İ.T.K. completed the
construction of a street network equaling a total length of 3,420 meters.
This network consisted of the three types of streets established in the
initial regulation. However, the classification was revised to conform to
the 1863 Street and Building Regulation, discussed above. The major
avenues (*büyük caddeler*), divided into two subcategories, 19.00 meters
and 15.20 meters wide, formed the first category. The second, the medium-
sized avenues (*orta caddeler*), likewise had two categories, 11.50 meters
and 7.60 meters wide. The third category covered the side streets (*yan
sokaklar*), which were only 6.00 meters wide.[46]

Topography and existing buildings influenced the planning schemes.
The Sirkeci and Cağaloğlu areas were not only hilly, but also dotted with
many monuments, such as mosques or other large-scale stone buildings.
The new street system was designed to conform to the topography, while
still preserving the monuments. For example, two big curves dictated
by the contours of the land were incorporated into Aziziye Caddesi just
before it reached Babıali. To the west of Aziziye Caddesi, Hamidiye
Caddesi and its intersection with two other roads were arranged so that
the two small mosques, and farther to the west, a large *medrese* (Mustafa
Ağa Medresesi), which had survived the fire, were not demolished in the
rebuilding process.

Construction of infrastructure accompanied the road building activity.
Sewage lines, equaling a total length of 2,660 meters, were built under
Mahmudiye Caddesi, Nuruosmaniye Caddesi, and Kumkapı Caddesi.[47]

The commission also took the initiative to help the residents rebuild
their houses and shops in brick. The reason for the persistent use of timber
construction despite the previous regulations was economic: timber was
much cheaper, whereas the taxes on brick and cement made these materials unaffordable for mass housing. To resolve this problem, the İ.T.K. set
up a factory to make bricks and cement, which were sold tax-free to those
rebuilding their houses. If bought from the İ.T.K.'s factory, 100 bricks
cost 135 *kuruş*, or 115 *kuruş* less than the open market price. The price
of cement was reduced from 9 *kuruş* per *kantar* to 5.5 *kuruş* per *kantar*.[48] Taxes on brick and cement produced by privately owned factories
were also abolished.[49] To help with transportation costs, certain roads at
strategic points were given construction priorities. The İ.T.K. was of the

opinion that the connection of the Sirkeci quay and Babıali (via Aziziye Caddesi), for example, facilitated the transport of materials.[50]

The 1868 Report. In this follow-up report two years later, the İ.T.K. focused on future projects. The most urgent problems outlined in the 1866 report had been dealt with. The commission's success led to larger planning decisions in 1868, with the entire city becoming a design project for the İ.T.K., whose concerns now went beyond the provision an efficient communication network. The İ.T.K. directed its attention to the accentuation of main monuments by clearing their immediate surroundings. A proposal was put forward to tear down the wooden houses adjacent to Hagia Sophia and around the Süleymaniye complex in order to provide unobstructed views of these monuments.[51] This was an idea borrowed from contemporary Western urban preservation concepts, and in particular from Haussmann, who claimed that monuments were glorified by isolation.[52] The rules of Haussmann were not rigorously applied, but preservation of buildings with historic value did become a goal of the İ.T.K., as illustrated by the policy pursued during the enlargement of the Divanyolu.[53]

Because the Divanyolu's projected width was 19.00 meters, a considerable amount of the built-up area on both sides had to be demolished. The presence of many monuments along this artery, the oldest in Istanbul, made the took difficult and incremental.

Until the Hocapaşa fire, Constantine's Column, which once marked the center of Constantine's elliptical forum, was hidden amid a dense residential fabric. Julia Pardoe, an English traveler, described its sad state in 1839:

> ... its beauty is entirely gone, as it has suffered so severely from the repeated conflagrations in its immediate vicinity, that it is cracked in every direction, and merely kept together by a strong wirework, which has been carefully woven about it. The pedestal upon which it stands measures thirty feet at its base, and is rendered interesting by the fact, that several portions of the Holy Cross were built up within it and that the space amid which it stood consequently became a popular place of prayer, every mounted passenger reverently alighting from his horse as he passed before it; but the Moslem, not recognizing the divinity of the relics enshrined within its solid masonry, nor the sanctity of the spot thus hallowed, have surrounded the pillar on every side with mean and unsightly houses; and it is only in one solitary direction that the anxious antiquary can obtain a satisfactory view of this singular monument.[54]

These "mean" and "unsightly" houses, most of which were burned in 1865 anyway, were torn down and a small triangular space (Çemberlitaş Meydanı) was cleared around the column. The İ.T.K. did not elaborate on the historical significance of Constantine's Column, but it can be assumed that the attention Western scholars lavished on the city's Byzantine heritage had, by then, played an important role in the commission's decision.[55] Not only the houses, but also several shops and a

29

section of a *han* were demolished, along with part of the Çemberlitaş Bath (1583).[56] The sliced dome of the Çemberlitaş Bath survives as the hallmark of İ.T.K.'s activities on the Divanyolu. The commission proposed the construction of ten new three-story retail buildings. These new shops were expected to create a handsome (*yakışıklı*) and showy (*nümayişli*) environment.[57]

The Atik Ali Paşa complex, across the street from Constantine's Column, was a rare example of the fifteenth-century preclassical Ottoman style in Istanbul. The original ensemble consisted of a mosque, a *tekke*, an *imaret*, and a *medrese*—the mosque and the *medrese* being the monu-

29. The Divanyolu, circa 1900. On the right side of the street are the Çemberlitaş Bath with its sliced dome, Constantine's Column, and the Mosque of Atik Ali Paşa.

30. *The Hippodrome, upper left, viewed from Hagia Sophia, circa 1900.*
On the right is the beginning of the Divanyolu and the Firuzağa Mosque.
In the foreground is Hagia Sophia Square with its newly planted trees.

mental components. Part of the *medrese* was sliced off and its gate pulled
back so as not to encroach upon the Divanyolu.[58]

The Köprülü complex, built in 1659, had a *medrese*, a library, and
a mausoleum; only the mausoleum projected into the Divanyolu and
was therefore dismantled and reconstructed in its present location neatly
lining the enlarged Divanyolu.[59] Its form complemented the mausoleum
of Mahmut II built across the road in 1840.

The northern edge of the Hippodrome was obstructed by a number
of buildings added to the Firuzağa Mosque, another fifteenth-century
monument. These buildings were demolished, creating a more conspicuous
meeting point between the Divanyolu (referred to proudly in the 1868
report as the wide avenue [*cadde-i cesir*]) and the Hippodrome.[60] At the
same time, the Firuzağa Mosque was accentuated.

A very controversial issue was the destruction of cemeteries to make
way for roads. Because cemeteries occupied the gardens of mosques and
külliyes, they were distributed throughout the city and, in fact, often were
placed in the centers of neighborhoods. The decision to regularize the
urban fabric brought with it the inevitable question of whether to remove
the cemeteries or to build over them. Both alternatives were at odds with

30

the religious sentiments of the Muslim community. At one point, Grand Vizier Fuat Paşa was even accused of being "French-like" (*frenkperes*) for allowing disrespectful treatment of the dead.[61] His defense was that of a Westernized bureaucrat determined to bring modernization at all costs: he argued with his fundamentalist opponents that his constructive work would surely please the souls of the dead.[62] With the grand vizier's approval, sections of the Sinan Paşa and Atik Ali Paşa cemeteries became part of the Divanyolu.

The 1869 Report. Server Efendi, the mayor of the city and perhaps the most influential member of the İ.T.K., wrote the third report himself.[63] He described the work completed by the İ.T.K. and outlined the future planning targets on a map.[64] Once again, all municipal improvements (*tanzimat-ı belediye*) were to follow these guidelines and to conform to the general enlargement and embellishment principles spelled out by the commission.

The main difference between this report and previous reports was that the Hocapaşa fire was not even mentioned. The goal of the report was the creation of a general plan that would "add a further beauty to the existing beauties of Istanbul." The Hocapaşa fire and the area it defined, were no longer a matter of much consequence to Server Efendi, who began his report with a summary of the tasks to be undertaken on the north side of the Golden Horn.

There the road network around the royal headquarters at Dolmabahçe and Çırağan previously had been improved. But, the sultan's move to Dolmabahçe made the regularization of the streets through the Tophane hills a matter of some urgency. In addition, Server Efendi proposed to cut a 15.20-meter-wide road that would follow the coastline from the Dolmabahçe Mosque to Kabataş. This improvement would also involve clearing the small boats from the quay (they would use the new port near the Çırağan Palace) to provide space for a "wonderful and spacious park" on the water.[65] Server Efendi's last scheme for the northern side of the Golden Horn was to widen the roads that climbed the hill from Tophane to the Austrian Embassy. Server Efendi felt this road was especially significant, for as one of the main connectors from the shore to the Grande Rue de Pera, it was among the first places that foreign visitors would see. The concern to please the Western eye thus became a design criterion.[66]

In Istanbul, the enlargement of the Divanyolu was completed, and with the demolition of an irregular block, it was connected to Beyazit Square. The regularized Divanyolu consisted of a wide and straight vehicular strip with pedestrian sidewalks, which prompted Server Efendi to exclaim happily, "just like in the European cities."[67] At the eastern end of the Divanyolu, the buildings adjacent to Hagia Sophia were demolished and a square was created in front of the church.

Server Efendi's lowest priority was repair of street surfaces. Although he noted the miserable state of the streets in the burned neighborhoods, he

31

31. Hagia Sophia Square, circa 1900

did not refer to specific locations. The general tone of his report suggests that the goals of the İ.T.K. were to give the city a certain monumentality according to European styles and values; providing services to the burned residential neighborhoods reads as a secondary concern. The İ.T.K. had substituted its initial goal of rebuilding the entire Hocapaşa quarter with that of creating European-inspired arteries in the prestigious parts of the capital. It was around this same time, in 1869, that the commission disintegrated.[68] Nonetheless, the four-year period from 1865 to 1869 was the most active phase of urban planning in nineteenth-century Istanbul. The İ.T.K. established the main arteries of the city on both sides of the Golden Horn, cleared the areas surrounding the most outstanding monuments, and provided extensive infrastructure.[69] The commission's work serves Istanbul even today, in a sense supporting the historian Osman Nuri Ergin's controversial statement that "the big fire of Hocapaşa brought more happiness than disaster to Istanbul."[70]

32. *Extent of the 1870 Pera fire*

The 1870 Pera Fire and the Grand Plan

In June 1870, the great fire (*harik-i kebir*) of Pera destroyed more than three thousand buildings. The fire originated in a house on Feridiye Sokağı near Taksim; a strong wind spread the flames toward the west, where the area defined by Tarlabaşı, Taksim, the Grande Rue and Galatasaray was destroyed.[71]   32

In an effort to cope with the disaster, the government created a commission of engineers and architects to determine the best method of rebuilding the suburb.[72] The commission responded with an ambitious and financially unrealistic plan for a "nouvelle ville."[73] The proposal projected onto the burned site an urban design plan with large squares, wide boulevards, and modern edifices, such as theaters and hotels. Realizing the immense financial commitment required to effect the scheme, the government asked for modifications. A second plan was prepared by the commission in which all monuments and most of the public squares were eliminated. Furthermore, road widths were reduced from 20.00 meters to 11.50 meters and from 12.20 meters to 9.00 meters. Even the width of the Boulevard Tarla-Bachi, formerly envisioned as 30.00 meters, was reduced to 20.00 meters, the scale of the Divanyolu.[74]   33

Two public squares were preserved from the first plan, however. The central square, where seven arteries met, served as a magnet. The spacious Boulevard Tarla-Bachi and its western extension, the Boulevard Toz-Coparan, both now wider than the Grande Rue, were foreseen as traversing the Place d'Armes in Taksim, ultimately connecting with the Boulevard Ayazma. Thus, an attempt was made to shift the main axis of Pera to the north, to the core of the "nouvelle ville." The total street surface was increased from 83,220 square meters in the pre-fire "ancienne ville" to 143,070 square meters.[75] However, the plan had a serious shortcoming: it did not take into account the irregular topography of the area, but treated it as a flat surface.

Property owners heatedly protested the second plan, fearing that because the projected streets were so wide, their lot sizes would be substantially reduced. Also, they objected to the extensive and expensive construction process, which would take a long time and create hardships for the district's residents. Instead, they proposed the regularization of Hammalbaşı, Tiyatro, and Deveux streets only and claimed that the rest had already been satisfactorily regularized.[76] Acknowledging the complaints of the property owners, the government abandoned the project. Only the principal streets, those recommended by the residents, were rebuilt.

What transformations would Pera have experienced if this project had been realized? The Grande Rue would have become a secondary artery as the Boulevard Tarla-Bachi and its extension, Boulevard Toz-Coparan, were designed to become the monumental spine of Pera. Shifting the

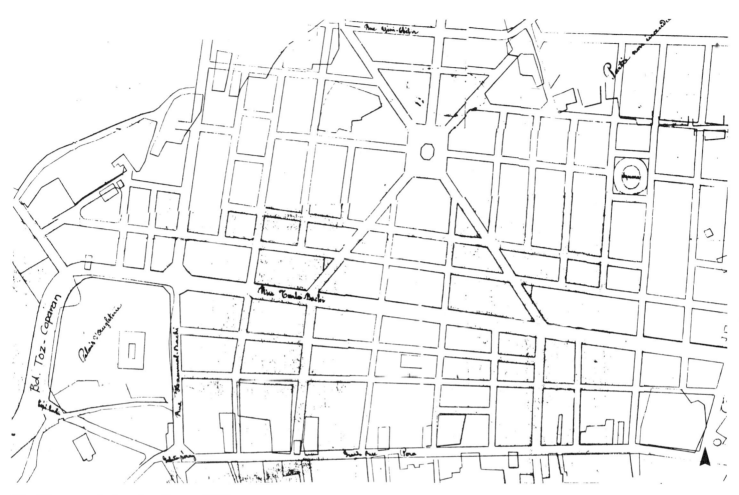

33. The grand plan for Pera, 1870

crowds away from the long and narrow Grande Rue was, in fact, not a bad idea. However, by 1870, the Grande Rue was flanked with the finest European-style buildings in the capital. To create another monumental strip was neither financially justifiable nor feasible.

The 1870 project proposed a second fundamental change in Pera by the introduction of two public squares. These would bring some breathing space to the tight fabric; but, as topography was not taken into consideration, the scheme would have to be revised again. Finally, a comprehensive regularization of the street network was proposed. However, this did not mean a substantial reorganization of blocks. The scale of the residential blocks and streets would have remained unchanged—a phenomenon observed time and again in the replanned zones on both sides of the Golden Horn.

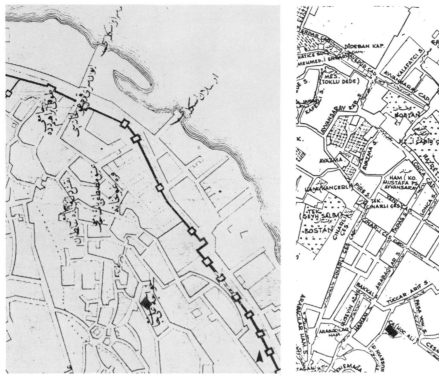

34. *Plan of Ayvansaray, circa 1850*

35. *Plan of Ayvansaray, circa 1870*

36. *Plan of Samatya, circa 1850*

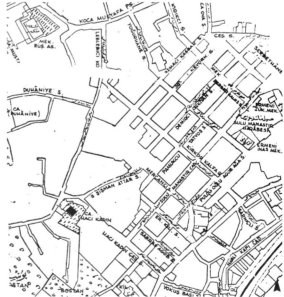

37. *Plan of Samatya, circa 1870*

Small-Scale Fires: Neighborhood Regularization

Fires that affected relatively small areas in the inner neighborhoods led to a patchy regularization of the urban fabric. The redesigned neighborhoods were not connected to each other or to major arteries, but stood as geometric entities amid the overall irregularity. In the absence of monuments, the *tarla* rule could be rigorously applied and grid patterns established. Nonetheless, topography and pre-fire lot sizes influenced the street layouts, and frequently resulted in grids that were not perfectly regular.

There are many of these reorganized neighborhoods scattered throughout the Istanbul peninsula and, to a lesser degree, in Galata. The replanning of the Golden Horn neighborhood of Ayvansaray after a fire in 1861 and of Samatya on the Marmara shore in 1866 clearly demonstrates the main trends. Before the fire in Ayvansaray, 219 houses and shops were packed into an area of very small blocks along a tight street fabric having many dead ends. These shops and houses were rebuilt upon a new and geometric scheme, which led to a 28 percent loss from the pre-fire lot sizes.[77] The burned area of the Armenian neighborhood of Samatya was not as densely built up as Ayvansaray or other parts of the city—a feature typical of the southwestern parts of the peninsula, close to the Theodosian walls. The İ.T.K. created a new settlement in Samatya, which was much more compact and regular, and did not resemble the pre-fire pattern.[78] As in Ayvansaray, however, the connections to the rest of the city were not worked out. The straight, new streets of Samatya met the surrounding roads haphazardly. Still, the resulting design was considered an example of modernization in city planning. The İ.T.K.'s 1868 report described the new streets of Samatya as "a checker-board pattern, and very large—just as observed in the most recently designed places in the world" (dünyada en yeni tanzim olunan memleketlere şebi olmak üzere santrançvari ve pek müstekim).[79]

On the smallest scale, reorganization after a fire meant providing a few wider and straighter streets. The 1863 fire that destroyed nineteen buildings in Beşiktaş is a good example of small-scale regularization.[80] An imperial decree that ordered the replanning of this area emphasized the need for wide arteries here because of its prestigious location close to the Dolmabahçe Palace.[81] The new streets were made much wider and more regular than the pre-fire streets, but the lot sizes and shapes remained unaffected.

NEW ARTERIES

Istanbul's piecemeal planning in the wake of major fires throughout the second half of the nineteenth century was paralleled by a construction and regularization activity that encompassed its major arteries (those unaffected by fires) and its waterfront. Prompted primarily by necessity and, to a lesser degree, by image-making concerns, this operation did not

38. Small-scale regularization in Beşiktaş, after the 1863 fire

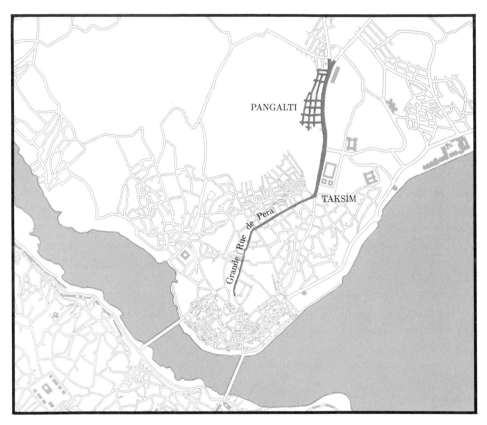

39. The new neighborhood of Pangaltı and its connection to Taksim

match in scale the reorganization that followed the fires. Nevertheless, it complemented the grander schemes and contributed to the creation of a more "orderly" image—at least, in the prestigious quarters of the capital. Planning and construction of new roads was almost exclusively limited to the northern side of the Golden Horn, following the needs of the area and the pattern of its growth.

The 1848 decision to create a new neighborhood in Pangaltı was the earliest step taken to promote orderly growth on the northern side of the Golden Horn. Population density in the mid-nineteenth century in Pera had reached intolerable levels, so in 1848 an imperial order was issued to develop the 272,800-square-meter area opposite the Military School (Mekteb-i Hayriye) into a residential neighborhood. The plan envisaged ten main avenues, each 15.20 meters wide with 2.30-meter sidewalks on both sides—a new concept for the city—and a 10.60-meter paved vehicular strip in the middle.[82] The secondary 6.80-meter streets would also be paved and would have 1.15-meter sidewalks. Infrastructure (water and sewage lines) was to be incorporated into the street network, and brick and cement construction was made mandatory for all buildings.[83]

39

The area defined by this 1848 decree roughly equaled eighteen to twenty residential blocks. Yet by 1870, only twelve blocks had been rebuilt. The resulting neighborhood, though noteworthy for its relative regularity, still did not match the ambitious guidelines given by the imperial order. But Pangaltı determined the direction of expansion from Taksim toward Şişli. It also established a spine that followed the main highway connecting Pera to Büyükdere, the seat of the summer residences for some European embassies on the Bosporus.

Between 1858 and 1870, the Sixth District assumed all replanning activities in Galata. The opening of Karaköy Square in 1858 marked the beginning of a new and intensive phase of activity in the district. By 1858, Karaköy was a densely populated and heavily traveled area, owing to its growing importance as an international commercial center. To ease congestion and aid police control, an imperial order was issued, giving the Sixth District the responsibility of creating a square in an orderly manner (*heyet-i muntazama*). Even though previous efforts in this direction had been met by the protests of property owners, expropiation was now seen as inevitable for the public good. The square was built at the foot of the Galata Bridge, possibly corresponding to the site of what was once the medieval city's piazzetta.[84]

Another significant task undertaken in this period was the connecting of the new neighborhoods of Pangaltı (planned in 1848) and Taksim, which was little more than a large open space covered with Christian cemeteries at the northern end of the Grande Rue. A wide road (*tarık-ı vaz*) between Taksim and the Military School in Pangaltı, first proposed in 1862, was completed in 1869.[85] This tree-lined artery was soon extended to Şişli.

The concept of public parks was introduced to the Ottoman capital during the 1860s. In 1864, when the road between Taksim and Pangaltı was under construction, the Christian cemeteries in Taksim were moved to Şişli, and a garden was planned for the area previously occupied by the cemeteries.[86] It took five years for the Taksim public park, the first of its kind in the Ottoman capital, to be realized. After the residents of Pera began pressuring the Sixth District Administration for the construction of this much-advertised breathing space, it was finally completed in 1869.[87] The park was a perfect rectangle, which had a symmetrical layout that combined formal Beaux-Arts principles in its central part with a looser and more picturesque scheme toward the edges.

40

Once completed, the Taksim Garden became the "promenade favorite" of the Pera community.[88] De Amicis wrote that: "... on Sunday afternoons it is crowded with people and equipages, all the gay world of Pera pouring out to scatter itself among the beer-gardens, cafes, and pleasure resorts."[89]

During the summer season, music was played every afternoon, and visiting French and Italian groups performed plays and operettas. This

40. Plan of Taksim Park. To the left of the park are military barracks.

41. *A gate in the Galata walls, circa 1926*

atmosphere must have been considered quite immoral by the police, who prohibited Turkish women from walking or riding in carriages in the park, further accentuating the dichotomy between the lifestyles of the indigenous population and the Europeans.[90]

The Sixth District Administration designed another picturesque public garden in Tepebaşı.[91] The Tepebaşı Garden also served the Pera community. The Istanbul peninsula, however, would have to wait another fifty years for its public park. Not until 1916, under the Young Turk government, did mayor Celil Paşa convert a section of the Topkapı Palace Garden into a public park.[92]

To facilitate communication in the dense fabric of Galata, the city walls (excluding the tower) were demolished in 1863, and, following the nineteenth-century European practice, the area gained was used to open new streets and widen the existing ones. As noted in chapter one, the independence of Galata as a Genoese suburb in the fourteenth century was symbolized by the construction of its own walls, which encircled an area defined by the Azapkapı-Şişhane-Galata Tower-Tophane line.[93] The growth of Galata and the development of Pera after the 1840s, however, turned the walls into a serious obstacle to efficient communication between Pera and Galata.   *41*

An 1863 imperial order, which described the useless and obstructive nature of the walls and ordered their demolition, argued that the building materials as well as the area gained could be auctioned to provide a considerable contribution to city coffers. In addition, the area previously occupied by the walls could be used for widening roads and providing much needed space for new buildings.[94] The Pera community approved the demolition decision. The *Journal de Constantinople* stated in 1864 that with the walls torn down, Galata would gain a "physionomie moderne."[95]

After demolition was completed in 1865, the Sixth District Administration oversaw a number of new road construction projects.[96] In the   *42* west, Galata Yenikapı Caddesi and Şişhane Sokak, in the north, Büyük Hendek Sokak, and in the east, Boğazkesen Caddesi were built on the wall line. In February 1865, the portion near Mumhane Street was taken down and the street, referred to as the "dirtiest" in Galata by the *Journal de Constantinople*, was turned into "one of the most beautiful" arteries of the suburb, the prostitutes expelled, and the old wooden houses replaced by brick houses. The *Journal de Constantinople* quaintly pointed out the Oriental elements of the scene when it described the minarets at the vista of Mumcular Sokağı as having "a picturesque effect."[97]

The other two streets that underwent enlargement and regularization during these years were Yorgancılar from Karaköy to Azapkapı at the foot of the Old Bridge, and Galata Caddesi from Karaköy to Tophane. The idea was to connect the Bosporus shoreline to the two bridges spanning the Golden Horn.   *43*

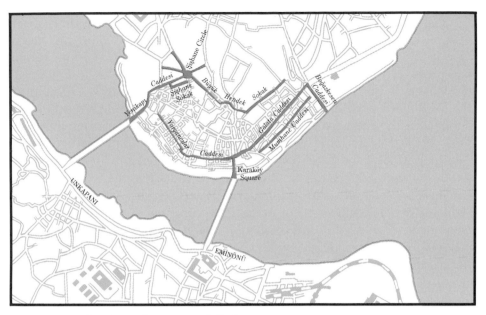

42. New and enlarged streets of Galata

43. The road connecting Karaköy to Tophane, circa 1900. On the right is the Nusretiye Mosque.

The last important planning task undertaken by the Sixth District Administration during this period was Şişhane Circle, along the main road leading from the Old Bridge to the Grande Rue. The administation had provided funds in the 1868 budget to build itself a new headquarters in Şişhane at the top of the southern slope of Pera heights.[98] Placed at the focal point of Şişhane Circle's major axis, the "Sixth District Palace" dominated the rond-point, which itself was a reflection of contemporary Parisian forms—perhaps, even inspired by the Place de l'Etoile (see fig. 24). In spite of the differences in the scale (the Şişhane Circle was much smaller), there are certain similarities with Haussmannian urban design schemes. For example, the Sixth District Palace, at the vista of the largest radial artery, is reminiscent of many Parisian avenues ending at modern monuments.[99] However, unlike their Parisian counterparts, the Şişhane arteries formed an isolated pattern, which had no main connections to the rest of the city network. Hence, as was often the case when European urban design models were imitated, the resemblance remained on the formalistic level—and then only to a limited degree (see fig. 42).

From the dissolution of the Sixth District Administration in 1870 to the Young Turk Revolution of 1908, there was a sharp decline in road-building activities. The city as a whole was neglected and a great portion of the available funds was spent on the street network serving the palaces in and around Beşiktaş.[100] The work undertaken elsewhere was insignificant and patchy in nature. In fact, the impact of the tramlines was stronger than any other planning decision during this period. The concession to construct and operate trams was given to the Tramway Company on the condition that whenever necessary, the roads would be enlarged and repaired by the city. Therefore, only main arteries where the tramlines passed underwent regularization.

The main emphasis, however, was once more on the road that connected the palaces along the Bosporus from Dolmabahçe to Ortaköy.[101] During this period, Yıldız Palace, on the Beşiktaş-Ortaköy hill, gained great importance as the main seat of Abdülhamit II. The road regularization and repair activities hence shifted toward the Yıldız Palace and toward Ortaköy.[102] At the same time, the Ortaköy River was drained and a road built on it.[103]

These projects marked the extent of construction under Abdülhamit II, whose reign was rich in imagination, if not in practice. (The most grandiose and utopian urban design projects for the capital were prepared during this period, as we shall see in chapter five.) The earlier efforts to improve and embellish the city faded during his long reign. However, a rather feeble attempt to improve the city's appearance came from Mazhar Paşa, mayor of Istanbul from 1878 to 1888, who ordered the planting of trees along the main avenues in the vicinity of Beşiktaş as well as on the Divanyolu. Under Rıdvan Paşa, mayor of Istanbul from 1888 to 1904, road-building activity consisted merely of surface paving in some central locations.[104]

CLEANING THE WATERFRONT

One of the most striking features of Istanbul is its relationship to water. The sea is everywhere in Istanbul. One comes face to face with it at unexpected turns, even in the midst of the densest quarters. Many major routes either lead to the water or follow its course, while hills on both sides of the Golden Horn afford spectacular views.

Water provides not only pretty scenery for the residents of Istanbul, but also a convenient and pleasant means of transportation. It acts as a recreational park: the daily commute on the deck of a ferry allows the inhabitants of the city to enjoy the fresh air and lovely views. At the same time, the water provides the setting for a marketplace: many goods, ranging from seafood to vegetables to clothing, are sold from boats to those along the embankments. Sidewalks end at the sea with no railings to separate pedestrians from the water.

This unique relationship of man to water created an additional challenge for the planners of nineteenth-century Istanbul. The waterfront had to be cleaned and regularized for three main reasons. First, the increase in trade and sea traffic called for orderly quays. In fact, foreign shipping companies, through their embassies, often put pressure on the city administration to rebuild the docks. Second, the unsanitary conditions—a public good concern—had to be ameliorated. Third, the city's urban image had to be improved. The waterfront was too chaotic, too dirty, and it embarrassed the order-conscious Ottoman elite, for whom beauty had come to mean regularity.

The waterfront in question involved the shoreline from Sirkeci to Balat on the Istanbul side of the Golden Horn and from Azapkapı to Tophane on the Galata side, including the harbor itself. In this area, the old wooden commercial quays were flanked by warehouses, shops, and *han*s. The customs offices were in Tophane and Sirkeci.[105] After the 1840s, the growth in international trade as well as in population led to a dramatic increase in sea traffic. The old quays could no longer adequately accommodate the transportation of huge quantities of commercial goods or the daily commute of the capital's residents between Istanbul, Galata, Üsküdar, and the Bosporus villages.[106]

The idea of coordinating operations to regularize the waterfront was first proposed in 1879. Before this date, quays needing repair were fixed individually upon imperial orders. The most crowded points naturally received the greatest attention. For example, the Karaköy quay, which, according to the complaints of its residents had turned into a genuine ruin, was repaired in 1848. An additional quay was built there the next year

44. *Eminönü quay, circa 1900. In the background is the Valide Mosque, to the right is the Galata Bridge.*

to meet the growing need of the customs.[107] From then on, the customs' quay underwent systematic repair.[108]

In a few cases, embankment construction transcended mere patching to become urban design. In 1846, for example, the coffee shops and an abandoned garden along the Tophane shore were expropriated to build a wide quay. All construction was forbidden on the new waterfront square, justified by the argument that the nearby sea traffic required extensive open areas.[109]

In 1855, in response to pressure from foreign embassies, an important decision was made to reorganize the harbor and the docks. A map of the harbor was prepared and a regulation concerning navigation was passed. The goal was to facilitate the operation of warships and commercial ships as well as commuter ferries.[110] In fact, the establishment of a regular commuter ferry service in 1851 contributed considerably to the waterfront improvement. After this date, the Bosporus villages started to acquire new quays. In an effort that paralleled the emphasis on road building in this area, the Beşiktaş and Dolmabahçe embankments were regularized following the completion of the Dolmabahçe Palace. The Beşiktaş quay was totally reconstructed in 1857 and the Dolmabahçe quay was built in 1864.[111]

On the Istanbul side, the area from Sirkeci to Eminönü, to the southern foot of the Galata Bridge, was repaired repeatedly. For example, the Eminönü quay underwent a major reconstruction in 1848. The section between Yalıköşkü in Sirkeci and Eminönü was substantially reorganized in 1858. Not only was this strip rebuilt, but also several large stone office buildings were erected for the customs.[112]

In 1863, the city passed a new regulation concerning privately constructed quays. This regulation stipulated that those who wanted to build new embankments in front of their properties on the waterfront would have to apply to the Ministry of Public Works (Nafia Nezareti) for permission. Permits would be issued only if proposals did not interfere with the public good. To encourage private involvement in city building, those who donated a portion of their privately financed quays for public use would be held exempt from taxation.[113] This was the first step toward regularizing the waterfront for public use.

In 1876, Eugène Henri Gavand, the French engineer responsible for construction of the Istanbul Tünel, proposed the widening of the embankment along the Sea of Marmara by filling in the sea to create an additional area of 2,200,000 square meters. Furthermore, he suggested building an embankment 2,760 meters long from Yedikule in the west to the Topkapı Palace Gardens in the east. His ambitious, but unrealized scheme was part of an even more grandiose plan, which included an extensive subway system for Istanbul and Galata.[114]

It was another Frenchman, Marius Michel (referred to as Michel Paşa in Ottoman documents), who was issued a seventy-five-year concession in

1879 to rebuild the waterfront in exchange for a certain percentage of the tax collected on imported and exported goods.[115] Although difficulties of construction in the soft soil of the Golden Horn delayed operations considerably, Michel Paşa obtained a second contract in 1890. This time the government urged him to establish a company in eighteen months and to complete all construction before 1904. Michel Paşa's contract called for the rebuilding of the strip between Sirkeci and Unkapanı on the Istanbul side, and Tophane and Azapkapı on the Galata side. In return, his firm was given the concession to establish and operate the docks and the warehouses for a period of eighty-five years. Providing rail transportation along the waterfront became another of the firm's responsibilities. Trams and omnibuses could be operated here jointly with the Tramway Company.[116]

This contract brought with it zoning and urban design decisions. A 20-meter strip was established between the new quays and the residential areas. This strip was to be divided into three parts: a 3.00-meter pedestrian sidewalk, a 9.00-meter vehicular road, and an 8.00-meter loading strip next to the quay.[117] As this operation was deemed to be for the public good, in cases of conflict between the company and property owners, the expropriation law was to be enforced.[118] In exchange, the firm was required to maintain the newly built docks, quays, and roads.[119]

The scope of the work undertaken by Michel Paşa's engineering firm and the benefit to be gained was warmly welcomed by the European community, who hoped for an increase in trade profits and land values. As one newspaper put it:

The creation of embankments will open large arteries in Galata and in Istanbul, along the two banks [of the Golden Horn] to the grand profit of public health. Communication will be facilitated, commerce will be expedited, smuggling will be prevented . . . property values will increase.[120]

Michel Paşa's firm began construction in 1892. Galata was given priority and by the end of 1895, the work on the Galata side was completed: a 758-meter quay and several new buildings were erected between Tophane and Karaköy for the customs.[121] The portion of road passing in front of these custom-houses was 280 meters long and 19.00 meters wide. The area in front of the quay was 8.00 meters wide, and there was a spacious concrete yard at the back.[122]

The construction of the embankment on the Istanbul side took longer. Work started in 1894 and was completed in 1900. A 370-meter quay was built from Sirkeci to the foot of the Galata Bridge in Eminönü.[123]

According to the 1890 contract, Michel Paşa's firm was responsible for the building of the embankments between the two bridges on both sides of the Golden Horn. These areas created immense difficulties because of the soft soil and the high concentration of workshops and produce quays. The firm was not enthusiastic about undertaking such a demanding

45

45. The regularized quay between Karaköy and Tophane, circa 1900

task, and in 1897, the government decided to postpone the embankment construction between the two bridges.[124] Later, a few futile attempts *46* were made to regularize these quays. For example, in 1902, a four-person commission, formed by the representatives of the cadastral office and the prefecture, inspected the shores of the Golden Horn between the two bridges with the intention of demolishing the illegally constructed quays and buildings. A few months later, another commission, this time including the chief engineer of the Ministry of Commerce and Public Works, Monsieur Leclerq, and architect Vallaury, estimated the cost of the proposed work, but no further action was taken.[125]

The 1890 contract stated that Michel Paşa's firm was to build new custom-houses, stores, warehouses, and administrative offices on both sides of the Golden Horn. But government engineers were to control and approve the plans and construction methods. All buildings were to be *kargir* and constructed in a perfect manner (*heyet-i mükemmeliye*).[126] A dispute erupted over the *kargir* construction, which strictly meant either stone or brick to the Ottoman inspectors. Michel Paşa's firm insisted on using reinforced concrete, a construction method successfully employed in Europe and America since the 1880s. In 1907, after a two-year debate, both parties agreed upon the use of reinforced concrete. Construction took three years and was finally completed in 1910. In Galata, the new warehouses and offices—multistoried buildings in a spare, neoclassical style—occupied an area of 7,000 square meters; in Istanbul the area was 13,436 square meters. However, the cost of the Galata buildings was twice as much as those of Istanbul. Construction costs in Galata amounted to 1,242,797 francs while in Istanbul the figure was only 620,000 francs.[127]

46. The waterfront between the bridges on the Golden Horn, circa 1900

Post-Tanzimat urban planning in the Ottoman capital was, therefore, determined first by the fires that periodically leveled portions of the city, and second, by the necessity to provide access to the now fashionable and newly developing areas. The neighborhoods razed by fires conveniently eliminated the controversial demolition process and facilitated expropriation.

The new schemes were based on the concept of bringing order to the irregular street pattern. The rationale was practical: fire prevention and police control, so difficult to provide in the pre-fire fabric, would be greatly facilitated by an efficiently communicating network. In addition, infrastructure could be incorporated easily and economically into the wide streets. But this was not all. The Westernized Turks were now acquainted with Europe. They had observed with admiration the rebuilding of the European capitals and wanted to fashion their own capital after European models.

47. Istanbul peninsula, regularized neighborhoods

For all these reasons the Ringstrasse of Vienna and especially the avenues of Paris became recurring points of reference. If the empire did not have the financial means to undertake Parisian-scale rebuilding operations, it could at least regularize its urban patterns. The terms used repeatedly in official documents define the word that most appropriately describes Haussmann's work in Paris, "regularization":[128] improvement (*islahat*), reorganization (*tanzimat*), regularizing (*tanzifat*), enlargement (*tevessu*), and regular pattern (*heyet-i muntazama*).

Because of the large-scale fires and the higher densities, the regularization efforts changed the urban fabric more noticeably in the Istanbul peninsula than on the northern side of the Golden Horn, which was still in an early growth phase during these seventy years. A number of previously mazelike neighborhoods in Istanbul acquired regular layouts, but, as mentioned earlier, their scale did not alter dramatically, and their communication with other parts of the city did not necessarily improve. Islands of regularized zones were created, yet their regularity did not affect the lifestyles of the inhabitants.

47

The housing patterns, scale, and even construction methods remained unchanged. For example, although *kargir* construction, encouraged from the 1830s on, was enforced in the 1882 Building Regulation, exceptions were made for the worthless (*değersiz*) and marginal neighborhoods, where the residents could not afford to rebuild their houses in *kargir*.[129] However, this provision of the Building Regulation found a much wider application, and, as an 1898 imperial order records, permission for timber construction was granted even in honorable (*şerefli*) and valuable (*değerli*) parts of the city,[130] such as the Kılıç Ali Paşa neighborhood in the vicinity of the Yıldız Palace, the residence of Abdülhamit II.[131] A large number of houses were thus constructed according to previous methods. Nonetheless, there was a difference: the houses now neatly flanked the edges of the new and straight streets; encroachments were largely eliminated.

48
49

When the situation in Istanbul is compared with Haussmann's rebuilding of Paris, we get a clearer understanding of why the regularization operations executed in Istanbul did not change the lives of the inhabitants. First, in Paris, Haussmann's avenues cut through the medieval fabric and formed an unobstructed citywide communication network. However, in Istanbul, fires determined the boundaries of regularization, and interconnections between the individually replanned neighborhoods were not addressed. The neighborhoods thus maintained their privacy to a large extent. Second, the new Parisian residential buildings on Haussmann's arteries constituted a sharp break from dense, organic patterns that existed before the 1850s. These residential structures were restricted to the same height, depending on the width of the streets. They followed similar layouts, and shared the same architectural language.[132] As we have seen above, Istanbul's housing patterns did not undergo such homogenizing changes.

Also, unlike in Istanbul, where the owners themselves rebuilt their houses in the regularized neighborhoods, private developers undertook the construction of the new Parisian structures. Consequently, the lower

49. A regularized street lined with wooden houses on the Istanbul peninsula

48. A crooked street on the Istanbul peninsula

income groups that lived in these neighborhoods prior to the replanning of the city's circulation network were pushed elsewhere, and the new Parisian bourgeoisie moved into the spacious flats lining Haussmann's avenues. No such displacement took place in Istanbul because the intrinsic qualities of the neighborhoods did not change radically. Nevertheless, the physical transformations in Istanbul affected to some degree the relation of the inhabitants to their neighborhoods. This was most striking in the improved communication in the residential areas. With the opening up of the street network in the replanned neighborhoods, and especially the abolition of culs-de-sac, the streets lost their semiprivate character and became "thoroughfares."

The communication network in the commercial and administrative core of Istanbul improved significantly. Connection of the Eminönü quay via the commercial zones to Beyazit and the Divanyolu was achieved. Beyazit was also linked to the Marmara shore, and the widened Divanyolu was given a new monumentality. In fact, with the area cleared around Constantine's Column, the punctuated entrance to the Hippodrome, and the newly opened Hagia Sophia Square, this artery now regained some of the glory that it had once possessed as the *mese* of Byzantine Constantinople.

The transformation of Galata's street network was relatively unimportant. The suburb acquired a few wide and straight arteries, but since they were scattered unevenly, there was not much overall improvement. Curiously, even though it was Istanbul's fabric that was to be pierced by straight arteries and broken by patches of grids—patterns adopted from contemporary European trends—Galata still remained the most European city. The change in the street layout and the fabric did not affect Istanbul's urban image significantly. The lifestyle in the Istanbul peninsula maintained older patterns, whereas residents of Galata now tried to imitate the lifestyles in European cities. Hence, the symbols of modern living—office buildings, banks, theaters, hotels, department stores, and multistory apartment buildings—were abundant in Galata. These buildings, in contrast to Istanbul's Ottoman monuments, with their domes and minarets against a down-played residential fabric, gave the old Genoese suburb a strikingly different and definitely more nineteenth-century European appearance.

4.

Transportation

The introduction of modern transportation systems acted as a major catalyst in nineteenth-century cities. Facilitated by broad, new arteries, smooth and fast communication was now possible between different urban neighborhoods. Better transportation also provided room for physical expansion, while at the same time enhancing it.

Istanbul's geographical setting called for the extensive use of water transportation in the form of steamboats, in addition to the more common land transportation systems. The city's communication network developed as four interconnected systems: water transportation, horse-drawn tramways, a short subway, and trains.

The empire had neither the capital nor the technical expertise to undertake the construction of these systems. Therefore, the government issued concessions to private investors, who were granted monopolies to operate the systems they constructed for a specified number of years. The government guaranteed profits, agreed to meet any deficits from the state budget, and helped the investors deal with problems such as expropriation. Private enterprise had a great advantage in these projects: it did not run the usual risks of capitalist investors in the West, because its deficit was to be met and its operations facilitated by the Ottoman government. However, issuing concessions, which seemed to solve the initial capital investment problem for the Ottoman government, resulted in long-term losses to the state budget.

WATER TRANSPORTATION

Istanbul, Galata, Üsküdar, and the Bosporus villages had been densely populated for many centuries. For example, the 1477 population outside Istanbul's walls was estimated between 185,000 and 195,000; in the sixteenth century, it was almost 400,000. The need for communication across the water, and especially to and from the administrative center in Istanbul, resulted in the development of an early transportation system. Rowboats and barges connected the shores of the city before regular steamboat

50. Sea traffic in the harbor, circa 1836

service was established in 1851. From the focal point of Eminönü, there were three main lines followed by the rowboats: one to Galata, one to the Golden Horn villages, and one to the Bosporus villages on the European and Asian sides. The busiest line was between Galata and Eminönü.[1]

Each commuter boat was affiliated with a certain quay and was designated for transportation of local passengers and cargo. Collection of passengers and cargo from other locations was subject to permission from the customs officer. The operation worked as a jitney system with fares regulated by the city. Depending on the average number of passengers, the size of the commuter boats ranged from two- to eight- to twelve-oars. There was also a large number of private boats, usually owned by high government officers who resided along the Bosporus in summer. The size of a boat and the number of its oars indicated the owner's social status. The grand vizier, the *şeyhülislam*, and high-ranking bureaucrats had boats with twenty oars. In the eighteenth and nineteenth centuries, foreign ambassadors had four-oared boats, the number being increased to twenty by the mid-nineteenth century, paralleling the growing influence of the Western world.[2] The main advantage of sea travel was speed. For example, from Büyükdere to Eminönü was only an hour and a half by rowboat, but the same trip on horseback took four hours.[3]

By the mid-nineteenth century, Istanbul's sea traffic had grown quite heavy. In 1844, the number of rowboats used for public transportation 50 was 19,000, up from 1,400 in 1680 and 3,996 in 1802.[4] This increase led to a search for a better solution to sea travel. In 1850, two foreigners started operating a steamboat on the Bosporus, and in 1851, an imperial order set the conditions under which it would operate: it was to leave İstinye on the Bosporus every morning to go to Istanbul and return to İstinye in the evening, where it would remain overnight.[5]

An 1851 government report supporting the establishment of a company to regulate water transportation examined the situation. The report found that one steamboat was clearly insufficient for the large number of commuters. Many people were forced to take rowboats home if they missed the single steamboat. Providing more boats would lead to a more convenient schedule, which, in turn, would benefit larger groups of people. Besides, if the Bosporus were more conveniently connected to Istanbul, the villages could develop into year-round residential areas, instead of mere summer resorts. Consequently, the expense of keeping two houses, one in the city, the other on the Bosporus, would be reduced—an obvious economic advantage for residents.[6]

Şirket-i Hayriye, the first Ottoman corporation, was founded a few months after the 1851 report was issued. All Ottoman citizens could buy its shares; and Ottoman citizenship was required of all employees with the exception of the engineers. The first shareholders were, nevertheless, the members of the ruling elite: among them were the sultan himself, the *valide* sultan (the sultan's mother), Grand Vizier Reşit Paşa, Minister of War Mehmet Ali Paşa, banker M. Camondo, and the mayors of Bursa, Aydın, and Silistre. The first concession period was twenty-five years, but the corporation was given a ten-year extension in 1873 and a thirty-year extension in 1884.[7] Immediately after its formation, foreign boats were prohibited from carrying passengers between Istanbul, Üsküdar, and the Asian and European sides of the Bosporus—the routes of Şirket-i Hayriye's first six boats.[8] The Şirket-i Hayriye's boats were all made of wood with 60-horsepower engines and were named after villages along the Bosporus.[9]

The three successive regulations of Şirket-i Hayriye, dating from 1852, 1871, and 1888, provide valuable information about the company, its operation, and the evolution of water transportation in Istanbul during the second half of the nineteenth century. According to the 1852 regulation, the six boats operated only on the Bosporus line.[10] In addition to these six boats, Şirket-i Hayriye was asked to develop a boat design to be used for the transportation of carriages and animals. The corporation was also held responsible for building and maintaining its own quays, which an imperial order decreed were to be constructed of "massive wood."[11]

The 1888 regulation, which remained in effect until 1919, outlined seven routes. According to the schedules specified in this regulation, a boat would run every twenty or thirty minutes on the lines between Üsküdar and Eminönü, and between Istanbul (departing from Eminönü) and the villages along the Bosporus, the most heavily traveled routes. The

51
52

51. The Galata. *One of Şirket-i Hayriye's first boats.*   *52. The* Sahilbent. *Şirket-i Hayriye's first ferryboat.*

establishment of this transportation network finally linked the previously isolated Üsküdar to the capital. This new ferry system now permitted many people residing in Üsküdar to commute to Istanbul for work. The schedule of the boats to the Bosporus villages was not as frequent as the Üsküdar-Eminönü line, although in the summer more scheduled runs were added to handle the considerable increase in traffic.[12]

The Üsküdar-Beşiktaş and Harem-Kabataş lines, firmly established by 1888, also show that communication was developing rapidly between the Asian and the European sides. The remaining routes, the majority of which had to be regulated according to fluctuating needs, were between Eminönü and the Golden Horn villages, Eminönü and Yeşilköy, and finally, Eminönü and the Princes' Islands on the Sea of Marmara. The link to the Golden Horn villages facilitated access to workshops and factories, as well as to the area's crowded neighborhoods. The lines to Yeşilköy and to the Prince's Islands served the upper-class non-Muslims, who favored these places as summer resorts. In addition to the regular schedules, additional boats were operated on Fridays, Sundays, during Islamic religious feasts, and Ramazan nights, and on Easter day. There were also ferryboats that transported carriages and animals between Üsküdar and Kabataş, Üsküdar and Sirkeci, and Büyükdere and Hünkar.[13]

Although regular water transportation was begun with the intention of serving high government bureaucrats and Europeans residing seasonally on the Bosporus, as the extent of the 1881 schedule indicates, it soon turned into a mass transportation system that benefited everyone. Its public service character was enhanced further by the policy of fare reductions for children, soldiers, and students. Security agents working for the police, the gendarmery, and city government employees were issued free passes.[14]

To make the journey as pleasant as possible, the comfort of passengers was carefully considered in the 1888 regulation. The maximum number of people permitted in each compartment was determined; both classes (there were two classes on every boat) were to have comfortable seats; heating would be provided by stoves; gas lamps would be used in the evenings and on dark, cloudy days; boats would be ventilated after passengers disembarked at the last stop and before the return trip; and, special attention would be paid to the cleaning of bathrooms.[15] Given the length of the trip on the majority of Şirket-i Hayriye's routes, these services were all vital. Social and religious values were carefully accommodated as well: the company had to provide separate sections for men and women on both boats and in the waiting areas to avoid mixing (*ihtilat*) and hence to facilitate obedience to moral codes (*usul-u edebiyeye riayet*).[16]

Creating the proper ambiance was another major concern. To this end, "ugly furniture" was not to be allowed in the compartments; the crew was urged to wear clean uniforms (*bir temiz kıyafet-i mahsusa*);[17] tables and shelves were to be provided for small parcels, but larger packages had to be stowed in the hold along with dogs and sheep; coffee and other beverages would be sold by waiters in uniforms; and, beggars would not be allowed on the boats.[18]

The concern over image sometimes reached exaggerated levels (and proportionally exaggerated expenses). For example, the boats purchased in 1894 for the Istanbul-Princes' Islands line were very luxurious and ornately decorated. Nevertheless, they pleased the reporter of *The Levant Herald*:

The new steamers have been built to the highest requirements.... The principal saloon is on deck above the engine space, and is a magnificent compartment. It is about 45 feet long by 18 feet broad. The fittings are in oak and walnut, with blue velvet cushions and yellow window curtains. The walls and ceiling are paneled in white, blue, and gold—a combination which produces a beautiful effect. The ladies saloon is a continuation of the main saloon, and is upholstered in the same luxurious manner.[19]

Always a colorful feature of urban life in Istanbul, water transportation was now developing into a broad network that would become a major public service during the second half of the nineteenth century. The Şirket-i Hayriye, which started with only six boats in 1851, possessed sixteen by 1864, thirty-four by 1872, and thirty-six by 1909.[20] Unlike the other transportation systems operating concurrently in Istanbul, water transportation was managed by an Ottoman company—Şirket-i Hayriye was the first imperial transportation enterprise of the Ottoman state and a successful one. However, its dependence on Western technology was typical of all major projects undertaken by the empire during this period: the boats were fabricated in England, and foreign engineers were hired for their maintenance.

53. *The first bridge across the Golden Horn between Unkapanı and Azapkapı (1836)*

Boats have always been a major means of communication in cities built on a network of canals or islands, such as Venice and Stockholm, and in those divided by a large river, such as Paris. However, with the evolution of alternative transportation systems, their importance declined.[21] But in Istanbul there was no substitute for water transportation—the distances across the water were too great for bridges and underground transportation systems to provide an effective alternative to sea travel. The situation has not changed much in the last century. Even though a bridge was built across the Bosporus in 1973, ferryboats still continue to connect the separated parts of the city.

BRIDGES OVER THE GOLDEN HORN

Connecting the two shores of the Golden Horn by bridges was another element of the nineteenth-century effort to improve overall communication in the capital.[22] The first bridge built in the nineteenth century across the waterway dates from 1836. This timber structure, connecting Azapkapı to Unkapanı, had two arches that provided the necessary height for the passage of small boats. It was about 600 meters in length and 10 meters

53

in width.[23] The main reason for constructing the first bridge across the Golden Horn at this point was the location of the imperial shipyards in Azapkapı. Besides, Pera and Beşiktaş were not developed enough in the 1830s to justify a connection between Karaköy and Eminönü, nor was Karaköy the busy trade center it would become after 1838.

The growing importance of Galata as a commercial center and the increase in its population after 1838 necessitated a fast and convenient connection between Karaköy and Eminönü. The first Galata Bridge was built at this point in 1845 under the patronage of Bezmi Alem Valide Sultan, Mahmut II's mother. This 500-meter timber structure served the city for eighteen years.[24] In 1863, it was replaced by another larger and sturdier timber bridge. It was probably not coincidental that an international exposition was held at the Hippodrome in this same year, to which many important foreign statesmen, including Napoleon III, were invited (only Empress Eugènie came). The desire to present a respectable façade to the eminent guests may have been the motivation behind the replacement of the old bridge. A toll was charged for carriages and pedestrians to meet part of the maintenance costs. The risk of fire was taken seriously: an imperial order was issued prohibiting smoking on the bridge and it was closed to traffic at night.[25]

The 1863 bridge served Istanbul for twelve years. Discussions about replacement of the wooden bridge with a more permanent iron structure began in 1869, when an English firm proposed a new bridge, 460 meters long and 18 meters wide. Pedestrian walks 1.5 meters wide would be built on both sides, leaving a vehicular road of 13 meters in the middle. Fourteen iron pontoons would support the structure. An iron frame consisting of components 80-centimeters thick was calculated. In addition to the bridge, the English company proposed building wide quays at both ends.[26]

The government agreed to the construction of this project. However, the initial plans underwent some transformations. When the bridge was almost finished in 1871, the English company submitted a report to the sultan suggesting that the structure be moved to the site of the old bridge between Unkapanı and Azapkapı. The reason was financial: the embankment construction was unexpectedly costly in Karaköy and Eminönü. This report maintained that the second location, which badly needed a new bridge in any event, was more appropriate. The English company advocated the construction of another iron bridge, regular and wider, between Karaköy and Eminönü. The government agreed and in 1872 the structure was transported to the site of the old Unkapanı Bridge, which it replaced.[27]

The construction of a new Galata Bridge according to revised specifications began in 1875 and was completed in 1878. This iron structure with wood planking was 480 meters long and 14 meters wide, the width consisting of two 2.15-meter sidewalks and a 9.70-meter vehicular strip. The

bridge, supported by twenty-four pontoons, could be opened in the middle
to allow the passage of sea traffic. Toward either end, shops, restaurants,
and coffeehouses were built.[28] There was even a sea bath near Eminönü,
facing the Golden Horn.[29]

This bridge connected Istanbul to Galata until the construction of
the 1912 bridge, which is still standing (see figs 117, 118). At the turn
of the century, several unexecuted projects were submitted by European
designers to Abdülhamit.

In 1902, three projects were proposed to replace the Galata Bridge,
none of which were implemented. In February 1902, a bridge design
was sent from Paris that called for an elaborate iron-frame structure
incorporating a number of eclectic architectural features.[30] It was divided
into three parts, the divisions were marked by pairs of minarets, each pair
joined by a balcony, which elegantly merged with the structural iron arch
and, at the same time, helped to form a visually impressive gate. The
sections near the Karaköy and Eminönü quays were lined with shops on
the main level. Two sets of stairs on each side connected the shop level to
the platform on the water level, which acted as a landing quay as well
as a promenade. A touch of Venice was added by the architecture of these
shops and the form of the stairs. Abdülhamit II scuddled this project, not
for practical or aesthetic reasons, but for security reasons. He feared that
during a revolt, rebels might take shelter in the shops on the main level
and open fire on his soldiers from both sides.[31]

Another project for the reconstruction of the Galata Bridge was prepared as part of a larger face-lifting scheme by Joseph Antoine Bouvard in
April 1902. Its birthplace was again Paris; this time, the projected image
was totally European.[32]

54

54. Proposal for a new Galata Bridge (1902)

In the fall of 1902, a third project was drafted by a German firm.[33] Although the contract was signed in 1906, construction was not commenced under Abdülhamit II. In 1909, the Young Turk government signed another contract with the same German firm for construction of the Galata Bridge that stands today.[34]

For a very short time there was also a bridge in a third location on the Golden Horn. Built in 1863 between Ayvansaray and Piripaşa, it stood only ten days until it was torn down by angry rowboat owners who had provided transportation between the two banks and whose livelihood it destroyed.[35] Though insignificant as a structure, the bridge is important because it is a further representation of the general goal of defining a larger metropolitan area by uniting Istanbul and Galata.

HORSE-DRAWN TRAMS

The Şirket-i Hayriye's boats improved communication considerably. However, on land, the inner parts of the Istanbul peninsula, as well as its Marmara shore, were still quite isolated. Also, the hills of Galata and the new neighborhoods toward Şişli desperately needed a land transportation system.

During the 1860s, several proposals were submitted to the government by entrepreneurs who wanted to build and operate a tramway system.[36] For example, in 1863, a contract was drafted to give a Mr. Huchiadson the right to construct and run trams along the main arteries of Istanbul and its suburbs.[37] This project was not implemented and, one year later, in 1864, an Englishman applied to obtain the tramway concession for Istanbul, Galata, and Beşiktaş. The government report, prepared after an analysis of the proposal, was receptive. Citing examples from similar systems in European countries, it advocated the construction of a tramway in the Ottoman capital. At the same time, this meant demolition along certain arteries, once again for the public good.[38]

The 1864 regulation draft provided the groundwork for the principles later put into practice, and it determined the routes to be followed by other companies (see fig. 57). The first route connected the Eminönü end of the Galata Bridge to the Hippodrome and Beyazit Square via the Divanyolu. From Beyazit Square it led to Aksaray, where it bifurcated; one branch followed Samatya Caddesi and reached Yedikule (the Golden Gate), the other linked Aksaray to Topkapı on the Theodosian walls. This network proposed for the first time the connection of the inner neighborhoods to each other and to the Byzantine walls forming the western boundary of the peninsula. The starting point of the other line in Istanbul was once more in Eminönü; this route was to run along the Golden Horn shore, pass the Theodosian walls in Ayvansaray, and reach Eyüp. The idea was to provide access to the workshops and the neighborhoods along the water as well as to the religious center in Eyüp—a function only partially met by the Şirket-i Hayriye boats. These lines, which cut the peninsula longitudinally, did not have north-south connections to facilitate communication in the western (and wider) part of the triangle. The initial concern must have been to connect major neighborhoods to each other. Unfortunately, this rather shortsighted policy was the basis for later projects, and, as we shall see, interconnecting tracks were never considered for Istanbul.

The final line proposed in the 1864 draft was in Galata. It connected Karaköy through Tophane, Beşiktaş, and Ortaköy to Arnavutköy, thereby proposing an alternative public transportation system on land for these still developing neighborhoods on the Bosporus.[39]

The technical aspects of construction were carefully outlined: the rails would be one meter apart, a minimum distance of one meter would be left between the trams and the buildings on either side of the streets; and a 3.00-meter strip on one side of the tram line would provide room for the passage of other vehicles. Slopes would not exceed 1/24, and finally, damaged water and sewage lines would be repaired by the company.[40]

Comfort and convenience were elaborately addressed. Trams would operate from dawn to midnight, and schedules and fares were to be posted in several languages at all stops. Only small parcels would be accepted inside the cars, larger items were to be loaded on top for a fee. At major intersections, shelters for waiting passengers would be built for protection against sun and rain. Women's privacy was accommodated by designating two types of cars, painted in different colors, for male and female travelers.[41]

Though worked out in such fine detail, the concession did not come through. In 1868, a third unsuccessful attempt was made at building a tramway, this time by a Turkish inventor, Rüstem Bey, who demanded a one-year concession. Rüstem Bey's proposal was a monorail system, which, he claimed, was more economical than the classical double-rail track.[42] Finally, in 1869, a forty-year concession was given to Krepano Efendi, who formed the Istanbul Tramway Company (Istanbul Tramvay Şirketi).[43] Three successive regulations, dating from 1869, 1881, and 1907, give us the basic information on the growth and efficiency of the system.

The 1869 regulation outlined four routes: the first connected Azapkapı at the foot of the Unkapanı Bridge on the Golden Horn via Tophane and Beşiktaş to Ortaköy; the second line led from Eminönü through Babıali and the Divanyolu to Beyazit and then to Aksaray; the third went from Aksaray to Yedikule (the Golden Gate); and the fourth from Aksaray to Topkapı (see fig. 57). The construction was to be completed in four years.[44] A comparison of this regulation with the unapplied 1864 regulation shows that the same area was covered with the exception of the third route in the 1864 proposal that ran parallel to the Golden Horn.

A Golden Horn line from Eminönü to Eyüp was proposed again in the 1881 regulation in addition to two new routes on the Galata side.

55

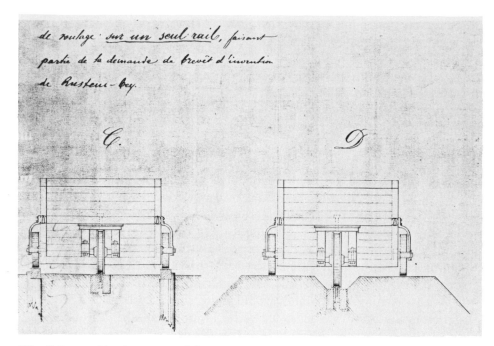

55. *Rüstem Bey's proposal for a monorail tramway system (1868)*

The first of the Galata lines was designed to follow Voyvoda Caddesi in Karaköy, pass through the Kabristan and Tepebaşı streets, and to meet the Grande Rue in Galatasaray. From there, it would go to Taksim, to Pangaltı, and finally to Şişli, serving Pera and the new neighborhoods along the Taksim-Şişli axis. At a location to be determined later, a line to Tatavla would branch off from the Karaköy-Şişli route. Krepano Efendi's company was responsible for operating as many cars as needed. It was also granted a concession to run omnibuses to make the necessary connections between the outlying neighborhoods and the tram lines.[45]

The Eminönü-Eyüp and Tatavla lines were never constructed. The 1907 contract, which extended the concession for another seventy-five years still mentioned these connections, as well as proposing three other routes. On the Galata side, the southern portion of the Grande Rue between Galatasaray and the Tünel Square was to be railed and connected to the Karaköy line and the Karaköy-Bosporus line extended from Ortaköy to Arnavutköy. In Istanbul, the foot of the Unkapanı Bridge needed a link to Fatih, the neighborhood around the *külliye* of Mehmet II; though not elaborated upon, a final connection between Fatih and Edirnekapı was also mentioned.[46] These lines would communicate to some degree with the inner parts of the peninsula. Though rather feeble, this was a unique, first attempt to link the Golden Horn to the Marmara shores.

Again, the Galata side of the Golden Horn was given preference in the effort to modernize. Even though an extensive transportation network was proposed for Istanbul, it was built only in part. An 1896 map shows only three short lines on the Istanbul side: Eminönü-Aksaray, Aksaray-Yedikule, and Aksaray-Topkapı. The Golden Horn line had still not been constructed.[47] But the two routes outlined in the 1869 and 1881 regulations for the Galata side, the Azapkapı-Bosporus line and the Karaköy-Grande Rue-Şişli line, were already in service.

Istanbul's population was 389,545 in 1885, compared to the Sixth District's 237,293.[48] Hence, demographic concentration was not an overriding concern in the distribution of tram lines. The orientation of growth and the general tendency to supply services to the favored residents of the city again determined the locus of investment. The completion of the first line between Azapkapı and Beşiktaş in July 1872 exemplified this attitude;[49] the Eminönü-Aksaray line in Istanbul was opened to service in November of the same year.[50]

It is true that the width and condition of the roads determined to a large extent the pace of the construction process. The Istanbul Tramway Company was responsible for widening the roads to a minimum of 11.50 meters (about the same width as proposed in the 1864 draft), as well as paving the surfaces and repairing the damaged water, sewage, and gas lines. All construction was to follow the current modes and standards applied in France. If conflicts occurred between property owners and the company during street-widening, the municipality and the Ministry of Public Works would mediate negotiations.[51] In the dense, old neighborhoods of Istanbul, such as Eminönü and Aksaray, construction was incremental and slow, whereas the wide, new streets on the northern side of the Golden Horn, such as the Taksim-Şişli and the Karaköy-Bosporus arteries, easily accommodated the tram tracks.[52] But even the denser areas of Galata, like parts of the Grande Rue, Tepebaşı Caddesi, and Voyvoda Caddesi, all of which needed widening for the installation of rails, were given immediate priority, while similarly dense areas in Istanbul, for example, Unkapanı and Fatih, were neglected.[53]

Fares, schedules, and the comfort of passengers were concerns that were resolved on the basis of the principles established in the 1864 regulation draft; they also paralleled the rules of Şirket-i Hayriye. For example, children under six traveled free; mailmen, soldiers, and policemen traveled at reduced fares; and large parcels were not permitted in the cars, but a luggage space was provided on top of the trams.[54]

The new transportation system had a distinctly modernizing effect on Istanbul's urban image. At major centers and intersections, shelters built for passengers and company employees were a new element in the city.[55] Trams pulled by horses added to the liveliness of the streets and were reminiscent of contemporary European cities even though each vehicle was preceded by stick-wielding men who chased the notorious dogs of

Istanbul off the tracks. De Amicis observed a striking duality between the new transportation system and the old city:

In another street, entirely Turkish and silent, you are suddenly startled by the sound of a horn and the stamping of horses' feet; turning to see what it means, you find it difficult to believe your eyes when a large car rolls gayly into sight over some track which up to that moment you had not noticed, filled with Turks and Europeans, with its officials in uniforms and its printed tariff of fares, for all the world like a *tramway* in Vienna or Paris. The effect of such an apparition, seen in one of these streets, is not to be described; it is like a burlesque or some huge joke, and you laugh aloud as you watch it disappear, as though you have never seen anything of the kind before. With the omnibus the life and the movement of Europe seem to vanish, and you find yourself back in Asia.[56]

The trams matched the Westernized lifestyle of Pera much better. They added a further touch of Europe to the Grande Rue, already bustling with cafés, restaurants, theaters, and department stores. According to *The Levant Herald*, a carnival, organized by the European community in 1896, made an interesting showpiece of a mock tram car:

56

A gaudy vehicle of the shape, size and color of Chichli trams, drawn by four gaily caparisoned horses—which by the way, looked as though they had been just imported from Wonderland—was yesterday morning seen slowly wending its way along the Grande Rue de Pera. Inside were lady passengers gracefully fanning themselves, while they helped, unseen by spectators, to supply motive power, and aristocratic-looking gentlemen did the rest of the work, while they smoked Manila cigars of the "Made in Germany" brand.[57]

Trams were in fact well integrated into the lives of Pera residents. For example, an agreement was made in 1900 between the Istanbul Tramway Company and the director of the Taksim Municipal Garden to issue free entrance to the holders of tram tickets for the Şişli-Taksim and the Sixth District Palace-Taksim lines. The rationale was that free admission would help families who could not afford to go to a summer resort by providing them with a place where they could breathe "the pure and healthy air of the Bosporus in the shadow of the beautiful trees of the garden."[58] The families in consideration were Pera residents. It was not likely that the inhabitants of Istanbul would travel several hours in the horse-drawn vehicles through tortuous streets in order to catch a breath of fresh air in the Taksim Garden.

Tram service for the residents of Istanbul who lived in the inner parts of the peninsula was quite different from service in Pera. Hüseyin Rahmi, a novelist and social critic who wrote during the late nineteenth and early twentieth centuries, recorded the state of the cars that ran between Aksaray and Topkapı:

The Tramway Company operates its most rotten cars on this line. The dust and mud of the street hid the green paint of the cars.... The four horses were so weak and lifeless that they could very well be used for a course in skeleton structure while still alive.[59]

56. *Street view from Pera, circa 1913. Trams are in the background.*

This description dates from the same decade as the two previous quotations, but the image conveyed is much grimmer and does not evoke the tramways in Vienna or Paris. When a modern urban service was brought to a low-income neighborhood, it functioned according to different rules. The level of efficiency and even the image of the cars running along the Aksaray-Topkapı line were not comparable to those in the "better" parts of the city.[60]

57. *Tramway routes as outlined by the 1864, 1869, 1881, and 1907 reg-ulations and the route of the Tünel*

THE SUBWAY

In 1869, an imperial decree gave Eugène Henri Gavand (the engineer who had proposed widening the embankments along the Sea of Marmara) a concession for a period of forty-two years to construct and operate a subway system between Karaköy and Pera. The growing importance of trade in the Galata area made better transportation imperative.[61]

The tram line did not provide a direct connection from Galata and Pera to the south end of the Grande Rue. For economy, its long and meandering route followed the existing roads. Yüksek Kaldırım, the only direct street leading from Karaköy to Pera, was steep and narrow and clogged daily with an average of 40,000 pedestrians (see fig. 6). The construction of a subterranean funicular, in Gavand's words, "a kind of elevator ascending and descending," was eminently practical. It reduced the journey to a few minutes and saved its passengers a lot of effort.[62]

It took Gavand three years, a great deal of commuting between Paris, London, and Istanbul, as well as a considerable amount of negotiation, just to form his company.[63] Established in 1872 the company was called

57

the Metropolitan Railway of Constantinople, from Galata to Pera. Work started the same year, but construction, and especially the digging process, was delayed by the conflicts between the landowners and the company. As in the tramway concession, the government had promised to enforce expropriation laws in the event owners were reluctant to sell.[64] However, the government was rather cautious and dilatory in its intervention between Gavand and the landlords.[65] Construction thus moved slowly and the steam-operated Istanbul Tünel did not open for service until January 1875, three years after construction began.

The system consisted of a tunnel, 554.80 meters long, 6.70 meters wide, and 4.90 meters high, stations at either end, and rooms for mechanical equipment. There was a 61.55-meter difference in level between the Galata and Pera ends; the slope varied from 2 percent to 15 percent. A two-car train ran on each of the two parallel tracks. One of the cars was reserved for passengers and divided into two classes; each class had, in turn, two compartments, one for men, the other for women. The second car carried merchandise, animals, and even horse-drawn carriages.[66]

The opening of the Istanbul Tünel was a big event for the city. The inaugural ceremony began with the conveying of distinguished guests between Galata and Pera in the upward and downward trains; a band playing music accompanied each train. *The Levant Herald* tells us that:

Shortly after one o'clock, the assembled guests sat down to a sumptuous *dejeuner à la fourchette*, with champagne and other choice wines, served by Messieurs Vallauri, the Pera confectioners, on several elegantly arranged tables on both sides of the Pera station. At the dessert, Mr. Albert, the general manager, proposed "The Health of His Imperial Majesty Sultan Abdul-Aziz." He said that the Sultan, having deeply at heart the welfare of his vast empire, had always, from the beginning of his reign, encouraged the extension and development of roads and railroads, means of communication which were a chief element in the prosperity of the nations. It was in that spirit that His Majesty had granted the concessions for this Underground Railway which now brought together the shores of ancient Byzantium. It was also to be hoped that the Metropolitan Railway would prove a new link of fraternity to cement the friendship between the Eastern and Western elements which met in Constantinople. Mr. Albert's remarks were greeted with much applause. The band played "The Turkish National Anthem." Baron Foelckershamb, as representative of the company, proposed "The Health of the Queen of England," the most ancient ally of the Sultan. The Company which had executed the railway was, he observed, formed in England and it was the result of British initiative and enterprise, applied to an undertaking of practical utility in Turkey, which had gathered them that day.... The band played "God Save the Queen".... Baron Foelckershamb again rose and proposed "The Health of all other Sovereigns" who had their representatives there. All, he said, had a common interest in the universal mission of civilization and progress, and that the dignitaries present on that occasion had manifested their sympathy with a work of improvement and public utility, which would, he trusted, prove of advantage to persons of all nationalities settled in Constantinople.[67]

This account crystallizes the elements of power and the goals of the mission. Power belonged to the English financiers and, as the tone of the speakers indicated, the "common interest" was that of the Europeans residing in the capital. Istanbul's European community loved this element of "progress and civilization." The company, in turn, tried to please its clients. In February 1875, glass was installed in the windows of the cars and lamps were brought from London to provide better light. An editorial, published in *La Turquie* a few months later, approved of other improvements intended for the two stations: stands designed to exhibit posters, announcements, and advertisements would bring the ambiance of the terminals up to the standards of European stations. *La Turquie* also advocated the creation of a "charming buffet at the Pera terminal" for the same purpose.[68]

In 1900, a new contract urged the Metropolitan Railway of Constantinople to demolish the existing terminals and replace them with *kargir* buildings, the plans and façades of which would first be approved by government engineers. The Pera station was to occupy a total area of 900 square meters, have four stories, incorporate shops, and have a regular (*muntazam*) exterior. The Galata terminal would occupy 700 square meters, have three stories, with shops at street level; and its shape was also to be "regular."[69]

In 1904, the Metropolitan Railway's concession was extended for another seventy-five years, to run from the date of expiration of the first concession.[70] The company thus provided transportation between Galata and Pera until the nationalization of all public transportation systems after the formation of the Turkish Republic in 1923.[71]

The success of the Istanbul Tünel led to several other subway proposals. Although none of these projects were realized, they provide valuable insights into the goals and rationales of the nineteenth and early twentieth-century planners of Istanbul.

Gavand, persistent entrepreneur of the Istanbul Tünel, submitted another proposal to the Ottoman government in 1876. This was a north-south railway system, a major part of which was to be underground. Starting from Kumkapı on the Marmara shore, the projected subway would cross the peninsula, and surface in Eminönü, where the Istanbul terminal was to be built. Its cars would traverse the Golden Horn by means of a new Galata Bridge, but immediately go underground once on the Galata side. The system was designed to run parallel to the shoreline from Karaköy to Ortaköy with stations in Karaköy, Tophane, Fındıklı, Dolmabahçe, Beşiktaş, and Ortaköy. Although Gavand referred to a extension along the Bosporus shore, he did not elaborate further. The estimated length of the railway was about 4,300 meters from Kumkapı to Beşiktaş.[72]

Gavand's major contribution here was his proposal for a short and direct connection between the Marmara and Golden Horn shores of the Istanbul peninsula. The lines for the Galata side of the Golden Horn duplicated the route of the tramways already in service, but had the advantage of unobstructed speed underground.

Gavand's proposal went even further. In addition to a project to widen the embankments along the Sea of Marmara, he suggested the construction of another subway, which would cross the Bosporus, possibly between Sarayburnu and Üsküdar. This would allow the trains coming from Europe to continue their journey on to the Asian continent.[73] The details of this ambitious project, called the "New City Project" by its designer, were not worked out. However, Gavand's transcontinental subway proposal has been the inspiration for many similar proposals—none of which have been realized.

Between 1838 and 1908, two other subway projects were drafted. In 1890, a line connecting Eminönü to the Grand Bazaar, serving a portion of the same area as Gavand's scheme, was presented to the Ministry of Public Works, accompanied by a concession demand. The proposal was turned down.[74]

In 1902, three American engineers, Fredrik E. Strom, Frank T. Lindman, and John A. Hilliker, proposed a subway system between Sarayburnu and Salacak (near Üsküdar), duplicating yet another portion of Gavand's scheme. The goal of of this new plan was to provide uninterrupted rail communication between the Asian and European sides.[75] A tube would be anchored to the bottom of the sea by means of sixteen piers, through which a three-wagon train two wagons for passengers and one for baggage—would travel. The design was not developed in detail, however, and even the exact location of the terminals was not worked out. But, a monumental station projected for the Asian side indicates the intention to create focal points at both ends of the tunnel. The government considered the project pure fantasy.[76]

The motivation behind these proposals was undoubtedly money. The technologically undeveloped empire provided excellent profit potential for Western investors offering "progress" and "civilization." However, the Ottoman government, perhaps not trusting the credibility of these large-scale and technically sophisticated schemes, turned down the majority of the proposals. Whether put into practice or not, the urban planning principle underlying all of the projects was to provide good communication between the scattered parts of the divided city, thereby creating a greater Istanbul out of Istanbul, Galata, Üsküdar, and the villages along the the Bosporus on both Asian and European sides.

THE RAILROAD

The first railroad that connected Istanbul to Sofia (with a branch to Alexandropolis) was opened in 1874. The route to be followed in Istanbul was a controversial topic. The project, prepared by a company owned by the Belgian banker, Baron Hirsh, called for constructing tracks along the Marmara shore, which would cut through the gardens of the Topkapı Palace. The proposal was heatedly debated by the palace bureaucracy until Sultan Abdülmecit put an end to the controversy when he expressed his enthusiasm for the new technology by stating that the trains must come to Istanbul, even if they had to pass over his own back. The relocation of the imperial residence to Dolmabahçe in 1856 naturally played a major role in this decision. As the railroad passed through the residential quarters along the Sea of Marmara, local trains soon started to operate on an urban/suburban route. In 1875, there were six stops: Istanbul (the terminal in Sirkeci), Kumkapı, Yedikule, Bakırköy, Yeşilköy, and Küçük Çekmece.[77] An 1896 map shows two more stations, one in Yenikapı, the other in Samatya. Therefore, the neighborhoods along the shoreline and the more distant suburbs of Bakırköy and Yeşilköy on the Sea of Marmara outside the Theodosian walls were finally connected to the city center.

58. Strom, Lindman, and Hilliker's proposal for a subway system under the Bosporus (1902). The Istanbul end.

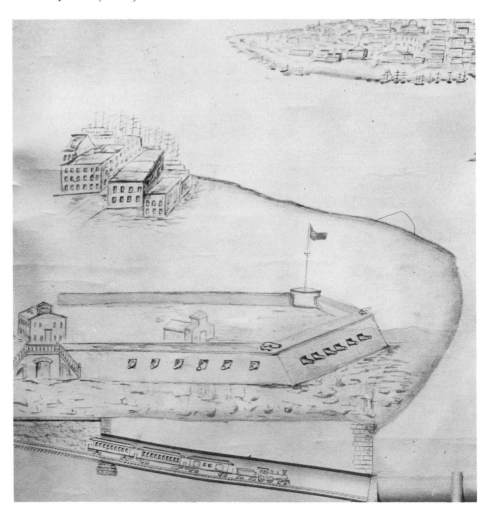

59. The Üsküdar end of Strom, Lindman, and Hilliker's proposed sub-
way system

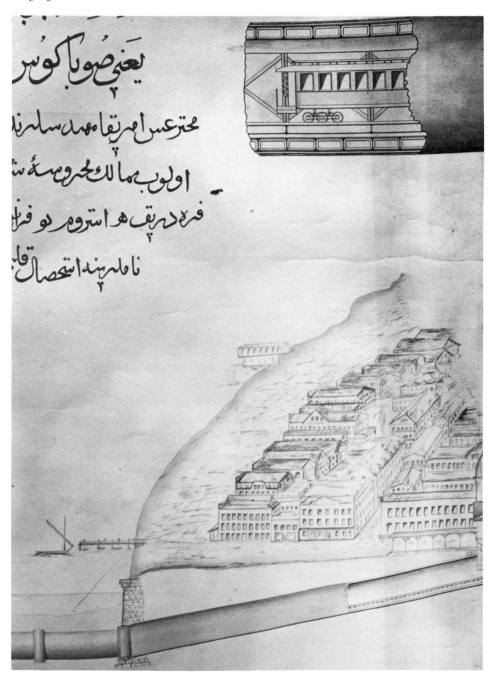

In 1888, the Istanbul-Vienna line was completed, an event that a European observer interpreted with mixed feelings:

> The completion of the railroad between Constantinople and Vienna . . . may be regarded as the conquest of the city by foreign thought and enterprise. . . . [This is] the annexation of Constantinople to the western world. New ideas, new fashions now rule, for better or for worse, and soon the defects and charms of the Oriental city will be a dream of the past.[78]

In fact, by 1888, the "conquest of the city by foreign thought and enterprise" had already been accomplished. The "defects and charms of the Oriental city" still existed in the neglected Istanbul peninsula, but a European urban image accommodating a European lifestyle had been constructed across the Golden Horn. And, on both sides of the waterway, European enterprise controlled almost all aspects of economic life. The uninterrupted connection to the heart of Europe further facilitated communication and at the same time symbolically reinforced the Westernization that had already taken place.

In contrast to the big European cities, where a number of train stations formed a perimeter around an old core, the Ottoman capital had only two stations—one on the European, the other on the Asian side of the Bosporus. The terminal in Istanbul, conveniently placed in Sirkeci at the meeting point of other transportation systems, provided fast connections to the boats and the trams. The architectural style of the Istanbul train station expressed the dichotomy of Western and local values already well incorporated into the late nineteenth-century urban image. Designed by a German architect named Jachmund and completed in 1887, it combined the principles of Beaux-Arts design with an Islamic revivalist style, thus housing modern technology within a framework that attempted to evoke the local tradition (see figs. 106, 107).

The terminal on the Asian side was not built until 1909 even though the Haydarpaşa-Izmit railroad dated from 1873. Designed by two Germans, Helmuth Cuno and Otto Ritter, the terminal was in an imposing neoclassical style. While the station on the European side met the travelers coming from Europe with an Oriental façade, the one on the Asian side met those arriving from Asia with a Western one, complementing the romantic notion of the capital as the place where East and West merged.

By the late 1800s, the different modes of public transportation met at convenient points where connections could be made easily. Boats left from the Istanbul side of the Galata Bridge; Eminönü was the "major mode mixer," the terminal point for the trains, boats, and trams. In Galata, Karaköy, at the northern end of the bridge, acted similarly: at this key point were located the main tramway stop and the lower terminus of the subway. Today these two locations still provide the main transportation connections.

The transportation network built during the mid and late 1800s provided the framework for twentieth-century systems. The majority of public transportation lines, the steamboats, the trains, and the Istanbul Tünel operate today as they did one hundred years ago. Horse-drawn trams, however, have been replaced by buses and trolleybuses. The major change in the twentieth century came with the automobile—a phenomenon that blossomed after the first decade of the twentieth century. However, its introduction to the Ottoman capital was made earlier, during Abdülhamit II's reign, when an automobile was exhibited in a shop window on the Grande Rue, attracting the attention of the whole capital for many months.[79]

5.

The Grand Schemes

During the seventy years from the declaration of the Tanzimat reforms in 1839 to the Young Turk Revolution of 1908, three ambitious urban design schemes were drafted for Istanbul. Their aims were modernization of the communication network and creation of an urban image based on European technology and cultural values. Foreign engineers and architects were commissioned for all three plans.

The first scheme, Helmuth Von Moltke's plan of 1839, completed under Abdülmecit, followed on the heels of the Tanzimat fervor. The other two, those of F. Arnodin and Joseph Antoine Bouvard, were proposed during Abdülhamit II's reign. And, as typical of many other projects of the era, they were ambitious schemes that were never actually implemented. Both plans hoped to embody the past power of the empire and to express that power symbolically in grand-scale rebuilding schemes for the capital.

THE CITY CONSIDERED AS A WHOLE: VON MOLTKE'S PLAN

A key element of the Tanzimat reforms was centralization, which was reflected in the urban planning scene as early as 1839. The incrementally built city was, for the first time, considered as a whole. Helmuth Von Moltke was commissioned by Mahmut II to draw a detailed map of Istanbul and to propose a plan to improve the street pattern. Von Moltke's map has been published several times although a redevelopment plan has yet to be found. There is, however, a detailed description of the project in an 1839 document, published by Ergin.[1] In fact, Von Moltke's proposal might have been nothing more than a verbally articulated set of urban design principles, since no evidence of a plan has surfaced.

Von Moltke's main goal was to provide an uninterrupted communication network throughout the Istanbul peninsula by the creation of wide arteries connecting the heart of the city—the administrative and commercial regions—to the old Byzantine gates. At the same time, the residential architecture gradually would be converted from wood to *kargir* for fire protection. Von Moltke proposed five major arteries. The first

60. H. Von Moltke's plan (1839)

connected Bab-ı Hümayun, the outer gate of the Topkapı Palace, to Aksaray; it thus followed the Divanyolu (the Byzantine *mese*) and passed
by Beyazit Square. The second route was between Aksaray and Topkapı
on the Theodosian walls. The third, which linked Beyazit Square to the
Fatih neighborhood, branched into two routes at Mehmet II's *külliye*;
with one branch leading to Edirnekapı and the second to Eğrikapı, both
major Byzantine gates. The fourth connection was along the Marmara
shore, between Kadırga and Yedikule (the Golden Gate). Finally, the
fifth artery originated in Eminönü, in front of the Valide Sultan Mosque,
ran parallel to the Golden Horn, and ended in Eyüp, the most important
Muslim shrine in the city.

Von Moltke's project recalled the road network of the Byzantine city, with its main artery, the *mese*, which connected the forums, and led to the gates on the Theodosian walls after branching off at Forum Tauri (Beyazit Square) and Forum Bovis (Aksaray). Von Moltke also proposed two major roads running parallel to the shoreline on the Sea of Marmara side of the peninsula and the other along the Golden Horn side, but he did not provide for connections between the Golden Horn and the Marmara shores, which would have linked his east-west arteries. His goal was merely to allow access to the major neighborhoods and gates.

The projected width for the main arteries in Von Moltke's plan was 15.20 meters. Three-meter sidewalks would be built on either side, reducing the vehicular strip to 9.20 meters. All other roads would be 11.50 meters, 9.00 meters, or 7.60 meters depending on their location and importance; dead ends were eliminated entirely. Rows of trees would be planted along roadways, and public squares would be opened at "appropriate" locations, as often as possible in front of mosques or other monumental buildings.

The waterfront on both sides of the Golden Horn was to be cleaned up and reorganized. The two areas of particular concern were, on the Istanbul side, the strip from Sirkeci to the southern end of the Unkapanı Bridge (the only bridge spanning the Golden Horn at the time); and on the Galata side, the strip from Tophane to the northern end of the same bridge. Von Moltke projected 15.20-meter stone quays to replace the wooden ones. Like the other major arteries, these would have 3.00-meter sidewalks and rows of trees on both sides.

Regularity in the streetscape was another important concept promoted by this plan. The street line would determine the absolute boundary of the buildings and no projections were allowed. Fountains and other public structures that formed obstacles to the orientation of the new streets would be moved to appropriate locations. However, mosques could not be touched; the orientation of the streets had to be modified to accommodate their preservation.

Von Moltke's scheme attempted to correct some of the city's physical problems, the solutions to which have been the goal of all subsequent schemes up to the present day. The problems to be overcome were the provision of direct and easy access through the dense fabric of the old city; regularization of the streets and the quays; creation of public squares; and, conversion of wooden construction to *kargir*. Von Moltke proposed practical solutions to the pressing problems of Istanbul's urban pattern. However, there was also in his plan a strong concern with image: Istanbul was to be converted into a European city in keeping with the Tanzimat philosophy.

The lack of north-south arteries—the main shortcoming of this project—was repeated in later schemes; not much attention was paid to the connection of the Golden Horn and the Marmara shores when opening new arteries or widening the existing ones. As discussed in chapter four the issue became especially apparent in the planning of the tram routes, which had only east-west routes but no provision for north-south lines.

DEFINING A METROPOLITAN AREA: ARNODIN'S RINGROAD

The first stretch of the railroad leading to the Ottoman capital was completed in 1873 on the Asian side of the Bosporus. It ran from Haydarpaşa on the Sea of Marmara, just south of Üsküdar, to the town of Izmit, about 100 kilometers to the east. On the European side, the link between Istanbul and Edirne was completed in 1875. During Abdülhamit II's reign, and especially after the 1880s, there was a boom in railway construction throughout the country, which was made possible by foreign concession-holders and companies. One such company, the Compagnie Internationale du Chemin de Fer de Bosphore, proposed a ringroad project for Istanbul that would encircle the city and connect the Asiatic and European shores by means of two bridges. The project was prepared by French engineer Arnodin and presented to the sultan with a written explanation in March

61 1900. It consisted of a map of the city showing the new road and the location of the bridges, as well as a drawing of each bridge.[2]

The main objective of the scheme was to establish rail communication between Europe and Asia. However, the plan also outlined improvements for pedestrian and vehicular traffic. The project thus extended beyond the limits of a new railroad and became an urban, almost regional, design scheme.

Arnodin's first bridge was to connect Üsküdar on the Asiatic side to Sarayburnu on the tip of the Istanbul peninsula. The railroad that ended in Haydarpaşa was to be extended to Üsküdar and from there connected to the Istanbul-Edirne line by means of this bridge. Bostancı on the Haydarpaşa-Izmit line and Bakırköy on the Istanbul-Edirne line were large suburbs on the Asian and European sides respectively. Arnodin's ringroad, which circled the northern section of the city, would link these two suburbs with a second bridge at a point between Kadilli and Rumelihisar. Hence, a metropolitan boundary was determined that defined a large undeveloped area outside the main concentrations of Istanbul, Galata, Üsküdar, and the Bosporus villages. Future growth must have been envisaged as limited to this area—a prediction that was to be proved wrong within fifty years.[3]

The impressive scale and unusual architecture of Arnodin's bridges would have added striking new elements to the city's skyline. The bridge between Sarayburnu and Üsküdar would act as an imposing gate to

62 Istanbul. It was a suspended cable structure with three pairs of iron pylons, two at each end, 130 meters from each shore, and one in the middle. Rather bare of ornament, the bridge was, more than anything else, a feat of engineering. Nevertheless, it did incorporate a few Islamic

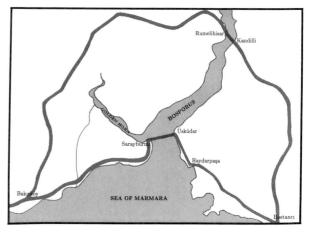

61. Arnodin's proposal for a ringroad (1900)

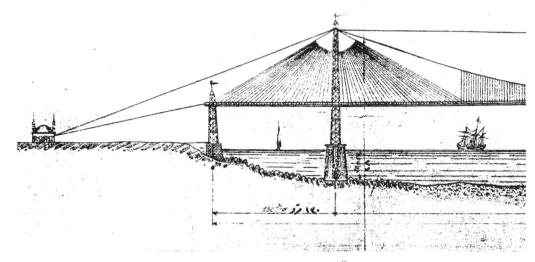

62. *Arnodin's proposal for the Sarayburnu-Üsküdar bridge (1900). The Sarayburnu end.*

revivalist features: the pylons were topped with tiny domes and were anchored by structures resembling mosques with minarets. The minarets were about sixteen meters high, so that the effect did indeed create the illusion of small mosques.

The second bridge was much more ambitious in its architectural style. Again, it was a suspended bridge with three pairs of pylons. In contrast to the more functional-looking iron-and-steel bridge at the gate of the Bosporus, the Hamidiye Bridge, named after the sultan, had more romantic connotations. Its stone pylons became mosques at the passage level. Each mosque had a central dome and four minarets. According to the description that accompanied the project, its architecture was inspired by "Seljuk" and other Islamic styles: "The domes are reminiscent of the palaces of Muslim Caliphs and symbolize and glorify the religious and political power of the Sultan, the Caliph of Muslims. They are adorned with colorful bricks, tiles, and glittering metals according to the 'Arabic' style; they embody all the beauty of the 16th and 17th centuries' northwest African architecture." The Hamidiye Bridge would acquire a more mystical image at night: "when the thousands of electric lamps illuminate the bridge with holy light, the Arabic style embroideries appear in all their delicacy, the bridge turns into a beauty from one end to the other, forming a view that embellishes the city and from which one cannot divert his eyes."[4]

This magical effect was precisely what Arnodin wanted to create. Conformity to an Islamic architectural heritage was a main theme; however, the sources of inspiration were not local, perhaps because of the designer's simplistic view of a uniform and undifferentiated Islamic architecture. The domed structures placed over the pylons were copies of the late Mamluk

63

63. Arnodin's proposal for the Kandilli-Rumelihisar bridge (1900)

sepulchral architecture of Cairo, even though the description accompanying the project called them "Seljuk" and their ornaments "Arabic," terms that Arnodin defined as northwest African architecture from the sixteenth and seventeenth centuries. The symmetrical placement of the four minarets reflected the organizational principles of some Ottoman mosques (for example, the Selimiye Mosque in Edirne), but their architectural style was again late Mamluk. It is just possible that Arnodin's source of inspiration was simply the *Description de l'Egypte* (Paris, 1820–26), a monumental survey carried out under Napoleon I's orders, where Mamluk architecture was richly illustrated.

The architectural implications of Arnodin's design may have been weak, but his scheme, which incorporated provisions for growth with the introduction of a transportation network, was the first of its kind for Istanbul.[5] Perhaps because of the novelty of the idea, but more likely for financial reasons, Arnodin's project was not viewed with enthusiasm. No imperial orders were issued on the topic; no action was taken for its implementation.[6]

BEAUX-ARTS PLANNING IN ISTANBUL: BOUVARD'S BOULEVARDS

At the turn of the century, when City Beautiful plans in the United States attempted to bring a new order and pattern to American cities, a similar scheme was prepared for Istanbul. Its author was the Beaux-Arts trained Joseph Antoine Bouvard, inspector-general of the Architectural Department of the City of Paris.[7] Paris had represented the pinnacle of beauty and culture to the ruling Ottoman elite since the beginning of the eighteenth century, and the selection of this highly-regarded Parisian architect was made with the total confidence that he had the knowledge, refinement, and talent to improve Istanbul's outdated urban image.

Joseph Antoine Bouvard (1840–1920) replaced Jean Charles Adolphe Alphand as inspector general in 1900. Concurrently, he was appointed chief of the Architectural Department of the 1900 World Exposition.[8] Bouvard's reputation was based largely on exposition design. He first drew public attention with the Pavillon de la Ville de Paris, built to exhibit machinery in the 1878 Paris World Exposition. His second chef d'oeuvre was the Palais des Industries Diverses of the 1889 exposition, a huge building extending almost the entire width of the Champ de Mars, with two wings toward the Seine and a grand central dome. According to a contemporary account, "immeasurable praise was bestowed on the fine silhouette of the dome and its elegant contour."[9] The impressive scale and the general layout of this building, as well as Bouvard's infatuation with domes, are reflected over and over again in his project for Istanbul. The site-planning principles of the Parisian expositions also exerted a strong influence on Bouvard's scheme for the Ottoman capital.

Bouvard's reputation was at its peak in 1901, when the French government conferred on him the rank of commander in the Legion of Honor.[10] It was at this time that he was commissioned by the Ottoman government to prepare a plan for Istanbul. Abdülhamit II's ambassador to Paris, Salih Münir, who was directly involved in the selection process, later recorded the sultan's feelings, intentions, and rationale. During one of the ambassador's many visits to the palace, the sultan showed him a piece of paper and said:

This has been bothering me.... It is the translation of an article written on Istanbul by a European traveler. Some of his accusations are wrong and unjustified, but others are true. For example, he criticizes us vehemently for not planning and improving the places that catch a traveler's eye, such as the Eminönü Square, the Karaköy Square, and the Galata Bridge; for neglecting the coast from Sarayburnu [Topkapı Palace] to Yedikule [Golden Gate], which could be made even more attractive than the shoreline of Nice and that of the Italian seaside cities; and for not cleaning and repairing the streets of the city. What can we say against these well-founded words? We should either silently accept all the guilt and yield to every accusation or we should clean, embellish, and rebuild our capital. You are the perfect person to handle this matter. You have been living in Europe, you are familiar with it, and you have seen embellished cities, you know of beautiful things and of engineering. I bestow upon you the responsibility to bring here the experts from France.[11]

Salih Münir sought out Bouvard and asked him to develop a master plan for Istanbul. Although overloaded with responsibilities in Paris that prevented him from visiting the Ottoman capital, Bouvard did not turn down the offer. Instead, he ordered large-size photographs of the city as aids for the preparation of his *avant-projet*. Even though Bouvard was hired by the Ottoman sultan, in the end, the French government paid his expenses and presented the project as an official gift.[12]

Bouvard's *avant-projet* proposed a very novel image for Istanbul. He chose several notable locations and applied to the existing fabric his classical Beaux-Arts principles of regularization, symmetry, isolation of monuments, and creation of vistas. The drawings for four of the areas Bouvard selected for replanning (the Hippodrome, Beyazit Square, Galata Bridge, and Valide Sultan Square) are still available.[13]

In his attempt to modernize Istanbul, Bouvard disregarded some vital urban design principles. First, because there was no master plan, the drawings did not go beyond the stage of impressionistic sketches; connections between the replanned areas were not addressed. Second, the city's complex topography was totally ignored—an astounding oversight given that Byzantine and Ottoman planners had sensitively taken it into consideration for fifteen centuries in the siting of their monuments. Third, the particular character of urban life in Istanbul was not considered. On this matter, Bouvard shared the viewpoint of those who gave him the commission: indigenous social and cultural values of the Istanbul residents were not important, what really mattered was the creation of a modern, clean, and embellished city.

The Hippodrome

The Byzantine Hippodrome had remained an open space, if not always a ceremonial one, throughout the Ottoman period.[14] It attracted considerable public attention owing to the general interest in antiquity prevalent in Istanbul during the second half of the nineteenth century. In 1856, British archaeologists excavated the bases of both the Serpent Column and the Egyptian Obelisk, and discovered the original level of the Hippodrome.[15] Later a few attempts were made to improve the large square at the Hippodrome, but the results were not satisfactory. On 28 October 1890, *La Turquie* mentioned the imperial intention to create a public park at the Hippodrome and to build "two beautiful kiosks in each wing of the garden," but the project was not realized. In 1899, Kaiser Wilhelm II donated a fountain to the city, which was placed at the north end of the Hippodrome and the area around it was paved (see fig. 105).[16]

64
65   Bouvard's scheme attempted to lower the Hippodrome to its original level. Several sets of symmetrically placed steps leading up from the floor of the Hippodrome would connect it to the surrounding boulevard. At the north end, where it met the Divanyolu, a monumental entrance was to

64. Bouvard's proposal for the Hippodrome (1902)

be created by the erection of two free-standing columns on two sides of a stairway; Kaiser Wilhelm II's fountain was ignored.

The 1890 proposal for a park at the Hippodrome came alive in Bouvard's design, which consisted of a symmetrical French garden with well-trimmed landscaping, trees placed at corner points, and complementing fountains. The "spine" of the Egyptian Obelisk, the Serpent Column, and the Colossus conveniently accommodated symmetry and gave the square a slightly Parisian tone, even reminiscent of the central part of the Place de la Concorde. The two parallel rows of trees on the higher sidewalk formed an elegant edge to the park.

Regularizing the built side of the boulevard encircling the Hippodrome was more problematic because the 1616 Sultan Ahmet *külliye*—an imperial and religious complex—could not be altered in any way. Nevertheless,

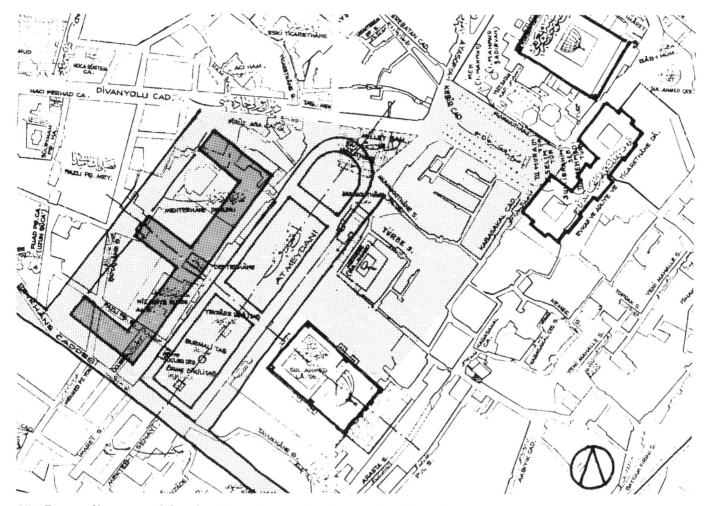

65. Bouvard's proposal for the Hippodrome superimposed on the urban fabric

Bouvard cavalierly proposed demolishing its *medrese* and ripping out its northern garden and garden wall to emphasize the axis perpendicular to the longer side of the Hippodrome. He created a perfect little French garden in the courtyard of the mosque, and even replaced the original domed fountain at the center with an open sculptural one.

The sixteenth-century palace of İbrahim Paşa on the west side of the Hippodrome was to be demolished and in its place was to be erected a "Préfecture de la Police," an oversized E-shaped building extending almost from one end of the Hippodrome to the other (a length of about 480 meters) and resembling in its scale and general layout the Palais des Industries Diverses. More gardens were planned for its west-facing courtyards, which opened up to a new north-south avenue parallel to the Hippodrome.

On the bottom left corner of the drawing, an observer is pictured, admiring the scene from the top of the building that should have been the Ottoman Law Courts.[17] The space between the law courts and the Sultan Ahmet Mosque is in reality much larger than is envisioned here— so much for working from photographs. In fact, to the south of Hagia Sophia Square, opened in 1868, lay a residential neighborhood extending as far as the mosque's garden wall. Bouvard suggested razing the neighborhood, incorporating the area into Hagia Sophia Square, and creating another French garden there.[18] The garden was to be mirrored by another symmetrical garden on the west side of the Hippodrome to the north of the police headquarters.

66

Topography was totally ignored. The grand avenue to the south of the Hippodrome could not be built in actuality since the Sultan Ahmet

66. View of the Mosque of Ahmet I from Hagia Sophia, circa 1900. There was a residential neighborhood adjacent to the mosque. Visible to the right of the mosque are the Egyptian Obelisk and the Colussus at the Hippodrome.

67. View of Beyazit Square looking toward the Ministry of Defense, circa 1900

Mosque and the Hippodrome are located on a man-made platform; the hill drops off at their southern boundary. Another question was where this avenue was to lead. Its scale suggested that it was a major artery. Its western portion, from Constantine's Column to the Hippodrome, perhaps deserved some monumentality, but there was no magnet along the coast to justify its extension in that direction.

Beyazit Square

While Bouvard's scheme for the Hippodrome followed the outline of the early twentieth-century fabric to some degree, he adopted a different approach for Beyazit Square. Disregarding its dominant character and treating it almost as a tabula rasa, he attempted to establish something that Istanbul had lacked for many centuries: a real civic center.

The entrance to Beyazit Square, on the site of the Byzantine Forum Tauri, was partially reorganized in 1867 in an attempt to create a monumental public space in front of the Ministry of War. The neo-Islamic gate 67 of the ministry and the kiosks flanking it on two sides, which were erected earlier in the century, formed the northern boundary of the square. The fifteenth-century Sultan Beyazit Mosque and its *medrese* loosely defined the eastern and western boundaries respectively.

Bouvard inflated the existing open space into a large rectangle and 68 placed a "Hôtel de Ville" on the axis of the Ministry of War. The new

68. *Bouvard's proposal for Beyazit Square (1902), looking south. The Beyazit Mosque is on the left. On the right are the Bibliotèque Impériale and Musée Industriel et Agricole. The building with a tower at the vista of the square is the Hôtel de Ville.*

square was divided into four islands by the north-south and east-west *69* axes, each symmetrically landscaped with identical fountains dotting the midpoints. The Hôtel de Ville was the dominant component of the ensemble; its huge, square central tower overshadowed the elegant, slender minarets of the Sultan Beyazit Mosque.

The Sultan Beyazit Medrese on the west side of the square was to be demolished and two identical buildings with inner courtyards and domes were proposed here. These were the "Musée Industriel et Agricole" and the "Bibliotèque Impériale," respectively the symbols of modernization and progress, and of learning and culture. They recalled Jacques Gabriel's two identical buildings on the Place de la Concorde, the Garde-Meubles. Furthermore, their arcades on the street level helped create an effect similar to the Rue de Rivoli.

The east side of the square posed a problem. The Sultan Beyazit Mosque was off axis with Bouvard's scheme and destroyed its integrity.

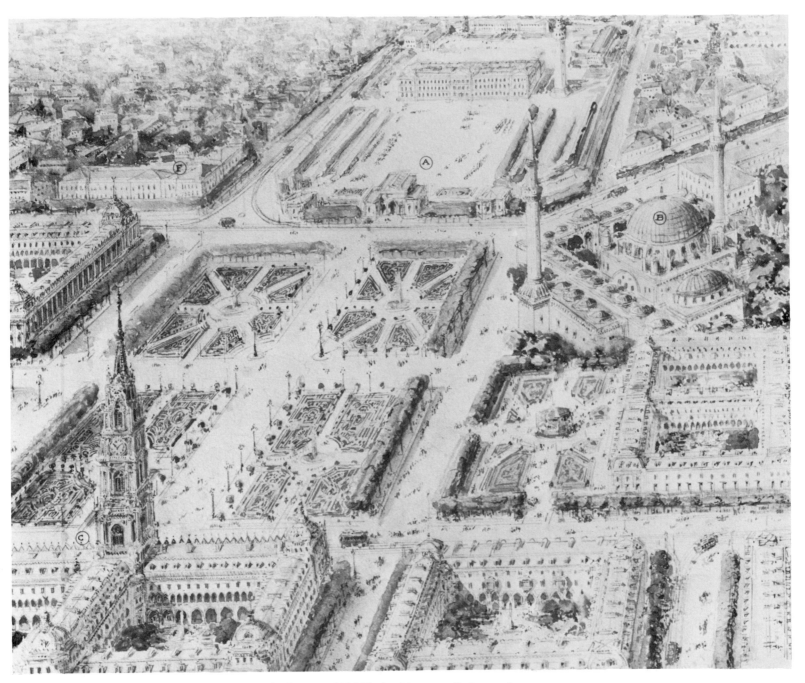

69. *Bouvard's proposal for Beyazit Square (1902), looking north toward
the Ministry of Defense*

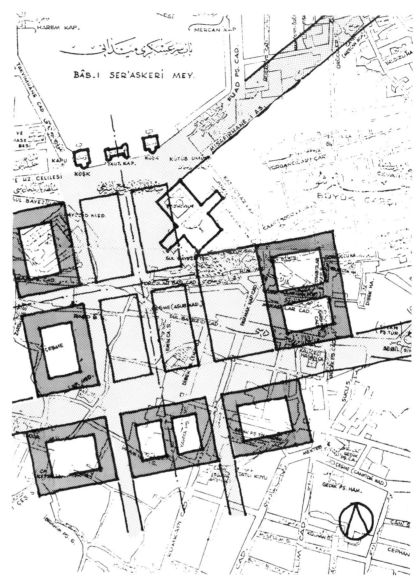

70. Bouvard's proposal for Beyazit Square superimposed on the urban fabric

Bouvard tried hard to bring a geometric order by using the southwest-facing entrance of the mosque to determine the orientation of a diagonal avenue. He blocked the rest of the mosque as much as he could with lush greenery.

At the southeast and southwest corners of the square were two more identical, unlabeled structures. They shared the stylistic language of the neighboring Bouvard buildings: they had arcades on the street level, two-story columns defining the main façades, Mansard roofs, and domes accentuating the corners.

Bouvard's cavalier attitude toward topography and the existing fabric made this ambitious scheme a mere illusion. The area of Beyazit is not flat as reflected in these drawings. With the entrance to the Ministry of War at the highest point, it slopes down toward the Sea of Marmara to the south and toward the Golden Horn to the north. Even the much smaller existing Beyazit Square had a considerable gradient between its north and south ends. Bouvard's scheme would lose its coherence if the slope were taken into consideration.

70 Bouvard's proposal becomes more impossible when projected over the existing city fabric. Given the dimensions and axiality of the plan, the western wing of the mosque and its courtyard would have to be partially amputated, and the Mausoleum of Sultan Beyazit would have to be completely torn down. Furthermore, the northeast and southwest corners of the Grand Bazaar would have to make room for two big structures. Regularizing the remainder of the Grand Bazaar would have presented a challenge, even for Bouvard.

Besides the inaccuracies in scale, Bouvard's boulevards and avenues created further problems. The ultimate destination of the diagonal avenue passing in front of the Beyazit Mosque is a mystery since the drawings do not extend beyond the immediate area being redesigned. The location of the main boulevard at the south end of the square was ill-advised because it cut through the Divanyolu, which led to the Hippodrome and to Hagia Sophia. In fact, here Bouvard betrayed his own scheme for the Hippodrome by not connecting it to Beyazit. Finally, Bouvard seems to have simply closed his eyes when it came to the street fabric in the south toward the Sea of Marmara. The orientation of his proposed arteries was fully thirty degrees off axis from the street network regularized in 1867.

The Galata Bridge and the Valide Sultan Square

In his scheme for the new Galata Bridge, Bouvard was directly influenced by the Pont Alexandre III, erected in Paris for the 1900 exposition. The Pont Alexandre III consists of a metal arch that spanned the Seine. With its pylons decorated by statues and the span itself adorned by elaborate candelabra and metal garlands, the Pont's profuse ornamentation matches the general spirit of the exposition (also embodied in the Grand Palais and the Petit Palais), for which Bouvard was the chief supervising architect.

71 Bouvard repeated the arch of the Parisian bridge four times in his proposal for the new Galata Bridge and added a half-arch to each end. Except for the length, everything else was derivative. The sculptural pylons at each end had forms similar to their French counterparts, but were crowned with an Oriental touch of tiny domes topped with crescents. The candelabra and the metal garlands were direct copies. Even the shape

71. Bouvard's proposal for a new Galata Bridge (1902)

and the placement of the lamps were reminiscent of the Pont Alexandre III.

The Galata Bridge that Bouvard envisioned for Istanbul was a grandiose structure. In contrast to the old and architecturally unsophisticated bridge it was to replace, Bouvard's bridge would present an image that the Western traveler, as well as the Westernized Ottoman elite, would easily associate with the finest in contemporary architecture. Bouvard used his excellent drafting techniques to give the design an exaggerated majestic tone. His bridge looks longer and the Golden Horn wider than in reality. The waterfront promenades helped to accentuate the monumentality of the bridge, and also reminded observers of the banks of the Seine.

While the Pont Alexandre III had the Hôtel des Invalides at its focal point on the Left Bank, Bouvard used the 1603 Valide Sultan Mosque to the south of his proposed bridge for that purpose. The waterfront at the south end of the bridge, in use since the Byzantine period as a produce quay, had always been a hub for sea traffic. Bouvard proposed cleaning the banks and opening a large public square in front of the Valide Sultan Mosque. He defined the boundaries of this square by two quadrant structures that framed the mosque. The scheme, with these two structures, is reminiscent of Davioud's Trocadéro Palace at the 1878 Paris

72
73

72. Bouvard's proposal for a Valide Sultan Square in Eminönü (1902)

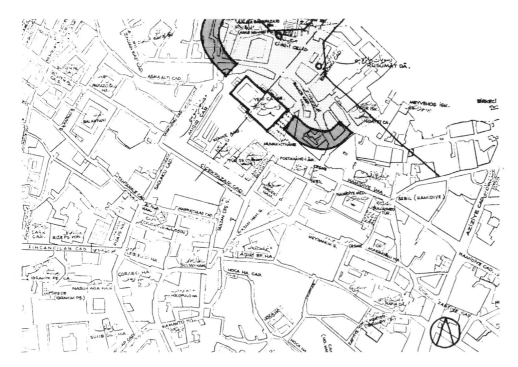

73. Bouvard's proposal for Valide Sultan Square superimposed on the urban fabric

World Exposition. The two buildings have tripartite end façades toward the Golden Horn, colonnades along the curves, and domes at the ends. However, the scale is smaller in Istanbul, the buildings are individual structures unlike the Parisian project, and the domes are derived from Istanbul's mosques.

The central dome of the Valide Sultan Mosque worked well conceptually with the new Galata Bridge, serving the same visual function as the Invalides at the end of the vista of the Pont Alexandre III and also recalling the central dome of the Trocadéro Palace (see fig. 117). But the building did not do justice to the symmetry of Bouvard's scheme. Its minarets, though resembling the two towers of the Trocadéro, did not symmetrically face the bridge. The courtyard to the west also damaged the symmetry. Bouvard tried to regularize this view by placing two pylons at the foot of the bridge.

The existing bridge that connected the two sides of the Golden Horn was one of the busiest spots in the city. A few years before Bouvard proposed his scheme, De Amicis described the scene on the bridge:

Standing there, you can see all Constantinople pass by in the course of an hour. . . . The crowd surges by in great waves of color, each group of persons representing a different nationality. Try to imagine the most extravagant contrasts of costume, every variety of type and social class, and your wildest dreams will fall short of the reality; in the course of ten minutes, and in the space of a few feet, you will have seen a mixture of race and dress you never conceived of before.[19]

De Amicis then gave a list of passersby: Turkish porters, an Armenian lady in a sedan chair, Bedouins, Greeks, a dervish in a conical hat and camel's-hair mantle, a European ambassador with his attendants, a Persian regiment in towering caps of black astrakhan, a Jew in a long yellow garment open at the sides, a gypsy with a baby on her back, a Catholic priest, ladies of a harem wearing green and violet in a carriage decorated with flowers, a sister of Charity from a Pera hospital, an African slave carrying a monkey, and finally, a storyteller in the garb of a necromancer.[20] He summed up: "It is an ever-changing mosaic, a kaleidoscopic view of race, costume, and religion, which forms and dissolves with a rapidity the eye and brain can with difficulty follow."[21] Whether Bouvard's bridge could accommodate this colorful crowd, at ease in the old setting, is questionable. The chaotic scene described above would most likely clash with the Parisian atmosphere, the ordered elegance, and the uniformity observed in Bouvard's drawings.

Bouvard's *avant-projet* was an exercise in form. It was not based on a preliminary program—many buildings were not even assigned a function in the drawings. The local culture and the existing urban living patterns were totally overlooked. The possibility of huge, barren open spaces did not seem to trouble Bouvard as he imposed his Beaux-Arts squares on the mazelike tissue. The architectural heritage was handled

74. *View of Galata Bridge looking toward Galata, circa 1913*

with the "isolate and preserve" mentality. No attention was paid to the urban texture that connected the monuments—a theme, which had found some popularity in Europe following Camillo Sitte's *The Art of Building Cities*, first published in 1889, and Charles Buls's *Esthétique des Villes* of 1893. Topography and existing major arteries were not considered, making the scheme rather utopian. Finally, the individually redesigned areas were not connected to each other. The Parisian-looking boulevards and avenues that dazzle in the drawings led nowhere.

75

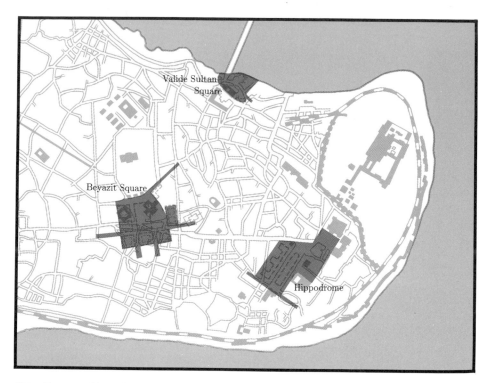

75. Bouvard's schemes for the Hippodrome, Beyazit Square, and Valide Sultan Square in relation to each other

In spite of its abstract context, the *avant-projet* was applauded by the Ottoman high bureaucracy. Imperial orders were issued to provide the funding for its realization.[22] However, like many other grandiose projects of the period, this one had to be given up too. The empire's financial resources could not meet the extravagant expenses of Bouvard's project.

The sultan and his entourage might well admire the new look. In Bouvard's drawings, Istanbul is no longer a run-down, disorderly Oriental town, but has the calm and self-assured elegance of Paris. This image might have appealed to the Westernized upper-class Turks and the Europeans residing in or passing through Istanbul. However, imposed from above and based on the aesthetic values of a different culture, Bouvard's scheme was likely to alienate the local inhabitants, who were living comfortably in an environment shaped over many centuries according to local needs.

The projects of Von Moltke, Arnodin, and Bouvard illustrate the main themes of urban planning in the Ottoman capital from 1838 to 1908. But, in contrast to the incremental and relatively small-scale applications surveyed in chapters three and four, they are more radical and daring proposals. To create a greater Istanbul out of the physically divided parts of the capital was the overriding concern of nineteenth and early twentieth-century transportation and bridge projects. Arnodin's plan, which drew the boundaries for a metropolitan Istanbul, was an ultimate step in this direction.

The technical aspects of city planning, such as the provision of good communication, a regularized street network, and an efficient transportation system, were other crucial issues. Both Von Moltke's and Arnodin's projects focused on such urban engineering challenges. Bouvard, however, did not work out the technical details of connecting the areas he redesigned. Yet the large avenues with electrical trams that he sketched in his proposals point to the absolute necessity for careful urban engineering.

Finally, as we have seen in the preceding chapters, the desire to build a novel and more regular urban image underlined almost all city-building activities between 1838 and 1908. The three schemes discussed here exemplify this trend in urban planning. In Von Moltke's and Bouvard's projects, the proposed image was European—one that was marked by straight, tree-lined boulevards leading to monuments, large public squares, and regularized embankments. On the other hand, Arnodin, certainly as image-conscious as Von Moltke and Bouvard, but perhaps more romantic in his Orientalism, attempted to contribute to the rich cultural heritage of the capital with his neo-Islamic Hamidiye Bridge, which would have dominated the urban image from Istanbul, Galata, and Üsküdar to the villages all along the Bosporus.

6.

Architectural Pluralism and the Search for a Style

Before the 1840s, the main monuments of the capital—the *külliyes*, the mosques, the bazaars, and the palaces—were concentrated on the Istanbul side. Galata was still a minor suburb with no buildings of outstanding size or importance. By the end of the nineteenth century the situation had changed; the northern side of the Golden Horn had become dotted with buildings that competed with Istanbul's monuments in their dimensions and stylistic aspirations.

These new buildings introduced contemporary Western architectural trends to the Ottoman capital and superimposed yet another layer over its already complex heritage. Although more prevalent in Galata, the Western-influenced architectural façade of the nineteenth century appeared in different parts of the Istanbul peninsula as well. The new urban image was created by two components: new building types and new architectural styles. Four major styles of the period illustrate the pluralism in the architectural language of the Ottoman capital. These new styles, classical revivalism, Gothic revivalism, Islamic revivalism, and Art Nouveau, commonly accompanied the new building types, such as office buildings, banks, theaters, department stores, hotels, and multistory apartment buildings.[1] They were also occasionally incorporated into the traditional building types, like mosques and mausoleums. When applied to the Western building types, the imported styles simply paralleled the European scene. However, when superimposed on a traditional building form, they created hybrid and interesting structures that deviated sharply from the established norms of classical Ottoman architecture.

ARCHITECTURAL STYLES

Classical Revivalism

Classical revivalism was undoubtedly the most frequently borrowed style.[2] The concept had a broad context in late nineteenth-century Istanbul: it ranged from Classical Greek to Renaissance to French Empire and its use was manifested by an eclectic, free-spirited borrowing from different peri-

76. *Karaköy Square, view toward Pera hills, circa 1900. In the background is the Galata Tower.*

ods and styles. Its abundant use helped to determine the overall urban image in the newly developing quarters on the northern side of the Golden Horn. A certain degree of natural zoning characterized the booming areas of the late nineteenth and early twentieth-century Ottoman capital: Karaköy at the foot of the Galata Bridge developed as a business center; the strip along the Bosporus shoreline from Karaköy toward Tophane and Kabataş evolved into a commercial waterfront; farther to the north, the Dolmabahçe-Beşiktaş axis following the waterway became the locus of imperial palaces; Pera, or Beyoğlu, turned into a Western-style cultural, shopping, and entertainment center that was home to much of the European community; and the bare hills of Taksim and Maçka were dotted with military barracks. Structures in other styles were scattered randomly in this fabric, but neoclassicism reigned.

Banks and other institutions associated with international trade were concentrated in Karaköy, conveniently close to the harbor. Karaköy Square at the foot of the Galata Bridge, opened in 1858, was barely as wide as the bridge itself. Most of the nineteenth-century streets that accommodated modern trade were merely the streets of the medieval town. De Amicis vividly described Karaköy's congested thoroughfares in the last decade of the nineteenth century:

76

Its streets, almost all of them narrow and tortuous, are dirty, ill-lighted, damp and narrow, like the streets of the lower parts of London. A hurrying, pushing throng of foot-passengers comes and goes all day long, now and then crowding to right and left to make room in the middle of the street for porters, carriages, donkeys, or omnibuses. Almost all the business conducted in Constantinople flows through this quarter.[3]

The new office buildings stood out in this chaotic fabric. The 1905 *Plan d'assurance de Constantinople* recorded a large number of office buildings that housed the institutions of international trade. Among them were the offices of numerous foreign insurance companies and many foreign banks.[4] The prototypical office building was a stone structure four or five stories high, imposing and heavy with lower stories of roughly textured rows of stone in the Renaissance manner and façades adorned with a variety of classical details. Though the classical elements prevailed,   *77* neo-Gothic, neo-Byzantine, and neo-Islamic features were also evident. This style has been justly identified with the "heavy-handed grandeur of Lombard Street classicism."[5]

77. Karaköy office building

78. A. Vallaury, Banque Ottomane, circa 1900

The most imposing structure of the business district was the Banque
78   Ottomane, designed by French architect Antoine Vallaury in the 1890s.
In 1896 the Banque Ottomane was described as the largest building in
the city.[6] It acquired an annex in 1899, which increased its dimensions,
giving it an even sturdier character. This building, which exemplified
many features of the commercial buildings in Galata, albeit on an enlarged
scale, was praised by *Le Moniteur Oriental* as being both beautiful and
solid.[7] Across the street, facing the Banque Ottomane, was a diminutive
79   replica of the Spanish Steps in Rome. This staircase did not fulfill an
important connecting function, but acted as an urban sculpture evoking
yet another image from Europe.

The waterfront from Karaköy to Tophane was regularized during
the second half of the nineteenth century. The new commercial buildings   custom houses and warehouses—were longitudinal stone structures,
erected parallel to the embankments. They were large, functional, and in
a matching stripped-down neoclassical style that strongly recalled their
80   contemporary counterparts in industrial European cities.

As we have seen in chapter three, the Tophane quay underwent a
major reorganization in 1864. A public square, "ornamented in the European manner," as the *Journal de Constantinople* wrote, was created here.

79. *Stairs opposite the Banque Ottomane*

80. *The shoreline between Karaköy and Tophane, circa 1900. Along the
waterfront are the warehouses and the custom houses. In the background
on the left is Sinan's Kılıç Ali Paşa Mosque.*

81. Tophane quay, circa 1900. In the center is the Nusretiye Mosque, to the left is the Tophane clock tower.

In 1888, Abdülhamit II ordered the erection of clock towers in several *81* locations of the capital.[8] One such tower was built on Tophane Square. The towers were considered "civic art," and symbols of Westernization and progress as they expressed the disassociation of time and religion.[9]

Farther up the Bosporus, the strip parallel to the shoreline between Dolmabahçe and Beşiktaş developed as a series of imperial residences during the second half of the nineteenth century. The first stages of this process began in the seventeenth century when an imperial garden was built in Dolmabahçe and a summer palace in a large garden was constructed at Beşiktaş by Ahmet III (1703–30).[10] But real change did not come until completion of the Dolmabahçe Palace in 1856 and the transferral of the imperial residence from Topkapı to the new palace. The Dolmabahçe Palace was the ultimate declaration of imperial preference for an architectural style imported from Europe.

The architect of the Dolmabahçe Palace was Karabet Balyan of the famous Armenian family that had served the court for several generations.[11] The palace is a longitudinal building with its principal façade *82* on the waterfront—a feature commonly observed in the *yalı*s along the Bosporus. A marble quay preceded by a wall broken by a curved railing separates it from the water. The structure consists of three sections: the *selamlık* (men's apartments), the throne room, and the harem. The overall organization adheres to the basic principles of Beaux-Arts design in symmetry, clarity, axiality, and regularity, but the interior organization of

82. K. Balyan, Dolmabahçe Palace, circa 1909. Dolmabahçe Mosque is on the left.

83. S. Balyan, Dolmabahçe clock tower

each component is based on the prototypical Turkish house plan arranged around a central hall on to which all other rooms open. The centralized quality of this traditional scheme meshed well with the main elements of Beaux-Arts design.

The palace's classical façades reflect many characteristics of the French Empire style: rows of delicate Doric and Ionic pillars are used next to twisted columns that frame the windows, flowers and foliage curl around the arches as well as intertwining with each other to form surface decorations, and innumerable sculptures, modeled on the standard French prototypes adorn the little balconies. No other building in the capital could equal Dolmabahçe in classical ornateness.

Karabet Balyan also designed the Dolmabahçe Mosque, built at the same time as the palace and facing its southern gate. The mosque complemented the palace stylistically with its French Empire details (see fig. 99). The extent to which Western fashions had penetrated the architectural vocabulary is apparent in the Dolmabahçe Mosque's slender minarets treated as Corinthian columns. In 1894, a clock tower was placed on the plaza between the palace and the mosque.[12]

83 Other palaces followed. Farther to the north and again on the waterfront, the Çırağan Palace, designed by Sergis Balyan, was built in 1871 for Abdülaziz. Although it was classical on the exterior, the interior was rich with Islamic decoration.[13] The Çırağan Palace was connected to the

*84. Fossati Brothers, Russian Embassy, annex on the Grande
Rue de Pera*

forested hills (the Yıldız gardens) by means of a bridge over the public
way, and several kiosks were erected inside the Yıldız gardens. The late
nineteenth-century extravagance of building a new palace for every sultan was further pursued by Abdülhamit II, who moved to Yıldız and built
there the neoclassical mansions of Şale Köşkü, Malta Köşkü, and Çadır
Köşkü to form his Yıldız Palace complex. A large library and a porcelain
workshop were among the many palace annexes. The planning principles of the Yıldız Palace were different from those of the Dolmabahçe
and Çırağan palaces. The buildings of the Yıldız Palace were individual
structures, reminiscent of the Topkapı Palace kiosks. They were almost
organically distributed throughout the large gardens and had no visual
connection with the city. They could not even be viewed from a distance

because they merged into the landscape. Only the high walls and the monumental entrances symbolized the presence of the imperial power in Yıldız.

Up the hills of Tophane, in Pera, the buildings on and in the vicinity of the Grande Rue de Pera conveyed an overall picture of the values, fashions, and social patterns introduced to the Ottoman capital following the Tanzimat reforms. Life in Pera was much different from life in Istanbul, and Pera's architecture reflected the difference. The Grande Rue, often referred to as the "Champs Elysées of the Orient," had no visual similarity to the famous French avenue, but was nevertheless a European-inspired urban artery. The attractions lining its two sides called for a strolling pace with many stops at shops, restaurants, and cafés. De Amicis described the Grande Rue as

... bright and cheerful.... It is the "West End" of the European colony, the quarter where are to be found the comforts and elegancies of life.... It is lined on both sides with English and French hotels, cafés of the better sort, brilliantly lighted shops, theaters, foreign consulates, clubs, and the residences of various ambassadors.[14]

85. *French Embassy, view from the garden*

Classical revivalism was the favorite style for Pera buildings. The embassies, which competed with each other in monumentality, must have played a crucial role in determining the neoclassical image of the quarter. In large gardens, often attached to religious and educational facilities, they formed integral units that dominated large sections of Pera's landscape. The neo-Renaissance Russian Embassy, designed by the Swiss Fossati brothers in 1839,[15] the Empire-style French Embassy reconstructed in 1838,[16] the neo-Renaissance British Embassy of 1845, constructed upon the original plan of Sir Charles Barry, but slightly modified by another English architect, W. J. Smith,[17] and the Dutch Embassy of 1855, again designed by the Fossati brothers (in the manner of a small French château), were the most outstanding examples.

The overwhelming majority of other Pera buildings—churches, hotels, department stores, restaurants, cafés, theaters, and so forth—adhered to the architectural styles imposed by the embassies. They also brought the amenities of a Western lifestyle to the capital. Along the Grande Rue, trade flourished in the shops and department stores stocked with luxury goods from all parts of Europe. These items were consumed not only by the foreign inhabitants, but also, and with great enthusiasm, by the Ottoman upper classes, including the court itself.

Clothing stores dominated the Grande Rue. Toward its southern end, an Englishman named Hayden sold fabrics imported from his native country; Madame de Milleville's Grande Maison de Couture dressed the "mondaines" of the city. Not far from Madame de Milleville's shop was Madame Vapillon's boutique, which specialized in Parisian accessories for women; the first ladies' gloves from Paris were sold here. The imperial harem was dressed by another "salon de mode": Paquin d'Istanbul.

86. *Buildings in Pera*

87. *Passage d'Europe, detail*

Among the many clothing stores, La Maison de Modes Françaises, La Maison de Modes et de Fournitures pour Dames, Salon de Modes, and Madame Trophe's millinery were the most popular.[18]

The names of the department stores, Maison Baker, Paris-Londres, Bon Marché, and Bazar Allemand, indicate the origins of their goods as well as their pretensions. The Bon Marché, for example, specialized in household articles, leather goods, stationery, hunting equipment, cosmetics, jewelery, bronze art objects, toys, optical instruments and eyeglasses, photographic equipment, drugs, gloves, hosiery, women's lingerie, umbrellas, clothing ("modes"), china, crystal, wines, and liquors. The Bazar Allemand had a collection of articles for all prices, but was famous for its clocks ("pendules") and "coucous."[19]

There were two galleries—the Passage d'Europe and the Passage Crespin—miniature models of their European precursors, replete with metal structures, glass roofs, and ornate neoclassical interior and exterior façades. Passage d'Europe housed a variety of shops, whereas only shoemakers were to be found in the Passage Crespin.[20]

87

European-style cafés, night clubs, restaurants, café-chantants, and chansonniers tried to duplicate another aspect of Western urban life: eating and entertaining outside the home. Their names demonstrate what Pera really wanted to be: La Maison le Bon Goût, Brasserie Suisse, Brasserie Strasbourg, Brasserie Viennoise, Brasserie de Londres, Café-Restaurant de Paris, Café-Chantant Parisiana, Concordia, and Trocadéro.[21]

With the increase in international trade after 1838, the number of transient Europeans escalated. This led to the emergence of many European-style hotels in Pera. Often, they became the long-term residences of European expatriates and were therefore forced to meet Western standards. The Hôtel des Ambassadeurs, for example, was praised in 1855 by *Journal de Constantinople* because it had magnificent apartments, furnished with all the desirable comfort and elegance as well as a dining room of "le plus grand luxe."[22]

In 1865, an imperial order gave James Missirie, the representative of Compagnie de l'Hôtel Impérial Ottoman, the right to construct and manage hotels that would provide convenient accommodation for foreign travelers and inhabitants. The sections of the city where hotels could be built were restricted to Pera, Büyükdere, Üsküdar, and Prinkipo (Büyük Ada) of the Princes' Islands.[23] Istanbul was not included, perhaps for the simple reason that foreigners preferred to stay in Pera.

The imperial order was not exclusive, so many other individuals obtained permits to run hotels. The 1905 *Plan d'assurance* presents us with a long list of hotels, again their names indicative of the type of establishments they aspired to be: Hôtel de Paris, Grand Hôtel Kroecker, Pera Palace, Hôtel Continental, Hôtel St. Petersbourg, Grand Hôtel de

Londres, Hôtel de Lyon, Hôtel Modern, Hôtel Royal, Hôtel Bristol. Neo-classical details dominated their façades.

The famous Pera Palace, the largest of the Pera hotels, was built and managed by the Compagnie Internationale des Wagons-lits et des Grands Expresses Européens. It was a multistory rectangular building with magnificent dining and reception rooms that hosted innumerable balls at the
88   turn of the century.[24] Another major hotel was the Hôtel Bristol, built in 1893 on Tepebaşı Caddesi. Perhaps not as majestic as the Pera Palace, but still among the best hotels in the city, the Hôtel Bristol had a spacious entrance hall, marble staircases, an elevator, large suites, apartments, drawing rooms, and a large dining room, which could accommodate about one hundred guests "on the 'separate table' system as at the grand hotels in Paris and Vienna."[25]

European-style multistory apartment buildings were introduced during the second half of the nineteenth century as well. Up to this time, the northern side of the Golden Horn had a residential fabric in wood. In the nineteenth century, legal restrictions based on fire prevention, resulted in a gradual conversion to brick and stone. Simultaneously, the new housing in Pera took as its model the European-style multistory apartment buildings. As the *Journal de Constantinople* reported in 1864, the wooden houses had almost totally disappeared in Pera having been replaced by "solid constructions of stone." Moreover, unlike in the past, these buildings no longer encroached upon the public way, but neatly defined the two sides of the streets with their regular façades as in European cities.[26]

Nevertheless, the apartment buildings constructed in the next decade, from 1864 to 1875, were not up to the standards of contemporary European examples.[27] In 1875, the number of "comfortable" flats with "commodious plans and well-studied façades" was very small.[28] Issues such as lighting, ventilation, and heating were not carefully addressed. But, *La Turquie* happily announced that a small number of well-educated architects had arrived in town and that they would be able to design the efficient interiors and the artistic exteriors observed in Europe:

For some time . . . we have been witnessing the arrival of architects from Paris, who are not only able builders, but also having completed a strong education at the Ecole des Beaux-Arts, are men of taste who know all the resources of their art, can estimate a site, distribute it without wasting an inch, meanwhile giving each room the importance that it deserves, and cover their façades with decorations, which give the buildings the seal of simplicity, grandeur, or mirth they must have.[29]

89   In 1876, the Cité de Pera building was erected on the site of the former Naum Theater, destroyed by the 1870 fire. This building, belonging to a wealthy Greek businessman, Chirtaki Efendi Zogrophos, occupied a surface area of approximately 4,600 square meters. The ground floor was reserved for commercial use: on either side of the monumental entrance

88. Pera Palace

89. Cité de Pera, view from the Grande Rue de Pera (under restoration after collapsing in the 1970s)

were two large stores; nineteen smaller shops lined the interior gallery, which connected the Grande Rue to a side street. From the courtyard, marble staircases led to the three upper floors where large apartments of five, six, and seven rooms were featured. The Cité de Pera incorporated all the amenities of modern European apartment living—running water, gas lighting (even on the staircases), and each unit was given a storage space in the basement for wood and coal.

Cité de Pera's architectural style was "Second Empire." *La Turquie* described it as "Renaissance mixed with Greek," resulting in a "monument elegant in its details, imposing in its ensemble." An editorial presented it as a turning point in the architecture of the Ottoman Empire:

The Cité de Pera is ... a monument that even Paris itself would be proud of. We can say confidently that Pera has been adorned with a monument that gives honor not only to its owner, but also to the entire city, and which marks the beginning of a new era for the architecture of the country.[30]

The Cité de Pera indeed became a landmark for the city (today the most popular tavernas are located around its courtyard) and a monumental prototype for the many apartment buildings erected in Pera during the last quarter of the nineteenth century. By 1900, the main arteries of Pera, Taksim, and Pangaltı were lined with large, luxurious apartment buildings.[31] However, there was still a serious housing shortage in both Pera and Istanbul. As *Le Moniteur Oriental* put it, there was no decent housing available at reasonable rates for the worker and those earning a modest income. The figures of the 1882 census also reflect the seriousness of the housing problem. According to the official numbers, approximately 26 percent of the capital's population did not reside in a private home. About 5 percent lived in mosques and *tekke*s (sufi convents), 8 percent were refugees without permanent residence, 1.5 percent Muslim students living in *medrese*s, 14 percent artisans living in their shops, and 2 percent artisans and merchants staying in *han*s.[32]

During the last twenty-five years of the nineteenth and the first decade of the twentieth century, an attempt was made to create moderate income housing in the form of rowhouses—a housing type foreign to the city until then. Its target population was small merchants, craftsmen, artisans, and low-level bureaucrats. The location of the rowhouses tells us more about the intended users. With one exception, they were all built in the modest neighborhoods and back streets of Istanbul, Pera, and Üsküdar.[33] The exception was the Akaretler project in Beşiktaş, where large and stylistically ambitious units lined the two main streets. In fact, this is the only instance in the capital of a rowhouse scheme being used as a form-giver in urban design. The proximity of the Dolmabahçe Palace no doubt played an active part in the relatively monumental treatment given to this scheme.

Formed under the influence of Western examples and depending on a land parceling that resulted from particular ownership patterns (*vakıf*s), the rowhouses had regular and prototypical layouts.[34] Their façades were simple, symmetrical, and adorned with some classical elements. Though they formed a contrast to the traditional houses of the city, some local elements, such as baywindows, were integrated into their design. The rowhouses hence added an unprecedented blend of Western and traditional elements to the urban image of the Ottoman capital.

The upper-class Muslim residential architecture also underwent a transformation after the mid-nineteenth century. This was manifested by an interesting usage of Western appliqué façades on traditional interiors. The new *konak*s (large mansions) built in *kargir* made extensive use of architectural features adopted from contemporary European styles, especially from classicism. However, the interior organization followed the principles of a traditional Turkish house with a series of rooms opening on to a large central hall. These new *konak*s were built on both sides of the Golden Horn.[35] In Istanbul, they often merged into the existing fabric,

90

91

90. *Apartment buildings in Pera*

91. *Rowhouses in Beşiktaş*

but on the northern side of the Golden Horn, erected along the recently opened straight, wide streets, they helped create a new cityscape.

The Nişantaşı neighborhood, which developed during the last decades of the nineteenth century, is a fine example of this new pattern. The streets were straight and wide, cutting each other at right angles; the two- or three-story mansions were built in the middle of the plots, their neoclassical façades often defining the boundary of the street. The spacious gardens of the mansions created an effect very different from the main arteries of Pera, where tall apartment buildings adjacent to each other formed a much denser fabric.

The wooden residential architecture of the city also made use of classical elements. Freely altered by the local craftsmen to match the traditional forms, they still display the current fashions in residential construction. Though the classical elements were more popular in the Bosporus villages, they also penetrated the Istanbul neighborhoods and adorned the entrances, windows, and cornices of many houses from the most humble to the most elegant.

92

To the west of Pera, the newly developing areas in the hills of Taksim and Maçka also acquired a neoclassical appearance. This new image

92. *Wooden houses on the Bosporus with classical details*

93. *Military barracks in Taksim, circa 1900*

was brought about by the construction of large military barracks, which accompanied the reorganization of the Ottoman army on Western models. The two barracks in Taksim, and those in Gümüşsuyu and Maçka (the last two designed by Sergis Balyan) were built in the 1860s under Abdülaziz. Others, farther up the Bosporus, in the vicinity of the Yıldız Palace, belong to Abdülhamit II's reign.[36] These overscaled structures that marked the otherwise bare hills of the Bosporus became conspicuous landmarks in the capital's nineteenth-century urban image. Rectangular, with large interior courtyards, the barracks had similar layouts. Their orderly and symmetrical façades were furnished with a severe and spare

93   classicism, befitting the military spirit.

Though not on a scale comparable to the northern sections of the Golden Horn, neoclassicism also penetrated the Istanbul peninsula. Here the neoclassical structures were concentrated near the southern end of the Galata Bridge. Immediately at the foot of the bridge in Eminönü and along the shoreline between Eminönü and Sirkeci were the *kargir* custom houses and warehouses, built in the 1850s and the 1870s in the same style as their counterparts along the Karaköy-Tophane strip.[37] A few office buildings, for example, the administrative office of the harbor, were also located on the Istanbul side of the bridge.[38] These large, multistory

94   structures echoed the office buildings of Karaköy.

Neoclassicism was also deemed appropriate for state architecture. An early example was the seat of the Sublime Porte (Babıali) inaugurated in 1843.[39] The monumental stone structure was composed of several interconnected offices. Fossati Brothers, the popular architects of foreign embassies, were responsible for the interior decoration. An 1878 fire destroyed most of the building, but the office of the grand vizier and the archives were saved, as well as the ornate and monumental entrance gate with baroque eaves.

94. Office building in Eminönü

As part of the Westernizing educational reforms, a university was

95   erected between Hagia Sophia and the Sultan Ahmet Mosque in 1846.[40] The architects were the Fossati brothers, who once more employed a neoclassical style. The three-story rectangular building had a powerful mass alien to the skyline of Istanbul. A neo-Greek portico dominated its eastern façade.

Another Western-inspired government building was the 1866 Ministry of War in Beyazit, constructed in stone on the site of an earlier wooden structure but following a more grandiose plan.[41] This Beaux-Arts structure was organized around an attractive glass-roofed central courtyard—the first of its kind in the city.

The Royal Museum of Antique Works (Asar-ı Antika Müze-i Hümayunu), designed by Antoine Vallaury, and built in the Topkapı Palace gardens in 1891, was another outstanding manifestation of the official adoption of Western cultural models.[42] The desire to build a museum went back to 1869, when an imperial decree was issued urging the construction

95. *Fossati Brothers, university, view from the Sea of Marmara, circa 1900. On the left is the Mosque of Ahmet I; on the right is a minaret of Hagia Sophia.*

of a *müzehane* (museum) upon the "examples in European countries."[43] Vallaury's museum had six sections: the first housed the Greek, Roman, and Byzantine artifacts; the second, the Assyrian, Egyptian, Phoenician, Hittite, African, and Asian (other than Arab) collections; the third, the Islamic collection; the fourth, antique coins; the fifth, natural history specimens; and the sixth was a library replete with a large collection of books on historical and scientific topics.[44] Compartmentalizing in this fashion reflected the museum arrangement that had developed in Europe from the beginning of the nineteenth century. Vallaury's neoclassical museum also conformed to the universally accepted museum style, and this choice worked especially well with the rich collection of antiquities exhibited.[45]

    These buildings imposed a novel tone on the multilayered historic fabric of Istanbul. Their concentration on the Western part of the peninsula, however, resulted in the creation of a modern, nineteenth-century

96

appearance restricted to a relatively small area. There were other neo-classical buildings, mainly some *kargir* mansions, scattered throughout Istanbul, but their small number and their distribution throughout the urban landscape did not contribute to a significant alteration in the general appearance of the city.

Classical revivalism was applied freely to traditional building types. Its champion in Istanbul was Karabet Balyan, the architect of the Dolmabahçe Palace and of Mahmut II's mausoleum on the Divanyolu, which dates from 1840. The latter is an octagonal building with grilled windows attached to a wall that forms a screen between the road and the cemetery—all common characteristics of an Ottoman mausoleum complex. However, this building also exhibits themes foreign to Ottoman architecture. It is oversized relative to the classical Ottoman examples, and a variety of imported forms—pilasters with elaborate Ionic capitals adorned with floral reliefs, arched windows with decorative keystones, floral decorations on the frieze and the iron grilles in the French Empire style—are applied to the façades.

Karabet Balyan pursued the same approach in his 1864 Ortaköy Mosque, where he used the traditional spaces and typical components of

96. A. Vallaury, museum, annex

97. K. Balyan, Mausoleum of Mahmut II, circa 1900

98. K. Balyan, Ortaköy Mosque

99. K. Balyan, Dolmabahçe Mosque

100. G. E. Street, Crimean Memorial Church

Ottoman mosques, meanwhile incorporating a large collection of neoclassical elements into the building. His Dolmabahçe Mosque shared similar characteristics. The Mausoleum of Mahmut II, the Ortaköy Mosque, and the Dolmabahçe Mosque present a variation on the French Empire style. Architectural historians attempted to distinguish this hybrid style from French Empire by labeling it "Turkish Empire." Motifs such as swords, bunches of flags, and musical instruments were integrated into the Turkish Empire style, but there were no animal or human figures as in the French.[46]

Gothic Revivalism

Victorian neo-Gothic was introduced to Istanbul through the Crimean Memorial Church designed by G. E. Street and built in 1869.[47] This

98
99

100

101. *Church of St. Stephen of the Bulgars, circa 1900*

102. *Pertevniyal Valide Mosque, Aksaray, circa 1900*

large and handsome structure, reminiscent of Street's London Law Courts, did not find a following. The only other outstanding example of Gothic revivalism (although with some neo-Romanesque details) is the Church of St. Stephen of the Bulgars, erected in 1871 when the Bulgarian church declared its independence from the Greek Patriarch. This church, located close to the Greek Orthodox Patriarchy in Fener on the Golden Horn, was built entirely of cast iron. It was prefabricated in Vienna and shipped down the Danube to Istanbul.[48]   *101*

Gothic revivalism accompanied Islamic forms and classical Ottoman scapes in two imperial nineteenth-century mosques, creating striking, but not uniformly pleasing results. The 1873 Pertevniyal Valide Mosque in Aksaray made use of Gothic revivalism in its general verticality, which was also repeated in the proportions of its various components, for example, its window details.[49] The second example is Nikogos Balyan's 1886 Hamidiye   *102*
Mosque, adjacent to the Yıldız Palace. Here the verticality is accentuated again with the longitudinal proportions of the building parts. The pointed arch is now boldly used, and the window treatments are overtly more Gothic than those of the Pertevniyal Valide Mosque.[50]   *103*

Two nineteenth-century neo-Byzantine buildings should be recalled in this context. The Greek Church of the Holy Trinity, completed in 1882, created, with its high dome and towers, a powerful focus from Taksim toward the Grande Rue; its style was metaphorically appropriate. The   *104*
other neo-Byzantine structure, Kaiser Wilhelm II's fountain, erected on the Hippodrome in 1899, paid homage to the nearby Hagia Sophia in its decorations, especially in the intricately carved capitals.   *105*

Islamic Revivalism

Ironically, Islamic revivalism was brought to Istanbul, the seat of the caliphate, by European architects. Interest in this "exotic" style had grown in the West in the nineteenth century, paralleling the expanding colonialism.[51] To Western architects, the value of Islamic architecture lay in its decorative elements, which could be applied to their thoroughly Western buildings as a mere surface veneer. The Ottoman capital made an especially appealing setting for an Islamic revivalist style.

Among the most striking examples of a neo-Islamic style was the Sirkeci Train Station, completed in 1889 under the supervision of the German architect Jachmund. Its design principles followed the classical   *106*
ideals of regularity, symmetry, axiality, and clarity, but the structure was clad in an Oriental style based on Mamluk and Moorish sources. Jach-   *107*
mund's purpose must have been twofold: to find an appropriate symbol for the terminus of the Orient Express and to conform to the urban image of classical Ottoman Istanbul. His design achieved the first objective, as the Orientalism of the building is unmistakable. However, Jachmund's unawareness of the stylistic differences between various regions of Islam and periods of its history caused him to fall short of his second goal.

103. *N. Balyan, Hamidiye Mosque. Opening ceremony in 1886.*

104. *Greek Church of the Holy Trinity, view from Taksim Square*

106. *Jachmund, Sirkeci Train Station. Opening ceremony in 1889.*

105. *Kaiser Wilhelm II's fountain at the Hippodrome, dedication ceremony in 1899. In the background is Hagia Sophia.*

107. Main entrance of the Sirkeci Train Station

In the end, his design was simply another foreign-looking structure that contributed to the fin-de-siècle architectural pluralism in the capital.

Antoine Vallaury applied a similar style to the Office of the Public Debt Administration (Düyun-u Umumiye Binası) in 1899. Located prominently on the hill behind the Sirkeci Train Station, this building combines Beaux-Arts design with elements taken from local architecture. The roof form with its large eaves, the baywindows, and the window details were borrowed from Turkish house design. The use of materials, the monumental entrances, and the organization of the fenestration repeated the themes of monumental Ottoman buildings. Vallaury's revivalism was a Turkish-Islamic one, and it is ironic that the seeds of a neo-Turkish style were planted in Istanbul by a Frenchman in the very building that symbolized the absolute economic control wielded by Western powers over the Ottoman Empire.   *108*

The birth of Islamic revivalism in the Ottoman Empire is often associated with Abdülhamit II's commitment to the ideology of Islamism. There is, however, no evidence to support this thesis.[52] On the contrary, Abdülhamit's appreciation of Bouvard's grand designs for Istanbul indicates where his preference lay. Islamic revivalism, as practiced by foreign architects in Istanbul during the later decades of the nineteenth century, is simply a logical development of the contemporary European eclecticism.

Islamic revivalism made a strong impact on Turkish architecture and evolved into a style referred to by architectural historians as the "First National Architectural Movement." Its pioneers were Kemalettin Bey, a student of Jachmund, and the Beaux-Arts-trained Vedat Bey. Their practice flourished during the 1920s and the 1930s, bolstered by the young Republic's emphasis on nationalism.[53]

Art Nouveau

The origins of Art Nouveau in Istanbul are rightfully attributed to the Italian architect Raimondo D'Aronco, the outstanding practitioner of the Stile Floreale. D'Aronco was first invited to the capital by Abdülhamit II to design the 1893 Industrial and Agricultural Exposition. He then served as the chief architect to the imperial court between 1896 and 1908.[54] But, his professional activity was not restricted to royal structures. He established a large practice in the city, designing apartment buildings in Pera, and villas along the Bosporus and the Sea of Marmara.

Among D'Aronco's many buildings, the small complex of Şeyh Zafir, built in 1903 in Beşiktaş on the Bosporus, consisting of a mausoleum, a library, and a fountain, deserves a special place in the history of Art Nouveau architecture. It successfully combines the stylistic characteristics of the movement with non-Western forms and functions. The layout of its parts is modeled upon earlier Ottoman examples and the forms and relationships between them are repeated. The mausoleum is a square,   *109* symmetrical structure, covered with a dome. Attached to the mausoleum is a library—smaller in scale and more modest in its architectural treatment. To these, D'Aronco integrated curving eaves, triangular battered reliefs, floral decoration, and metalwork for the windows.

Casa Botter, an apartment house belonging to the Botter family on the Grande Rue, was one of D'Aronco's most admired buildings in Pera.

110

108. A. Vallaury, Public Debt Administration Building. Main entrance.

109. R. D'Aronco, Şeyh Zafir complex. Street façade.

110. R. D'Aronco, Casa Botter. Detail from façade.

111. Flora Han in Eminönü

Built in 1907, its nontraditional façade brought a novel liveliness to the main street. This façade was divided vertically by four huge pilasters decorated with medallions, abstract, curving floral and vegetal forms, and two, stone faces. The pilasters were connected by an elaborate frieze of floral texture above the fourth story, which was repeated on the entrance gate as well as on the turrets. The metal railings of the balconies made use of a universal Art Nouveau feature, the sinuous line.

Art Nouveau became a favorite style in the capital. Numerous turn-of-the-century buildings along and around the Grande Rue exhibit Art Nouveau traits, especially in the railings, window details, and floral friezes where the rose motif reigns. The fashion crossed the Golden Horn as well. For example, an office building in Eminönü, appropriately named Flora Han, makes extensive use of the rose motif in its friezes, upper levels, and as single elements that define the windows. Its window-frames and the iron railings are also unmistakably Art Nouveau. *111*

Art Nouveau spread to the Bosporus villages where D'Aronco built a rather flamboyant palace for Princess Emine Naciye in Kuruçeşme, a summer palace for the Egyptian Khedive in Bebek, and a summer residence for the Italian Embassy in Tarabya. Many features from these, as well as other Art Nouveau buildings in the city, found their way to the more modest houses of the Bosporus. In architectural historian Godfrey Goodwin's words, "Art Nouveau came to the Bosphorus like a gardener. House after house reflects this with its wrought iron daisies and convolvus guarding glass paneled front doors."[55] The new vocabulary seemed at ease with the traditional forms of residential architecture. The popularity of Art Nouveau perhaps can be attributed to its stylistic affinity to the familiar abstracted language of Islamic art.

THE SEARCH FOR A STYLE

Architectural pluralism in the Ottoman capital, defined by various imported styles, created a deep anxiety among Turkish intellectuals. Ottoman architecture, as represented in the works of earlier architects, such as Sinan, was a matter of pride. The developments during the nineteenth and early twentieth centuries, in contrast, were considered a decline, a degeneration. Solutions were attempted to "save" Ottoman architecture paralleling the general goal of saving the empire.

The Westernized Ottoman intelligentsia approached the question of style with a biased attitude: Ottoman architecture was to be explained by a vocabulary and a set of rules similar to those developed in European architectural treatises. This thesis was first ventured in a work titled *Usul-u Mimari-i Osmani* (or, *L'Architecture ottomane*), prepared at imperial command by Montani Efendi and Boghos Efendi Chachian for the 1873 Vienna Universal Exposition. It was published in Istanbul in Turkish, French, and German.

The goal of this work was to bring to light the superior qualities of Ottoman architecture and to re-introduce to modern architects its chefs d'oeuvre, such as the mosques of Istanbul, Edirne, and Bursa. In the "Précis historique" section, the decline of Ottoman architecture was discussed after a brief survey of the most important monuments. The influence of French architects, engineers, and artists was seen as a destructive force, which had led to a loss of purity in Ottoman architecture, as observed in examples such as the Nuruosmaniye and Laleli mosques.[56] The nineteenth-century architects of the capital were accused of experimenting with every known style and "trying in vain to adopt them, sometimes one by one, sometimes in a confusion that is ridiculous and powerless; to the requirements of Ottoman buildings—religious and other—they produce nothing but monstrous and dull designs."[57] If Ottoman architecture continued to imitate the European styles, it would soon terminate its own existence.

However, according to this treatise, with Abdülaziz's reign (the sultan under whose patronage the *Usul-u Mimari-i Osmani* was published), some positive tendencies had emerged and a "national art" based on a "renaissance" of Ottoman architecture was in sight. Ironically, the Aksaray Valide Mosque, with its neo-Gothic elements, and the Çırağan Palace, with its classical façades, were considered pioneers of an "école neo-turque."[58]

The chapter titled "Documents téchniques" attempted to outline the rules of Ottoman architecture. It used the model of the first-century Roman architect Vitruvius to establish a classification of the Ottoman orders into the ordre échafriné, ordre bréchiforme, and ordre crystallisé, corresponding to the Doric, Ionic, and Corinthian orders. These were described in detail, each description ending with a few Vitruvian statements. Hence, the ordre échafriné was categorized as appropriate for lower levels of galleries, for shops, and for every building type that required a great simplicity. The bréchiforme was very severe and heavy and was not used in civil architecture; the crystallisé displayed playfulness and refinement and was used in the interiors of civil buildings.[59]

112
113
114

The argument followed that the Ottoman orders had created many beautiful buildings in the past and that they should still be used, because "they presented more subtlety than the vulgarly known classical orders." By reorganizing the principles of Ottoman architecture in a doctrine, it was believed that a service was paid to art in general.[60] The main objective was to make a place for Ottoman architecture within the wide spectrum of Western architectural styles and to encourage the use of a neo-Turkish style with defined rules of application for contemporary buildings.[61]

An undated document from the reign of Abdülhamit II, catalogued in the Başbakanlık Arşivi as "Unsigned Summary Report on the Development of National Fine Arts and the Provision of Opportunities," discussed once more the state of contemporary Ottoman architecture.[62] According

112. Ordre échafriné from Montani Efendi and Boghos Efendi Chachian, Usul-u Mimari-i Osmani *(1873)*

113. Ordre bréchiforme

114. Ordre crystallisé

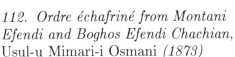

to this document, Ottoman architecture had entered a period of crisis because the profession had been taken over by Greeks and Armenians. The 1603 Valide Sultan Mosque in Eminönü was deemed the last true piece of Ottoman architecture. Like *Usul-u Mimari-i Osmani*, this report singled out the Nuruosmaniye and Laleli mosques as bad examples, because they were built in a "French style called 'rocaille'" (*rokay tabir olunan Fransız tarz-ı mimarisi*). However, contrary to the opinion expressed in *L'Architecture ottomane*, the buildings erected under Abdülaziz were not applauded and, for example, the Aksaray Valide Mosque was defined as "ugly" and accused of opening the way for a style that was neither Turkish, nor Arabic, nor Gothic!

The report also criticized the residential architecture done in the French style, *alafranga*, as it was called. It argued that neither the stone nor the timber *alafranga* houses were in fact *alafranga*, which, the report claimed, was attested by those who had been to Europe. The report considered this housing style very ugly and ill-suited to the climate and local needs.

The real cause of the architectural decline was attributed to builders (*kalfas*), the majority of whom were Christians who had taken the place of Islamic architects in the Ottoman Empire. With the establishment of a school of architecture in Istanbul, which would promote a systematic architectural education, it was believed that the problem could be resolved in about eight to ten years. The report, however, did not suggest an appropriate architectural style for the empire.

A document on the architectural styles to be used in the 1893 Industrial and Agricultural Exposition once again brought the debate over Western and Islamic styles to the fore.[63] Like the two previous discussions, this document began by criticizing the contemporary architecture of Istanbul, this time for not obeying any architectural rules (*kaide-i mimari*). The preferred styles for the exposition were expressed as "Ottoman," "Arabic," or "Moorish," hence Islamic. However, after negotiations (the document does not tell us who the negotiators were), an agreement was reached to use Islamic styles in some buildings and Western styles in others. Renaissance was chosen from European books as the appropriate Western style. The debate over the proper architectural style for the 1893 exposition reflects the architectural scene even better than the previous discussions on style, which remained on the theoretical level. In contrast, this was a debate whose resolution would be implemented. However, what was meant by "Renaissance" style, defined here as an offspring of the "Roman," "Greek," and "Gothic," was not clear. The choice of the architect-in-chief added to the confusion: the commission was given to Raimondo D'Aronco, whose work was neither neo-Islamic nor Renaissance.

The last discussion of the subject comes from the turn-of-the-century writings of the eminent Turkish art historian Celal Esat. Celal Esat's goal was to retrieve the legacy of Ottoman architecture and to revive it in contemporary practice. He began by criticizing the simplistic view, commonly shared by European art historians, that made no distinction between Persian, Arabic, and Ottoman art.[64] In order to clarify the differences between Ottoman art and other traditions, he first wrote a series of articles on the art and architecture of different cultures, comparing and contrasting them with Ottoman art.[65] He then proposed a method that would provide a better understanding of Ottoman art and architecture and thus improve contemporary practice. In an article titled "Osmanlı Mimarisi" (Ottoman Architecture), Celal Esat summarized some of the ideas of the nineteenth-century French architectural authority Eugène Emmanuel Viollet-le-Duc and, defending their universality, attempted to apply them to Ottoman architecture.[66] He argued that the only way to improve Ottoman architecture lay in the discovery of its underlying rules, which could be achieved by first taking careful measurements of major monuments and drawing them to precision. The fundamental principles (*kaide-i esasiye*) of Ottoman architecture would surface only after analyzing these drawings scientifically. As contemporary architects did not investigate and understand the science of architecture, they made random collages out of the various elements borrowed from Ottoman monuments. According to Celal Esat, this was pure imitation (*taklit*) and was doomed to remain so until the rules were scientifically discovered.

These discussions on architectural styles shared several views. Their point of departure was always the same: Ottoman architecture was in decline and had to be saved. The proposals agreed on the need for improvement of local architecture and condemned the direct adoption of Western models. But the employment of Western-type academic and scientific methods was strongly advocated to reincarnate the past glory of Ottoman architecture. Education was seen as the key in training Turkish architects.

The outcome was not an immediate recovery. Nevertheless, as an extension of the Tanzimat's educational reform program, a Western-style School of Fine Arts (Sanayi-i Nefise Mekteb-i Alisi) was founded in 1881. Two years later, the School of Civil Engineering (Hendese-i Mülkiye Mektebi), which included a program in architecture, was established. Architectural education thus gained a new importance, and took a sharp detour from the traditional professional training.

Until the Tanzimat reforms, architectural education was under the aegis of the Organization of Royal Architects (Hassa Mimarları Teşkilatı), the group in charge of the construction and repair of buildings that belonged to the palace, as well as all other government construction activities. At the same time, the organization acted as an educational institution, based on a master-apprentice relationship within the practice. The organization disintegrated after the declaration of the Tanzimat reforms, when ministries, and, for that matter, the Ministry of Trade and Construction (Umur-u Ticaret ve Nafia Nezareti), were created.[67] The result was an interruption in architectural education for four decades, until the establishment of the School of Fine Arts.

In the School of Civil Engineering, architectural education was not differentiated from engineering, but in the School of Fine Arts it became a distinct discipline. The School of Fine Arts consisted of three departments: painting, sculpture, and architecture. The initial enrollment was twenty students; the number increased rapidly, and reached 198 in 1895. Antoine Vallaury was its main instructor.[68]

The description by *The Levant Herald* of a year-end exhibition in 1893 reveals the Westernized nature of the education:

... on the other side is exhibited the work of the pupils of the well-known architect Mr. Vallaury. They are all striking; twenty students are represented, two of whom are Turks, two Greeks, and sixteen Armenians. The Turkish labels show that the first prize is given to Carabet Ehrachian for the plan and elevation of a Custom-House, the second goes to Totos Toromanian for that of a palace; noted also were works by Bogos Haberian, Suleiman, Leon Ekserdjian, Mehmet Alaeddin. There are about forty architectural works, which all denoted much talent and great merit; the neatness and the finish of the technical part of these works as well as the completeness of details is most remarkable when one takes into consideration that these plans are not copies, but are produced by the pupils to scale from the indication of the size and style of the buildings required, given by their teacher. There are plans of theaters, palaces, etc ... etc ..., all beautifully executed and most meritorious in point of conception.[69]

As in many other parts of the world at that time, the methods and values of the Parisian Ecole des Beaux-Arts were adopted. Eclecticism, in the process of gaining legitimate status within the Beaux-Arts tradition itself, became incorporated into the philosophy of the new institution.[70] Willingness to experiment with a variety of styles enhanced the study of the local architectural heritage, as well as its re-evaluation in current practice. The architectural education at the School of Fine Arts in Istanbul therefore responded favorably to the proposals put forward by the Ottoman intelligentsia. The architectural education offered was systematic in following the clarity of Beaux-Arts principles. It was academic and scientific in the study of architecture. And, finally, rather than rejecting *115* Ottoman architecture, it embraced it as a colorful addition to an already *116* eclectic vocabulary.

115. *School of Fine Arts, student project for a mausoleum, first prize in the year-end competition (1909)*

116. *School of Fine Arts, student project for a mausoleum, second prize in the year-end competition (1909)*

7.

Epilogue

Istanbul approached from the water has always been an inspiring sight. Invariably, the accounts of travelers start with a dazzling description of the city viewed from the sea. Edmondo De Amicis's first impressions of his "beloved Istanbul" are perhaps overly emotional, but they do convey the glory of the city's urban image at the turn of the century:

> To the right, Galata, her foreground a forest of masts and flags; above Galata, Pera, the imposing shapes of her European palaces outlined against the sky; in front, the bridge connecting the two banks, across which flow continually two opposite, many-hued streams of life; to the left, Stambul, scattered over her seven hills, each crowned with a gigantic mosque with its leaden dome and gilded pinnacle ... the sky, in which are blended together the most delicate shades of blue and silver, throws everything into marvelous relief, while the water, of a sapphire blue and dotted over with little purple buoys, reflects the minarets in long trembling lines of white; the cupolas glisten in the sunlight; all that mass of vegetation sways and pulpitates in the morning air.... To deny this is the most beautiful sight on earth would be churlish indeed, as ungrateful toward God as it would be unjust to his creation; and it is certain that anything more beautiful would surpass mankind's powers of enjoyment.[1]

117   The image the city presented when viewed from the Sea of Marmara was deceptive—a fact that every traveler discovered as soon as he landed on the shore. Istanbul was run-down and neglected. Many neighborhoods destroyed by fires were not rebuilt for long periods. Upon closer inspection, the monuments that glittered so brilliantly from afar, were poorly maintained and badly in need of restoration. Many wealthy families had left the peninsula for the new quarters across the Golden Horn. The mansions they left behind were subdivided into smaller units and rented to low-income families. Building activity had shifted to Galata and, except for a small number of offices and *kargir konak*s, no new buildings were erected in Istanbul. The grand old city was gradually being abandoned to the working classes.

118   Galata's story was different—it was the center of the modern and Westernized life in the empire. Viewed from the sea, its skyline was

117. View of Istanbul from Galata Bridge, circa 1900. Valide Mosque is at the vista of the bridge.

dominated by tall and handsome new buildings with regular contours. A local author of the time noted the general character of the suburb: "As most of its buildings are *kargir* and new, its view is very beautiful from the sea; however, because its streets are narrow and tortuous, it is not so pretty from the inside."[2] A turn-of-the-century English traveler, W. H. Hutton, labeled the European appearance of Galata and Pera a "veneer of the West" and argued that Pera was a "poor outpost of civilization." He saw the nineteenth-century changes in the Ottoman capital as a thin layer over the reality: "Constantinople remains, with all its changes, a

118. View of Galata from Galata Bridge, circa 1900

city of the dark ages. At any moment, the curtain may be lifted on a scene of tragic horror, and meanwhile there is the grotesque mimicry of Western civilization."[3] Though based on the author's preconceptions of "horror" associated with an alien, non-Western culture, there is validity in his observations. The formal character of Galata and Pera was not in harmony with the living patterns of the majority of the capital's residents, let alone with life in the rest of the empire. Yet, the Western façade, with its imported social and economic models, and its values that were embraced by only a very small group, was so well established that it added a powerful new component to the image of the capital by turning it into a dual city—Istanbul on one side and Galata on the other side of the Golden Horn.

The Turks were outsiders and shy observers in Pera. De Amicis noted:

... here are Greek, Italian, and French dandies, merchant princes, officials of the various delegations, foreign navy officers, ambassadors' equipages, and doubtful-looking physiologies of every nationality. Turkish men stand admiring the wax heads in the hairdressers' windows, and the women pause open-mouthed before the showcases of the milliner's shops. The Europeans talk and laugh more loudly here than elsewhere, cracking jokes in the middle of the street, while the Turks, as if they were foreigners, carry their heads less high than in the streets of Stambul.[4]

The dichotomy between Istanbul and Galata had grown to such a striking extent that on several occasions it was brought to the attention of Abdülhamit II. For example, an 1879 document, titled "Some Thoughts and Observations on the Run-Down State of Istanbul as Compared to the Built State of Galata and Pera," read:

The difference between the city of Istanbul and Galata and Pera is very striking in both buildings and orderliness. For example, even though there are only three hundred *kargir* houses in Istanbul (most of them constructed in very simple ways), there are several thousands in Galata and Pera; most of these are valuable and the majority are ornamented. Many things that are regarded as signs of civilization and that exist even in the secondary and tertiary cities of Europe are present in Pera, but, for example, guest houses called hotels, which even the smallest countries must have, do not exist in Istanbul.... In this age of civilization, the streets of Istanbul are still in the dark and people walk around with lanterns as in China, whereas Galata and Pera are lighted with gas.... The areas in Galata and Pera that were repeatedly burned down by big fires are today all built in *kargir*; there are no empty lots left. In contrast, in Istanbul many empty lots are observed in the Cibali area, burned fifty years ago, and in Hocapaşa and Aksaray, burned later.[5]

The deterioration of Istanbul so troubled the rulers that many attempts were undertaken to bring the old city up to modern standards. As we have traced throughout this study, the post-Tanzimat Ottoman reformers agreed that their capital had three major problems: it had an irregular street fabric, it was divided, and it was dilapidated. These problems were in sharp contrast to contemporary cities in Europe, which symbolized progress and refined culture to the Westward-looking Ottoman bureaucrats. In accordance with the general struggle to "save" the empire through European-style reforms, Istanbul had to be modernized along Western lines. The reformers agreed that modernization could be achieved by imposing a regular order on the urban fabric, by providing good communication between different parts of the capital, and by improving the urban appearance.

The solutions to the three problems went hand-in-hand. Regularization meant replacing the old street network, composed of short, crooked arteries and many dead ends, with well-connected roads—straight, spacious, and of uniform width. Also new building codes and regulations were passed that aimed at creating a uniform residential fabric. Regularization involved, at the same time, clearing the waterfront of dilapidated buildings and opening wide embankments.

These efforts helped to improve access to the major nodes of the capital. The introduction of modern transportation systems further enhanced accessibility. Trams, running along the newly opened or enlarged arteries, connected the scattered neighborhoods of Istanbul and Galata. The construction of two bridges across the Golden Horn facilitated communication between the two banks of the waterway. It was, however, by the ferryboats of the Şirket-i Hayriye that the physically divided parts of the capital—Istanbul, Galata, Üsküdar, and the Bosporus villages—were finally linked to each other. The wide, new embankments made water transportation easier.

Improving the capital's urban image was the concluding order of business. The models most admired were the European capitals. The Tanzimat Council (Meclis-i Tanzimat) expressed this point clearly in an 1839 report: "If some artful embellishment is added to the natural beauty of Istanbul, which is unique in the world, there is no doubt it will become the most beautiful of the most beautiful cities of Europe."[6]

The Ottoman ruling classes associated beauty with regularity in city-building. Embellishment, regularization, and road enlargement were the key words used time and again in government reports advocating the renovation of the urban image.

The ultimate step toward creating a capital that would compete with, and even surpass, the beauty of European cities was reached in Joseph Antoine Bouvard's project that proposed renovating prominent areas of the city according to European architectural and urban design prototypes. That Bouvard's plan remained on paper was not only a matter of financial constraints but also indicated the capital's unwillingness to undergo such sweeping change overnight. When introduced in increments, urban design principles imported from Europe were smoothly integrated into the existing patterns, but a more radical surgery was not yet possible in a city still clinging to its customs and heritage. The social change imposed by the Tanzimat reforms only gradually penetrated the more traditional sectors of the society, and the slow transformation of the urban fabric reflected this reality.

The redesigning and rebuilding done between 1838 and 1908 perhaps did not match the ambitious goals of the rulers, but nonetheless some long-lasting changes were introduced into the urban fabric. The most intensive building activity took place from the late 1850s to the 1870s under the supervision of the İ.T.K. in Istanbul and the Sixth District Administration in Galata. It was during these years that the capital acquired some of its main connectors—the Divanyolu in Istanbul, the Karaköy-Ortaköy road that follows the Bosporus shoreline, and the Taksim-Şişli route on the northern side of the Golden Horn.

The majority of the remaining street regularization operations took place after fires. Their scale was restricted to the burned areas, and often the replanned neighborhoods were not adequately connected to the main arteries. They formed, in the midst of the overall labyrinthian fabric, isolated islands with orthogonal streets but fuzzy boundaries. Another aspect that affected the city form was the introduction of modern urban services, such as street lighting and cleaning, made possible by new laws and regulations.

The two sides of the Golden Horn did not benefit equally from urban reform: Galata, flourishing as an international commerce center, collected the greater share and acquired a more modern appearance. The duality of the Ottoman capital's urban image, with the more traditional Istanbul peninsula to the south and the Western-looking Galata to the north of the Golden Horn, recalled the pattern of many colonial cities from Saigon and Delhi to Cairo and Rabat. The common colonial practice was to create a Western city next to the indigenous one, the latter being left exclusively to the "local" people. In many cities, a barrier zone, referred to as the "cordon sanitaire," separated the Western city from its indigenous counterpart.

Istanbul was not a colonial city. Nevertheless, the growing control of Western powers over the Ottoman Empire resulted in the reflection of some colonial urban design trends in its capital. At first glance, the nineteenth-century Ottoman capital appeared to have both a traditional and a European component. Yet, unlike the colonial cities, the indigenous populations were not locked into the traditional city. There were many Muslim neighborhoods to the north of the Golden Horn—a phenomenon that can be attributed to the fact that the "Western" city in Galata was not a newly planned one, but the expansion of an already existing settlement. For the same reason, Galata does not have a regular street pattern like the new annexes to the colonial cities.

The Golden Horn initially might seem to be a physical barrier between Istanbul and Galata, but it could never be considered a cordon sanitaire. The nineteenth-century bridges insured the vital connection between the two areas and contributed to the creation of a greater Istanbul. Furthermore, urban reform and modern amenities were not excluded from the Istanbul peninsula. An effort was made to bring the new services to at least the prominent quarters of the traditional city—a practice not typically observed in colonial cities.

Thus the nineteenth-century Ottoman capital did not conform to the development pattern typical of colonial cities, nor did it resemble contemporary European cities. First, Istanbul's architectural heritage gave it a unique skyline with many domes and minarets that had no comparison in Western cities (though not as conspicuous as in Istanbul, many mosques were also scattered throughout Galata, especially along the waterfront). Second, the street network was still not completely regularized. Even the newest arteries were not as spacious and continuous as the modern avenues in nineteenth-century European cities; nor were the buildings that flanked them homogeneous like the European five- or six-story buildings. Third, the construction materials were different: most of the residential architecture in the Ottoman capital, and particularly in Istanbul, was still made of timber.

The Ottoman capital hence followed a rather unique development pattern from 1838 to 1908. The nature of the work undertaken and the policies adopted during this period had a great impact on the city's future. First the Young Turks, then the cadres of the Turkish Republic continued to look to Europe as their source of inspiration. Immediately after the abolition of the sultanate, Emin Bey, the mayor of Istanbul, translated a book from the French, titled *Şehircilik* (Urbanism) on the reconstruction of Paris in the nineteenth century.[7] In his introduction, Emin Bey elaborated on the importance of studying Paris, one of the world's greatest cities, from an urbanistic point of view as a guide to the replanning of Turkish cities. The goal was once more to elevate the Turkish cities to the level of regularity (*seviye-i intizam*) observed in Paris.

The post-Tanzimat practice of appealing to Western expertise was pursued also under the Republic and many European specialists were invited to modernize the Turkish cities. The first attempt to control Istanbul's development by means of a "master plan" was made in the 1930s.[8] The consultants were German and French planners, Alfred Agache, Herman Elgötz, H. Lambert, and Martin Wagner, whose opinions on major planning issues, such as growth, transportation, historic preservation, and zoning were not implemented but survive as reports. On the other hand, French architect and planner Henri Prost played a crucial role. Prost's presence in Istanbul spanned the years from 1936 to 1951. Parts of the plan he developed for the city are still in application. Prost's plan is interesting for our purposes, because it combines the various points made in different contexts during the period studied in this book. For example, the main skeleton of the road network proposed for Istanbul is reminiscent of Von Moltke's 1839 plan; the artery that runs parallel to the Theodosian walls recalls the arguments for the creation of a Ringstrasse in 1900; and, the Galata Bridge-Beyazit connection was previously attempted by Gavand in his subway system project of 1876.

119

The second wave of planning occurred in the 1950s. Among the European consultants of this phase were Hans Högg, a German planner, and Luigi Piccinato, an Italian planner.[9] While Högg focused mainly on the importance of zoning, Piccinato's plan was of a regional character. During the second half of the twentieth century, Turkish planners and architects became more directly involved in the planning of Istanbul. The record increase in the city's population beginning in the 1950s contributed yet another major planning issue to the already existing ones.

Almost 150 years have passed since the declaration of the Tanzimat reforms. During this long period, the communication network of the city has improved, new roads and new squares have been opened, dead ends have

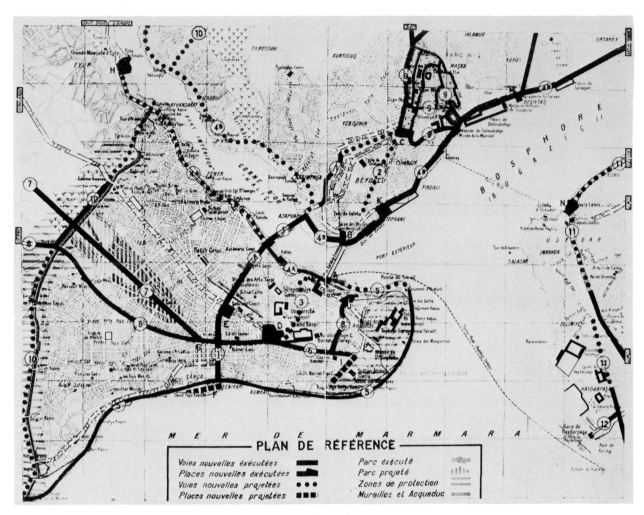

119. H. Prost's plan (1937)

almost been eliminated, a large section of the waterfront in both Istanbul and Galata has been regularized, modern transportation has penetrated to even the most isolated neighborhoods, and the built fabric has been almost completely converted into *kargir* (now meaning concrete). However, many irregular streets still exist, the waterfront along the Golden Horn is still crowded with warehouses, factories, and workshops, and the poor quality of the concrete construction gives even the newest buildings a run-down and unfinished look. The dichotomy between the two sides of the Golden Horn continues to the present day. Istanbul and Galata still present different images: Istanbul's skyline is dominated by the domes and minarets of the *külliye*s and mosques, whereas the Western look of the Galata side has become even more pronounced with the construction of several buildings over twenty stories high.

Today's city occupies a vast area. The Istanbul side is no longer defined by the Theodosian walls, but extends westward. The new quarters, built up over the last three decades, spread out on both sides of the Golden Horn for kilometers past the borders of the nineteenth-century city. Their development happened quickly and often organically, resulting once again in irregular settlement patterns.

The problems of the nineteenth-century city have thus survived to the present day and so have the goals of the early planners. Their twentieth-century counterparts are still struggling to establish a "regularity," following in the steps of Mustafa Reşit Paşa, the Tanzimat reformer who introduced the concept to the empire in 1836.

Notes

INTRODUCTION

1. See E. Hobsbawm and T. Ranger, eds. *The Invention of Tradition* (New York, 1983).
2. E. Hobsbawm, "Introduction: Inventing Traditions," in *The Invention of Tradition*, ed. E. Hobsbawn and T. Ranger, pp. 4–5.
3. E. Hobsbawn, "Mass-Producing Traditions: Europe, 1870–1914," in *The Invention of Tradition*, ed. E. Hobsbawn and T. Ranger, p. 263.
4. Terence Ranger studies this issue in colonial African societies in "The Invention of Tradition in Colonial Africa," in *The Invention of Tradition*, ed. E. Hobsbawn and T. Ranger, pp. 211–62.
5. E. Hobsbawm, "From Societal History to the History of the Society," in *Historical Studies Today*, ed. F. Gilbert and S. R. Graubard (New York, 1972), pp. 14–16.
6. S. J. Summerson, "Urban Forms," in *The Historian and the City*, ed. O. Handlin and J. Burchard (Cambridge, Mass., 1963), pp. 165–66.

CHAPTER ONE

1. Üsküdar and other settlements on the Asiatic side of the Bosporus will not be covered in this study.
2. H. İnalcık, "Istanbul," *Encyclopedia of Islam*, 2d ed. (hereafter *EI²*), vol. 4 (Leiden, 1978), p. 227.
3. The transformation from the straight and wide Byzantine *mese* to the irregular and narrow Divanyolu recalls the process, studied by Sauvaget, during which the geometric antique avenues of Damascus and Aleppo were replaced by irregular *suqs* under the Muslim rule (J. Sauvaget, "Esquisses d'une histoire de la ville de Damas," *Revue des études islamiques* 8 [1934]: 454; and J. Sauvaget, *Alep* [Paris, 1941], pp. 74, 104).
4. O. N. Ergin *Mecelle-i Umur-u Belediye*, 5 vols. (Istanbul, 1914–22), 1:1067–68. Ergin illustrated this point by citing ancedotes from Istanbul folklore in which women, living on opposite sides of the same street in houses facing each other, passed goods and even babies from window to window.
5. İnalcık, "Istanbul," *EI²* 4:236.
6. D. Kuban, "Anadolu-Türk Şehri Tarihi Gelişmesi, Sosyal ve Fiziki Özellikleri Üzerinde Bazı Gelişmeler," *Vakıflar Dergisi* 7 (1968): 69–70.
7. S. Eyice, *Galata ve Kulesi* (Istanbul, 1967), p. 19.
8. C. Stolpe, *Plan de Constantinople*, 1863, Topkapı Palace Library, no. MR712; and P. G. İnciciyan, *XVIII. Asırda Istanbul* (Istanbul, 1956), p. 83. Stolpe's plan used a color code to differentiate the neighborhoods of the capital according to ethnic groups.
9. C. Esat, *Eski Galata ve Binaları* (Istanbul, 1911), pp. 79–81. The medieval city also had a main square, the "piazzetta," close to the waterfront, possibly corresponding to today's Karaköy Square (S. Eyice, "Istanbul-Tarihi Eserler," *İslam Ansiklopedisi* [hereafter *İA*], vol. 5, pt. 2, sec. 1214–15 (Istanbul, 1950), p. 157.
10. G. Dagron, *Naissance d'une capitale* (Paris, 1974), p. 34.
11. Aside from Osman Nuri Ergin's *Mecelle*, there are only three scholarly essays on the historic development of Istanbul: İnalcık's "Istanbul" in the *Encyclopedia of Islam*; Eyice's "Istanbul-Tarihi Eserler" in *İslam Ansiklopedisi*; and D. Kuban's "Istanbul'un Tarihi Yapısı" in *Mimarlık* 5 (1970). As the issues discussed are somewhat different in each of these articles, they complement each other and together give a dependable, though rather concise and encyclopedic view of Istanbul's historic development. İnalcık focuses on settlement patterns, demographic structure, urban administration, and the impact of social and economic institutions on city-planning. Eyice chronologically surveys the building types in an art history approach. Kuban looks at the urban form. His essay conveys a clear image of the city's development from its foundation as a Greek

colony to the 1900s. In 1982, the Brussels-based *Archives d'architecture moderne* published a special issue on the history of Istanbul between 1453 and 1980, prepared by André Barey. Though much better illustrated than the three articles mentioned above, the text is poorly organized and full of factual errors.

There are only a handful of detailed analyses on specific periods of Istanbul's history. G. Dagron's *Naissance d'une capitale* and R. Janin's *Constantinople byzantine* (Paris, 1964) are the leading studies on the Byzantine period. Dagron surveys Constantine's city, whereas Janin focuses on the period from antiquity to the end of the reign of Theodosius II (408–50). R. Krautheimer's "Constantinople" in *Three Christian Capitals* (Berkeley and Los Angeles, 1983) again deals with the founding of the city by Constantine. R. Mantran's *Istanbul dans la deuxième moitié du XVIIè siècle* (Paris, 1962) is undoubtedly the most complete work done on the Ottoman capital so far. Mantran's main theme is the economic life even though he investigates the urban form as well. The seventeenth century is in fact one of the better documented periods, thanks to two writers of that time, Evliya Çelebi and Eremya Çelebi Kömürcüyan. In his *Seyahatname*, Evliya Çelebi provides some basic data, and, more importantly, draws a lively picture of daily life. Eremya Çelebi's *Istanbul Tarihi*, translated into Turkish from Armenian and annotated meticulously by H. D. Andreasyan, describes the different parts of the city.

For the eighteenth century, İnciciyan's *XVIII. Asırda Istanbul* is the only detailed survey. Again translated and annotated by Andreasyan, this work discusses the main monuments, urban services, and the neighborhoods of the capital.

12. The following discussion on the ancient city is based on Janin, *Constantinople byzantine*, pp. 9–20.

13. The following discussion on Constantine's period is based on Dagron, *Naissance d'une capitale*, pp. 77–92, 320–44, and 518–30; Janin, *Constantinople byzantine*, pp. 21–46, 154–55, 166, 184; E. A. Grosvenor, *Constantinople*, vol. 2 (Boston, 1895), pp. 374–76; J. E. N. Hearsey, *City of Constantine* (London, 1963), p. 82; and Krautheimer, *Three Christian Capitals*, pp. 41–67.

14. Galata was incorporated into the capital as the thirteenth region.

15. For a detailed discussion of urban administration, see Dagron, *Naissance d'une capitale*, pp. 214–94.

16. Quoted by Janin in *Constantinople byzantine*, pp. 44–45.

17. See L. M. E. de Beylié, *L'Habitation byzantine* (Grenoble, 1902), p. 30; and Dagron, *Naissance d'une capitale*, p. 528.

18. Today, a sports stadium stands on the site of the Cistern of Aetius; the Cistern of Aspar contains a little villagelike settlement; and the Cistern of St. Mosius is still a vegetable garden.

19. Procopius, *Buildings*, trans. H. B. Dewing (London, 1914), p. 13.

20. W. MacDonald, *Early Christian and Byzantine Architecture* (New York, 1979), p. 41.

21. De Beylié, *L'Habitation byzantine*, pp. 199–200; L. M. E. de Beylié, *L'Habitation byzantine, supplément* (Grenoble, 1903), p. 3; Celal Esat, *Eski Istanbul* (Istanbul, 1909), pp. 231–32.

22. The following discussion on foreign colonies is based on Janin, *Constantinople byzantine*, pp. 245–60.

23. Eyice, *Galata ve Kulesi*, pp. 12–25.

24. İnalcık, "Istanbul," *EI*² 4:224.

25. A. B. Schneider, "XV. Yüzyılda Istanbul Nüfusu," *Belleten* (1962): 1–39; Ö. L. Barkan and E. H. Ayverdi, *Istanbul Vakıfları Tahrir Defteri* (Istanbul, 1970), p. xiii.

26. İnalcık, "Istanbul," *EI*² 4:225; Barkan, *Istanbul Vakıfları*, p. xiii.

27. İnalcık, "Istanbul," *EI*² 4:243; Barkan, *Istanbul Vakıfları*, pp. xiv–xv.

28. H. A. R. Gibb and H. Bowen, *Islamic Society and the West*, 2 pts. in 1 vol. (New York, 1957), pt. 2, p. 164. The objects of *vakıf*s varied from religious buildings (mosques and sufi convents) to educational ones (*medrese*s, *mekteb*s, and libraries) to all kinds of public works (fountains, roads, aqueducts, pavements, and bridges) and to charitable institutions (hospitals, hostels, laundries, kitchens), thereby defining a very wide spectrum of building types.

29. İnalcık, "Istanbul," *EI*² 4:226–35.

30. İnalcık, "Istanbul," *EI*² 4:226–35.

31. Kuban, "Istanbul'un Tarihi Yapısı," p. 31.

32. Barkan, *Istanbul Vakıfları*, p. xi. Of these mosques, 112 are still standing and 92 of them are open to prayer.

33. İnalcık, "Istanbul," *EI*² 4:227.

34. İnalcık, "Istanbul," *EI*² 4:243, 321.

35. İnalcık, "Istanbul," *EI*² 4:235–36.

36. Sinan is the most studied Turkish architect. For further reference, see: E. Egli, *Sinan* (Zurich, 1954); Eyice, "Istanbul," *İA* 5:2:1214/57–75; G. Goodwin, *A History of Ottoman Architecture* (Baltimore, 1971), pp. 196–283; İ. H. Konyalı, *Koca Mimar Sinan ve Eserleri* (Istanbul, 1950); D. Kuban, "Sinan," in *Macmillan Encyclopedia of Architecture*, vol. 4 (New York, 1982), pp. 62–73; M. Sözen et al., *Türk Mimarisinin Gelişimi ve Mimar Sinan* (Istanbul, 1975), pp. 159–247.

37. Kuban, "Sinan," pp. 70–71.

38. Kuban "Sinan," p. 66.

39. Mantran, *Istanbul*, p. 47.

40. Eighty-thousand houses were estimated to amount to approximately 400,000 residents.

41. Kuban, "Istanbul'un Tarihi Yapısı," p. 35.

42. Quoted in N. Berkes, *The Development of Secularism in Turkey* (Montreal, 1964), p. 33.

43. Yirmisekiz Mehmet Çelebi, *Fransız Seyahatnamesi* (Istan-

bul, 1970), pp. 55–68.

44. For an analysis of the eighteenth-century architecture of Istanbul, see: D. Kuban *Türk Barok Mimarisi Hakkında Bir Deneme* (Istanbul, 1954); A. Arel, *Onsekizinci Yüzyıl Istanbul Mimarisinde Batılılaşma Süreci* (Istanbul, 1975).

45. Evliya Efendi, *Narrative of Travels in Europe, Asia and Africa*, trans. J. Von Hammer, 2 pts. in 1 vol. (London, 1937), pt. 2, p. 52.

46. Mantran, *Istanbul*, pp. 77–78.

47. İnciciyan, *XVIII. Asırda Istanbul*, p. 94.

48. İnciciyan, *XVIII. Asırda Istanbul*, p. 156n4.

CHAPTER TWO

1. "Anglo-Turkish Commercial Convention of 1838," art. ii, in *The Economic History of the Middle East, 1800–1914*, ed. C. Issawi (Chicago, 1966), p. 39.

2. B. Lewis, *The Emergence of Modern Turkey* (London, 1961), pp. 226–28.

3. Lewis, *The Emergence of Modern Turkey*, p. 228.

4. Lewis, *The Emergence of Modern Turkey*, p. 178.

5. S. Shaw, "Some Aspects of the Aims and Achievements of the Nineteenth-Century Ottoman Reformers," in *Beginnings of Modernization in the Middle East*, ed. W. Polk and R. Chambers (Chicago, 1968), p. 32.

6. Shaw, "Aims and Achievements," pp. 32–33.

7. M. A. Ubicini, "Decline of Ottoman Industry in the 1840s," in *The Economic History of the Middle East*, ed. C. Issawi, p. 41.

8. Quoted in O. C. Sarç "Ottoman Industrial Policy, 1840–1914," in *The Economic History of the Middle East*, ed. C. Issawi, p. 46.

9. D. Chevallier, "Western Development and Eastern Crisis in the Mid-Nineteenth Century," in *Beginnings of Modernization*, ed. W. Polk and R. Chambers, p. 218.

10. E. C. Clark, "The Ottoman Industrial Revolution," *International Journal of Middle East Studies* 5 (1975): 67.

11. Clark, "The Ottoman Industrial Revolution," p. 67.

12. C. MacFarlane, *Turkey and Its Destiny*, 2 vols. (London, 1850), 1:58.

13. G. Ökçün, "XIX. Yüzyılın İkinci Yarısında İmalat Sanayi Alanında Verilen Ruhsat ve İmtiyazların Ana Çizgileri," *Ankara Üniversitesi Siyasal Bilgiler Fakütesi Dergisi* 17 (1972): 139–46.

14. O. C. Sarç, "Tanzimat ve Sanayimiz," *Tanzimat* (Istanbul, 1940), pp. 437–38.

15. Ergin, *Mecelle* 1:748–49.

16. Clark, "The Ottoman Industrial Revolution," pp. 69–70.

17. MacFarlane, *Turkey and Its Destiny* 2:620–21.

18. Ergin, *Mecelle* 1:738–40.

19. Başbakanlık Arşivi (hereafter BBA), İrade, Dahiliye, no. 37141.

20. *The Levant Herald*, 6 March 1893.

21. *Düstur* (Ankara, 1939), vol. 6, p. 1435; *The Levant Herald*,

4 September 1893.

22. *The Levant Herald*, 12 March 1893, and 4 September 1893.

23. Clark, "The Ottoman Industrial Revolution," p. 75.

24. R. S. Suvla, "The Ottoman Debt, 1850–1939," in *The Economic History of the Middle East*, ed. C. Issawi, p. 95.

25. For a chronological chart showing the amounts, see Suvla, "The Ottoman Debt," pp. 100–101, 104–6.

26. See chapter six.

27. Çavdar, *Türkiye'de Liberalizmin Doğuşu* (Istanbul, 1982), p. 41.

28. S. Shaw and E. K. Shaw, *History of the Ottoman Empire and Modern Turkey*, 2 vols. (Cambridge, 1977), 2:241.

29. S. Shaw, "The Population of Istanbul in the Nineteenth Century," *International Journal of Middle East Studies* 10 (1979): 266.

30. During the fifty years from 1846 to 1896, the population of Paris increased 150 percent from 1,053,896 to 2,536,836. London grew by 220 percent from 1,873,676 in 1841 to 4,232,118 in 1891. Vienna almost doubled from 373,236 in 1843 to 798,719 in 1890 (E. F. Weber, *The Growth of Cities in the Nineteenth Century* [Ithaca, 1967], pp. 46, 73, 75).

31. Shaw, "The Population," p. 276.

32. Shaw, *History*, p. 241.

33. Shaw, "The Population," pp. 266–67.

34. These percentages are worked from the table titled "Population of Istanbul by Districts" in Shaw, "The Population," p. 268.

35. B. R. Davies, *Constantinople* (London, 1840).

36. İnciciyan, *XVIII. Asırda Istanbul*, p. 82.

37. İnciciyan, *XVIII. Asırda Istanbul*, pp. 78–79.

38. Mantran, *Istanbul*, p. 103.

39. İnciciyan, *XVIII. Asırda Istanbul*, pp. 108, 112.

40. The growth of the capital can easily be appreciated by comparing Davies's map with others from the late nineteenth and early twentieth centuries. For this purpose, we shall refer to two maps: (*a*) *Istanbul Haritası* (Map of Istanbul) by Mühendishane-i Berr-i Hümayun (The Royal Engineering School), 1871, Topkapı Palace Museum Library, no. YB3858 (see fig. 21); and (*b*) an undated map from Abdülhamit II's reign, circa 1900, Istanbul University Library, no. 92677 (see fig. 22).

41. Ergin, *Mecelle* 1:1327; S. Rosenthal, *The Politics of Dependency, Urban Reform in Istanbul* (Westport, Conn., 1980), p. 30.

42. Rosenthal, *The Politics of Dependency*, pp. 30–31; İ. Ortaylı, *Tanzimattan Sonra Mahalli İdareler, 1840–1878* (Ankara, 1974), pp. 108–9.

43. Ortaylı, *Tanzimattan Sonra*, pp. 95–96.

44. Ortaylı, *Tanzimattan Sonra*, p. 111.

45. Shaw, "Aims and Achievements," p. 33.

46. Rosenthal, *The Politics of Dependency*, pp. 34–35.

47. "Şehremaneti Nizamname Lahiyası" (1854), art. 2, in Ergin, *Mecelle* 1:1374.

48. "Şehremaneti Nizamname Lahiyası" (1854), arts. 3, 4.

49. Rosenthal, *The Politics of Dependency*, p. 37.

50. Ergin, *Mecelle* 1:1377–79.

51. Ergin, *Mecelle* 1:1378; text translated in Rosenthal, *The Politics of Dependency*, pp. 39–40.

52. "İntizam-ı Şehir Komisyonu Mazbatası" (1856) in Ergin, *Mecelle* 1:1389–91.

53. O. N. Ergin, *Şehreminleri* (Istanbul, 1929), p. 27.

54. "Dersaadet-i İdare-i Belediye Nizamnamesi," in *Düstur* (Istanbul, 1872), vol. 2, p. 450.

55. Ergin, *Mecelle* 1:1414–15; BBA, İrade, Dahiliye, no. 24593.

56. Ergin, *Mecelle* 1:1314; text translated in Rosenthal, *The Politics of Dependency*, p. 51. According to Ergin, the name given to this district was symbolic: it recalled the "sixième arrondissement" of Paris, the lively left bank district on the Seine that the Turks in Paris frequented and admired the most. Ergin's argument may have some validity. Yet, given the physical organization of the districts, one could also argue that the eastern half of the Istanbul peninsula was called the First District because of its utmost importance. Galata and Pera would logically fall into the sixth order when a clockwise configuration was followed.

57. Ortaylı, *Tanzimattan Sonra*, pp. 128–30; Rosenthal, *The Politics of Dependency*, pp. 51–52.

58. Ortaylı, *Tanzimattan Sonra*, p. 129. Foreign influences were so strongly established that French was accepted as the official language along with Turkish (Ergin, *Mecelle* 1:1322n1).

59. Ortaylı, *Tanzimattan Sonra*, pp. 131–32; Rosenthal, *The Politics of Dependency*, p. 55.

60. Ergin, *Şehreminleri*, p. 40.

61. Rosenthal, *The Politics of Dependency*, p. 196.

62. Ergin, *Mecelle* 1:1446.

63. Ergin, *Mecelle* 1:1482.

64. Ergin, *Mecelle* 1:1457–58.

65. Ergin, *Şehreminleri*, p. 44.

66. Ortaylı, *Tanzimattan Sonra*, pp. 156–59.

67. Ortaylı, *Tanzimattan Sonra*, p. 161.

CHAPTER THREE

1. Cevdet Baysun, "Mustafa Reşit Paşa'nın Siyasi Yazıları," *İstanbul Üniversitesi Edebiyat Fakültesi Tarih Dergisi* 11 (September 1960): 15, 124–25.

2. For a detailed discussion of Von Moltke's project, see chapter five.

3. Ergin, *Mecelle* 1:1340–43; O. N. Ergin, *İstanbul'da İmar ve İskan Hareketleri* (Istanbul, 1938), pp. 28–32.

4. Ubicini, *Letters*, p. 162. The fervor to welcome the "attendant train of Western civilization" resulted in the promulgation of a new penal code in 1849, largely influenced by French law, and a commercial code in 1841, also based on French models (Lewis, *The Emergence of Turkey*, p. 110).

5. The first was prepared by the Supreme Council of Judicial Ordinances, the second by the Sixth District Administration, the third by the Council of Laws, the fourth by the Council of State, and the fifth and sixth by the Parliament. For a detailed discussion of these councils, established after 1838, see S. Shaw, "The Central Legislative Councils in the Nineteenth Century Ottoman Reform Movement before 1876," *International Journal of Middle East Studies* 1 (1970): 51–84.

6. "Ebniye Nizamnamesi" (1848), art. 1, in Ergin, *Mecelle* 1:1098.

7. "Turuk ve Ebniye Nizamnamesi" (1863), art. 1, in Ergin *Mecelle* 2:86.

8. "Istanbul ve Belde-i Selasede Yapılacak Ebniyenin Suret-i İnşaiyesine dair Nizamname" (1875), art. 33, in *Düstur* (Istanbul, 1876), vol. 3, pp. 1044–45.

9. In 1848, 16.70 meters was judged appropriate for timber and 22.80 meters for *kargir* ("Ebniye Nizamnamesi" [1848], art. 10), whereas in 1863 these numbers were reduced to 10.60 and 15.20 respectively, thereby attempting to lower the densities ("Turuk ve Ebniye Nizamnamesi" [1863], art. 20, p. 92).

The Bureau Technique of the Sixth District found the 1863 restriction too confining and argued that it would be reasonable to increase the heights by a few meters, because the land was much too valuable in Pera for low densities. The Council of Public Works agreed, and raised the building heights in the Sixth District alone to 18.20 meters for *kargir* and 12.20 meters for wood buildings (BBA, İrade, Meclis-i Vala, no. 22533).

10. The 1882 regulation re-established a 22.80 meter height for *kargir* and a 15.20-meter height for timber buildings on the widest streets (those 11.50-meters wide) and 18.20 meters for *kargir* and 12.20 meters for timber on the narrowest streets (those 7.60-meters wide) ("Ebniye Kanunu" [1882], art. 33, in *Düstur* [Istanbul, 1882], vol. 4, pp. 1044–45.

11. "Turuk ve Ebniye Nizamnamesi" (1863), art. 5, p. 87.

12. "Turuk ve Ebniye Nizamnamesi" (1863), art. 9, pp. 88–89.

13. "Ebniye Kanunu" (1882), art. 22, p. 1042.

14. "Turuk ve Ebniye Nizamnamesi" (1863), art. 12, p. 89.

15. The French ordinances, for example, stated that "the interests of the private individuals must yield before the interest of the public," when the right of ownership was concerned (L. Benevolo, *The Origins of Town Planning* [Cambridge, Mass., 1971], p. 102).

16. "Turuk ve Ebniye Nizamnamesi" (1863), art. 3, p. 86. This article again reflects the French compulsory acquisition legislations based on the 1841 law and devised for public works (Benevolo, *The Origins of Town Planning*, p. 104). Its date slightly precedes similar legislation in other European countries. For example, a compulsory purchase law for the execution of public works was introduced in Italy in 1865 (D. Calabi, "The Genesis and Spatial Characteristics of Town Planning Instruments in Italy, 1880–1914," in

The Rise of Modern Urban Planning, ed. A. Sutcliffe [New York, 1977] pp. 56–57).

17. "Turuk ve Ebniye Nizamnamesi" (1863), art. 12, p. 89.

18. "Ebniye Kanunu" (1882), art. 22, p. 1042. These articles recall the 1865 planning law in Italy and the 1875 town planning act in Prussia, both of which empowered municipalities to prepare plans for town improvements and town development (S. D. Adshead, *Town Planning and Town Development* [London, 1923], pp. 181–91, 195). But, it was not until the 1902 German replotting law, the Lex Adicis, that the terms of replotting were clearly spelled out in Europe. The 1902 German law stated that in a replotting situation, the lots should be laid out at right angles to the streets, in the same location in which they were before replotting, and equal in size to the former lots (F. B. Williams, *The Law of City Planning and Zoning* [New York, 1922], pp. 110–11).

19. Ergin, *Mecelle* 1:1105–12.

20. *Journal de Constantinople*, 23 September 1864.

21. "İstanbul ve Belde-i Selasede Yapılacak Ebniyenin Suret-i İnşaiyesine dair Nizamname" (1875), art. 6, p. 519.

22. "Dersaadet Belediye Kanunu" (1877), in *Düstur*, vol. 4, p. 530.

23. Ergin, *Mecelle* 1:1258.

24. Ergin, *Mecelle* 1:1259–1309, and 1317–32.

25. E. de Amicis, *Constantinople*, 2 vols. (Philadephia, 1896), 2:98.

26. The mid nineteenth-century map of the Istanbul peninsula (sections of which are used as the base map throughout this chapter) does not show geometric street patterns. Regularization is, therefore, a post-1850s phenomenon.

27. According to BBA, İrade, Dahiliye, no. 20937, this number is 666; in *Mecelle*, it is given as 748; and the *Journal de Constantinople* estimates a more exaggerated number of 1,000 houses and as many shops.

28. Topkapı Palace Museum Archive, no. E9433.

29. BBA, İrade, Dahiliye, no. 23150.

30. *Journal de Constantinople*, 3 January 1856.

31. This crossroads was the location of Forum Bovis.

32. *Journal de Constantinople*, 3 January 1856.

33. *Journal de Constantinople*, 3 January 1856.

34. Even Eugène Haussmann's direct involvement was rumored. Ergin argued against Fazıl Halil Ethem, who insisted that Haussmann had personally drafted the actual plan (Ergin, *Mecelle* 1:1019). The plan in the Topkapı Palace Museum Archive bears L. Storari's signature, and there is no mention of such an involvement in Haussmann's *Mémoires*, 3 vols. (Paris, 1893).

35. Quoted in Ergin, *Mecelle* 1:1345.

36. Ergin, *Mecelle* 1:1313.

37. BBA, İrade, Meclis-i Vala, no. 24667. This official statement recalls Mumford's analysis of the rebuilding of Paris under Napoleon III. According to Mumford, Haussmann's geometric boulevards were designed to facilitate military control—so hard to achieve in the medieval fabric of Paris (L. Mumford, *The Culture of Cities* [New York, 1970], p. 96).

38. BBA, İrade, Meclis-i Vala, no. 24667.

39. BBA, İrade, Meclis-i Vala, no. 24667.

40. BBA, İrade, Meclis-i Vala, no. 24895.

41. "İslahat-ı Turuk Komisyonu Vezaifini Mebyun Talimatname," art. 1, in Ergin, *Mecelle* 1:995.

42. For a list of members, see Ergin, *Mecelle* 1:933.

43. "İslahat-ı Turuk Komisyonu," art. 2, in Ergin, *Mecelle* 1:995.

44. "İslahat-ı Turuk Komisyonu," art. 3, p. 995.

45. The first funds were provided from the palace budget and the government budget. A secondary income came from the sale of unclaimed lots or the leftover lots from the new plans (Ergin, *İmar ve İskan*, p. 42). On many occasions, government subsidy was used in addition to the sums gained from these sales. For example, the urgency of rebuilding the newly burned neighborhoods of Samatya and Balat led to an unexpected increase in costs, which the government was asked to offset in 1867 (BBA, İrade, Dahiliye, no. 41216). Whenever a main artery or a government building was in question, the state budget was used. Hence, the rebuilding of the Babıali walls, for example, was paid by the government (BBA, İrade, Dahiliye, no. 41216).

46. Ergin, *Mecelle* 1:1001.

47. Ergin, *Mecelle* 1:1002.

48. Ergin, *Mecelle* 1:1002.

49. BBA, İrade, Meclis-i Vala, no. 24866.

50. Ergin, *Mecelle* 1:1002.

51. Ergin, *Mecelle* 1:1006.

52. E. Haussmann, *Mémoires*, 3:28–29.

53. The İ.T.K. practiced historical preservation, but not in a systematic manner. It was fifty more years before the imperial government took the first step to systematize the preservation activities. In 1917, Halit Bey, the director of the Royal Museum, was requested to form a committee that would take the necessary measures for the conservation of historic monuments and the picturesque sites in the empire. The capital was the beginning point: a commission of engineers and architects was to prepare an inventory of the monuments and maintain their conservation. The goal was educational and touristic ("Sauve-garder des monuments d'art et des sites pittoresques," *Génie civil ottoman* [April 1917], pp. 80–81).

54. Julia Pardoe, *Beauties of the Bosphorus* (London, 1839), p. 118.

55. Among the early nineteenth-century contributions are J. Von Hammer's *Constantinopels und der Bosporus* (Pesth, 1822) and Compte Andreossy's *Constaninople et le Bosphore de Trace* (Paris, 1828). A number of books were published during the 1870s; their preparation must have gone

back to the 1860s. The most well-known are P. A. De-
thier's *Der Bosporos und Constantinopel* (Vienna, 1873);
W. Salzenberg's *Altchristhiche Baudenkmaler von Constantinopel* (Berlin, 1877); and F. W. Unger's *Queller der
Byzantinischen Kunstgeschichte* (Vienna, 1878).

56. Ergin, *Mecelle* 1:1007.
57. Ergin, *Mecelle* 1:1008.
58. Ergin, *Mecelle* 1:1009.
59. R. E. Koçu, *Istanbul Ansiklopedisi* (Istanbul, 1968), p.
    4625.
60. Ergin, *Mecelle* 1:1009.
61. This accusation sounds like a reference to Haussmann's
    urban planning principles concerning cemeteries. However,
    the popular term *frenkperes* is used to define the mentality
    that disregards the Islamic values; it does not necessarily
    refer to French attitudes. Besides, it was quite unlikely
    that Haussmann's work was known in such detail to the
    critics of the İ.T.K.
62. Koçu, *Istanbul Ansiklopedisi*, p. 4625.
63. BBA, İrade, Dahiliye, no. 41216.
64. I could not locate this map in the BBA.
65. BBA, İrade, Dahiliye, no. 41216.
66. According to Ergin, this is Boğazkesen Caddesi (*Mecelle*
    1:1014).
67. BBA, İrade, Dahiliye, no. 41216. Server Efendi's frame
    of mind is again reflected in this statement. After all, he
    had been a clerk in the Ottoman Embassy, first in St.
    Petersburg, and then in Paris between 1854 and 1859,
    and had personally witnessed the transformations in these
    European cities (Rosenthal, *The Politics of Dependency*, p.
    146).
68. Ergin, *Mecelle* 1:1013.
69. The city experienced a planning activity comparable in
    scale only much later, in the 1950s—this time with a much
    larger budget, but a ruthless and insensitive approach to
    the urban landscape.
70. Ergin, *Mecelle* 1:1310.
71. Ergin, *Mecelle* 1:1314.
72. Rosenthal, *The Politics of Dependency*, p. 186.
73. I could not locate this plan in the BBA.
74. BBA, İrade, Dahiliye, no. 43001.
75. BBA, İrade, Dahiliye, no. 43001.
76. BBA, İrade, Dahiliye, no. 43351.
77. BBA, İrade, Meclis-i Vala, nos. 20344, 23348.
78. BBA, İrade, Meclis-i Vala, no. 24981.
79. Ergin, *Mecelle* 1:1013.
80. Ergin, *Mecelle* 1:1322.
81. BBA, İrade, Meclis-i Vala, no. 22333.
82. Pedestrian sidewalks were first proposed by the German
    planner Helmuth Von Moltke, in 1839 (see chapter five).
    We come across the same concept again in the 1848 *irade*
    that ordered the planning of Pangaltı. Sidewalks became a
    common feature of all major arteries in the 1860s.

83. BBA, İrade, Meclis-i Vala, nos. 3776, 9351.
84. An 1858 report, quoted in Ergin, *Şehreminleri*, p. 38; BBA,
    Cevdet, Belediye, no. 5718; İrade, Dahiliye, no. 27332.
85. BBA, İrade, Meclis-i Vala, no. 21687.
86. The origin of this idea goes back to 1853 when the first
    investigation was made to move these Christian cemeteries
    outside the city boundaries (BBA, İrade, Hariciye, no.
    4665).
87. BBA, İrade, Dahiliye, nos. 40886, 42291.
88. *Le Moniteur Oriental*, 17 July 1899.
89. De Amicis, *Constantinople* 1:97.
90. *La Turquie*, 13 May 1890, and 7 January 1875.
91. Ergin, *Şehreminleri*, p. 40.
92. Ergin, *Şehreminleri*, pp. 160–61.
93. Eyice, "Istanbul," *IA* 5:2:1214/145.
94. BBA, İrade, Dahiliye, no. 36789; Meclis-i Vala, no. 22492.
95. *Journal de Constantinople*, 5 November 1864.
96. *Journal de Constantinople*, 24 May 1865. The Galata
    Tower, which functioned as a fire tower, was preserved.
    But the reason for its preservation was not only practical;
    the tower had become the symbol of Galata. The numerous
    repairs it saw during the nineteenth century demonstrate
    its importance as an urban landmark: for example, the
    *irade*s of 1848 and 1854 ordered the restoration of its cone
    and in 1861 another imperial decree was issued to restore
    the whole tower (BBA, İrade, Meclis-i Vala, nos. 12083,
    20776).
97. *Journal de Constantinople*, 10 May 1865, and 21 May 1865.
    The Theodosian walls marking the western boundary of
    Istanbul on the south side of the Golden Horn were not
    demolished even though the idea was introduced several
    times.

    By the nineteenth century, the walls were in ruins.
    The patchy repairs done over several centuries were not
    adequate to preserve the 6.5-kilometer stretch for which
    the city had no practical use (the fifth-century walls could
    not resist modern siege techniques). An 1841 *irade*, typical
    of the lack of direction on the issue, merely points out
    that some parts of the walls need repair and orders an
    investigation (BBA, İrade, Dahiliye, no. 2180).

    A more radical stand was adopted in 1872 by the
    grand vizier, Mithat Paşa, who proposed tearing down the
    walls. The current sultan, Abdülaziz, known for his enthu-
    siasm for modernization, could easily agree with Mithat
    Paşa's decision. However, a group of "British protectors
    of antique works" (*İngiltere asar-ı antika taraftarları*) in-
    tervened before an *irade* was issued and the 1,400-year-old
    walls were saved ("Konstantiniye Surları," *Yeni Tasvir-i
    Efkar*, 28 October, 1909). After this intervention, the
    Byzantine walls enjoyed some attention. For example, in
    1891, a detailed map was drafted ("Istanbul Surları Hari-
    tası," Istanbul University Library, no. 93550). Alexander
    Van Millingen's *Byzantine Constantinople, The Walls and*

Adjoining Historical Sites (London, 1899) must have also exerted some influence on their preservation. Nevertheless, once the idea of demolition was introduced, the government no longer made large investments in repairs.

In 1906, upon the insistence of the minister of education, Haşim Paşa, an *irade* was issued for the restoration of the walls by the municipality (BBA, İrade, Şehremaneti, no. 7, Muharrem 1324/1906). However, nothing significant was done and in 1901, the demolition proposal was brought forward again, this time through a newspaper, *Yeni Tasvir-i Efkar*. The 28 October 1909 editorial, titled, "Konstantiniye Surları" (The Walls of Constantinople), argued that the walls had no historical, architectural, or defensive value. It gave Vienna's Ringstrasse project as an excellent example of what could be done with obsolete city walls and proposed the construction of a large new road, as well as a city hall, a parliament, and a "perfect and regular" (*mükemmel ve muntazam*) theater on the area cleared from the walls. This vision overlooked Vienna's concentric growth in the nineteenth century, which left its walls in the middle of the city. Istanbul's growth pattern was very different and, as we have seen in chapter two, the city had not expanded toward the west, that is, outside the land walls. The areas on both side of the walls were still agrarian zones and vegetable gardens. Unlike Vienna, there was no justification for placing a monumental strip here. Immediate opposition from both foreign scholars and from Halil Bey, the history-conscious mayor of the city, helped to restrict this proposal to the pages of *Yeni Tasvir-i Efkar*.

98. BBA, İrade, Dahiliye, no. 10514. Topkapı Palace Museum Library, no. MR712; Topkapı Palace Museum Libary, no. YB3858; Istanbul University Library, no. 91677.

99. One immediately thinks of the Avenue de l'Opéra with C. Garnier's opera at its focal point.

100. The streets in different neighborhoods of the village were repeatedly repaired as the following documents indicated: 1872 (BBA, İrade, Dahiliye, no. 45789); 1875 (BBA, İrade, Şura-i Devlet, no. 1369), and Dahiliye, no. 49663); and 1895 (BBA, İrade, Şehremaneti, no. 3, Recep. 1313).

101. Its portion in front of the Beşiktaş Palace, for example, was paved in 1876 (BBA, İrade, Dahiliye, no. 50558).

102. The roads in the vicinity of Yıldız Palace were regularized and paved in 1881 (BBA, İrade, Şura-i Devlet, no. 2381); 1892 (BBA, İrade, Şehremaneti, no. 2, Sefer 1310); 1892 (BBA, İrade, Şehremaneti, no. 1, Şevval 1313); and in 1897 (BBA, İrade, Şehremaneti, no. 2, Muharrem 1315).

103. BBA, İrade, Şehremaneti, no. 6, Cemaziyelahir 1310/1892.

104. Ergin, *Şehreminleri*, p. 173.

105. Mantran, *Istanbul*, pp. 93–94.

106. For the increase in the number of boats, see chapter four.

107. BBA, İrade, Meclis-i Vala, nos. 2849, 4276; Dahiliye, nos. 9676, 10401.

108. Major rebuilding activities were undertaken in 1856 (BBA, İrade, Dahiliye, no. 23807); 1860 (BBA, İrade, Meclis-i Vala, no. 19271); 1861 (BBA, İrade, Meclis-i Vala, no. 20480); and 1872 (BBA, İrade, Dahiliye, no. 45188).

109. BBA, Cevdet, Belediye, no. 3789; İrade, Dahiliye, no. 7404.

110. BBA, İrade, Meclis-i Vala, no. 14236.

111. BBA, İrade, Dahiliye, nos. 25148, 35311; Cevdet, Belediye, no. 1775.

112. BBA, İrade, Dahiliye, no. 10197; Meclis-i Vala, nos. 16910, 17477; *Journal de Constantinople*, 28 October 1864.

113. "Boğaziçinde ve İdaresi Doğrudan Doğruya Dersaadet'te Murebbar Olan Sevahilde Müceddeden Yapılacak Rıhtımlar Hakkında Nizamname," arts. 1, 4, 9, in *Düstur*, vol. 2, pp. 537–38.

114. O. Erinç, "92 Yıl Önce Istanbul Metrosu Çalışmaları ve Yeni Liman Projesi," *Belgelerle Türk Tarihi Dergisi* 4 (1968): 7, 50.

115. Z. Bilge, *Istanbul Rıhtımları Tarihçesi* (Istanbul, 1949), p. 1.

116. "Dersaadet Rıhtımları İmtiyazına Dair Mukavelename," arts. 1, 2, in Ergin, *Mecelle* 3:595–96.

117. "Dersaadet Rıhtımları," art. 3, in Ergin, *Mecelle* 3:596–97.

118. "Dersaadet Rıhtımları," art. 6, in Ergin, *Mecelle* 3:598–99.

119. "Dersaadet Rıhtımları," art. 11, in Ergin, *Mecelle* 3:606–7.

120. *La Turquie*, 13 November 1890.

121. Bilge, *Istanbul*, p. 9.

122. *The Levant Herald*, 31 December 1894.

123. Bilge, *Istanbul*, p. 10; *Le Moniteur Oriental*, 16 February 1900.

124. Bilge, *Istanbul*, p. 13.

125. *Le Moniteur Oriental*, 25 August 1902, and 29 October 1902.

126. "Dersaadet Rıhtımları," art. 22, in Ergin, *Mecelle* 3:701.

127. Bilge, *Istanbul*, pp. 34–36.

128. F. Choay, *The Modern City* (New York, 1969), pp. 15–19.

129. "Ebniye Kanunu" (1882), arts. 79 and 80, in *Düstur*, vol. 4, p. 1051. This provision led to appeals for permission to build in wood following almost every fire. For example, the burned neighborhoods of Samatya (BBA, İrade, Şehremaneti, no. 4, Cemaziyelevvel 1313/1895); Altımermer (BBA, İrade, Şehremaneti, no. 1, Rebiülevvel 1319/1901); Çukurçeşme (BBA, İrade, Şehremaneti, no. 3, Cemaziyelevvel 1323/1905); and Koca Mustafa Paşa (BBA, İrade, Şehremaneti, no. 2, Şevval 1323/1905) regained their wooden fabric.

130. These terms, so often used in government documents, are not defined. However, "worthless" is intended to designate the poorer residential quarters, whereas "valuable" and "honorable" are used to refer to the administrative and the commercial core, as well as the areas around the religious monuments and palaces.

131. BBA, İrade, Şehremaneti, no. 3, Zilhicce 1315/1898.
132. D. Pinkney, *Napoleon III and the Rebuilding of Paris* (Princeton, 1958), pp. 91–99.

CHAPTER FOUR

1. C. Orhonlu, "Osmanlı Türkleri Devrinde İstanbul'da Kayıkçılık ve Kayık İşletmeciliği," *İstanbul Üniversitesi Edebiyat Fakültesi Tarih Dergisi* (March 1966), pp. 109–10.
2. Orhonlu, "Osmanlı Türkleri," pp. 111–29.
3. Orhonlu, "Osmanlı Türkleri," p. 128.
4. Orhonlu, "Osmanlı Türkleri," p. 126.
5. BBA, İrade, Dahiliye, no. 14062; Şirket-i Hayriye, *Chirket-i Hairié, Annuaire de la société* (İstanbul, 1914), p. 23.
6. "Şirket-i Hayriye'nin Bedayet ve Suret-i Tesisi Hakkındaki Mazbata Sureti," in Şirket-i Hayriye, *Annuaire*, pp. 5–6; Ergin, *Mecelle* 1:14–15.
7. Şirket-i Hayriye, *Annuaire*, pp. 5–12.
8. BBA, İrade, Meclis-i Vala, no. 8142; Dahiliye, no. 16493; Hariciye, no. 4465.
9. Şirket-i Hayriye, *Annuaire*, p. 9.
10. "Şirket-i Hayriye ile Vapur Mültezimleri Beyninde Akid Olunan Kontrato Sureti," arts. 2, 4, 18, in Şirket-i Hayriye, *Annuaire*, pp. 139, 142.
11. BBA, İrade, Meclis-i Vala, no. 7419.
12. In summer, boats ran from the Bosporus to Eminönü once every forty-five minutes during the morning hours and once every sixty minutes during the late afternoon. In the winter, the schedule was reduced to a boat every ninety minutes. In the Eminönü-Bosporus direction, the schedule was a boat per hour during the day and a boat per forty-five minutes during the busy summer afternoons.
13. "Hükümet-i Seniye ile Şirket-i Hayriye Beyninde Akid ve Tati Olunan Mukavelename," arts. 40, 41, 42, and 46, in Şirket-i Hayriye, *Annuaire*, pp. 156–57.
14. "Hükümet-i Seniye," arts. 37, 51, and 54, pp. 147–48 and 159. The upper classes and the Europeans, regarding themselves as the true patrons of the boat service, were not always happy to be treated like the "common folk." A letter of complaint, published in *The Levant Herald* on 25 September 1899, voiced this view:

The Shirket administration is highly proficient in the art of causing discomfort and inconvenience to its customers; but it isn't merely so brilliantly successful as it was on Saturday morning. By loading up the early steamers coming from the upper Bosphorus by the Asiatic shore with disbanded soldiers and their baggage, there was scarcely standing room for the regular passengers.... We congratulate the Shirket at having been able to occasion discomfort to several hundred of its clients in the course of one forenoon.

15. "Hükümet-i Seniye," arts. 23, 25, 26, 28, 29, pp. 154–55.
16. "Şirket-i Hayriye ile Vapur Mültezimleri," art. 20, p. 143.
17. "Şirket-i Hayriye," art. 7, p. 140.
18. "Hükümet-i Seniye," arts. 27, 30, 35, p. 155.
19. *The Levant Herald*, 6 August 1894.
20. Şirket-i Hayriye, *Annuaire*, pp. 7, 16.
21. The service became established during the Middle Ages, when there were few bridge connections. Evolving according to new technologies, it continued to function up to our day in cities like Venice and Stockholm, whereas the development in cities on riverbanks followed a different path. In Paris, for example, even though transportation on the Seine by means of small steamers became widespread during the second half of the nineteenth century (by 1886, 105 steamers served the interior of Paris and its suburbs), the number of passengers declined dramatically after 1900 because of the competition from the new Metro (N. Evenson, *Paris, A Century of Change, 1878–1978* [New Haven, 1979], p. 90).
22. The fifth-century *Notitia Urbis Constantinopolitanae* mentions a wooden bridge across the Golden Horn situated in the Fourteenth Region at the extremity of the land walls. In 528, Justinian replaced this with a stone bridge that did not survive into the Ottoman period (A. Van Millingen, *Byzantine Constantinople*, pp. 174–76).
   A proposal to construct a bridge that would connect Pera to Istanbul came from Leonardo da Vinci in 1503. Leonardo's unbuilt design consisted of a single arch 240 meters long. The translation of the letter he wrote to Sultan Beyazit II describing the project is in the Topkapı Palace Museum Archive. His sketches are in the Bibliothèque Nationale in Paris (İ. İlter, *Boğaz ve Haliç Geçişlerinin Tarihçesi* [İstanbul, 1973], pp. 49–52).
23. Eyice, "Istanbul," *İA* 5:2:1215/157.
24. Eyice, "Istanbul," *İA* 5:2:1215/157.
25. İlter, *Boğaz ve Haliç*, pp. 70–71.
26. BBA, İrade, Meclis-i Mahsus, no. 1540.
27. BBA, İrade, Meclis-i Mahsus, no. 1743; Dahiliye, no. 45389.
28. İlter, *Boğaz ve Haliç*, p. 74.
29. BBA, İrade, Şehremaneti, no. 16, Sefer 1310.
30. BBA, uncatalogued. I could not decipher the signature of the engineer.
31. Sait Paşa, *Sait Paşa'nın Hatıratı*, 2 vols. (İstanbul, 1910), 1:212.
32. See chapter five. Among the unrealized projects for the reconstruction of the Galata Bridge, a sketch by Raimondo D'Aronco should be mentioned. D'Aronco's framed drawing decorates a wall in the section of the Dolmabahçe Palace not open to the public.
33. *Le Moniteur Oriental*, 2 October 1902.
34. Ergin, *Mecelle* 2:859–63.

35. Eyice, "Istanbul," *İA* 5:2:1215/157.
36. The word "tramway" is used synonymously with a horse-drawn street car in Turkish documents.
37. BBA, İrade, Meclis-i Vala, no. 23412.
38. BBA, İrade, Meclis-i Mahsus, no. 1265.
39. BBA, İrade, Meclis-i Mahsus, no. 1265, art. 1.
40. BBA, İrade, Meclis-i Mahsus, no. 1265, arts. 2, 4, 6, 7.
41. BBA, İrade, Meclis-i Mahsus, no. 1265, arts. 12, 13, 16, 17, 18, 53.
42. BBA, Şura-i Devlet, no. 443.
43. "Dersaadet Tramvay Şirketi Tesis ve İnşasına dair Mukavelename" (1869), arts. 1, 2, in Ergin, *Mecelle* 3:141.
44. "Dersaadet Tramvay Şirketi" (1869), arts. 1, 2, p. 141.
45. "Dersaadet'te İnşa Olunacak Tramvay Hatlarına dair Şartname" (1881), arts. 1, 16, in Ergin, *Mecelle* 3:167, 194.
46. "Dersaadet Tramvay Şirketi Müddet-i İmtiyaziyesinin Temdidi ve Bazı Hatt-ı Cedide İnşaşı Hakkındaki Mukavelename" (1907), art. 1, in Ergin, *Mecelle* 3:172–73.
47. BBA, Harita, no. 323.
48. Shaw, "The Population," p. 268.
49. BBA, İrade, Dahiliye, no. 44205.
50. Ergin, *Mecelle* 1:1015.
51. "Dersaadet Tramvay Şirketi," arts. 4, 6, p. 146; "Dersaadet'te İnşa Olunacak Tramvay," art. 5, p. 168.
52. BBA, İrade, Meclis-i Mahsus, no. 1592.
53. "Dersaadet'te İnşa Olunacak Tramvay," art. 5, pp. 168–69.
54. "Dersaadet'te İnşa Olunacak Tramvay," arts. 10, 11, p. 148.
55. "Dersaadet Tramvay Şirketi," art. 14, p. 148.
56. De Amicis, *Constantinople* 1:63–64.
57. *The Levant Herald*, 17 February 1896.
58. *Le Moniteur Oriental*, 28 June 1900.
59. Hüseyin Rahmi, *İffet* (1896; Istanbul, 1973), p. 17.
60. Istanbul's use of trams did not match the rapid developments in the West. The horse-drawn tram had originated in New York City in 1832 and spread to other major cities in a couple of decades. Electric traction, which was first tried out in Richmond, Virginia in 1888, was applied very rapidly in the United States and Europe. As we have seen above, Istanbul made use of the horse-drawn trams only after 1870; the conversion of the system to electricity was proposed in 1910 and realized only in 1912. (*Réseau de tramways urbains et suburbains de Constantinople, projet présenté par la Société Générale d'Entreprises* [Paris, 1910], p. 49; "Metropoliten Demiryolu Şirketinin Mukavelenamesi" [1912], art. 5, in Ergin, *Mecelle* 3:296).
61. BBA, İrade, Meclis-i Mahsus, no. 1533; "Tünel İmtiyazı Hakkındaki Ferman-ı Ali," in Ergin, *Mecelle* 3:246.
62. P. Oberling, "The Istanbul Tünel," *Archivum Ottomanicum* 4 (1972): 220.
63. Oberling, "The Istanbul Tünel," pp. 222–25.
64. "Tünel Şirketi Mukavelenamesi" (1869), art. 9, in Ergin, *Mecelle* 3:249.
65. Oberling, "The Istanbul Tünel," pp. 228–36.
66. Oberling, "The Istanbul Tünel," p. 237.
67. *The Levant Herald*, 18 January 1875, quoted in Oberling, "The Istanbul Tünel," p. 239.
68. *La Turquie*, 6 February 1875, and 16–17 May 1875.
69. "Tünel İmtiyazının Elli Sene Müddetle Temdidine Dair Mukavelename," arts. 5, 7, in Ergin, *Mecelle* 3:280–81.
70. "Tünel Şirketi İmtiyazının Yetmişbeş Sene Müddetle Temdidi Hakkındaki Ferman-ı Ali," in Ergin, *Mecelle* 3:283.
71. The Istanbul Tünel was among one of the earliest examples of underground transportation. The pioneer was the London subway, going as far back as 1862. The Lyon funicular was built in 1863; those in Budapest, Vienna, and the Clay Street Railway in San Francisco followed in 1873. According to Gavand, the Lyon funicular served as his model. However, the Istanbul Tünel was completely underground, thus it became the second subway in the history of transportation after the subway of London (Oberling, "The Istanbul Tünel," p. 220n72).
72. Erinç, "92 Yıl Önce," p. 48.
73. Erinç, "92 Yıl Önce," p. 51.
74. *La Turquie*, 13 November 1890.
75. Istanbul University Library, no. 93295.
76. İlter, *Boğaz ve Haliç*, p. 24.
77. *La Turquie*, 11 March 1875.
78. Van Milligen, *Constantinople*, p. 205.
79. S. Naum-Duhani, *Vieilles gens, vieilles demeures, topographie sociale de Beyoğlu au XIXème siècle* (Istanbul, 1947), p. 39.

CHAPTER FIVE

1. Ergin, *Mecelle* 1:1340–43; Ergin, *İmar ve İskan*, pp. 28–30; see also chapter three.
2. BBA, Yıldız, Kısım 35, Evrak 2370, Zarf 43, Kutu 110.
3. Though not developed to the same degree, Arnodin's project recalls two important late nineteenth-century urban design schemes: Otto Wagner's winning project for Vienna in the competition of 1893 and Arturo Soria y Mata's 1894 linear city scheme for Madrid. Both of these were dominated by the idea of transportation, and in both cases, rail transportation was the key to growth. With the premise of indefinite growth, Wagner proposed four circumferential rail belts for Vienna, the Ringstrasse being the first. They were intersected by radial arteries (C. Schorske, *Fin-de-Siècle Vienna* [New York, 1981], p. 73). Soria y Mata, on the other hand, planned only one belt, a fifty-five kilometer railway circling Madrid. It was flanked on both sides by Ciudad Lineal settlements (C. R. Collins, "The Ciudad Lineal of Madrid," *Journal of the Society of Architectural Historians* [May 1959]: 43). F. Arnodin's scheme, like the proposals for Vienna

and Madrid, was based on rail transportation and pursued the same formal characteristic—a ringroad defining a large area for growth. However, the communication from the old city to the ring and the nature of the settlements along it were not projected.

4. BBA, Yıldız, Kısım 35, Evrak 2370, Zarf 43, Kutu 110.

5. Similar ringroad projects were proposed and realized in part much later, after the mid twentieth century, but the mode of transportation taken into consideration was always the automobile.

6. H. Mutluçağ, "Boğaziçi Köprüsünün Yapılması Yolunda İlk Çabalar," *Belgelerle Türk Tarihi Dergisi* 1 (1968): 34.

7. A version of this section was published as "Bouvard's Boulevards: Beaux-Arts Planning in Istanbul," *Journal of the Society of Architectural Historians* 43.4 (December 1984): 341–55.

8. The first Ottoman ambassador to Paris, Mehmet Çelebi Efendi, glorified Paris in his *Seyahatname* of 1727. This account became one of the most influential references in the history of Westernization of the Ottoman Empire.

9. R. de Cuers, "J. A. Bouvard," *The Architectural Record* (July 1900–1901): 242–44, 291, 298–304; L. Hautecœur, *Histoire de l'architecture classique en France*, 7 vols. (Paris, 1957), 7:386, 394–95. Among Bouvard's other noteworthy buildings were the Bourse du Travail, the Caserne Louviers, and the Municipal Disinfection Ovens near the Canal de Saint-Martin. Bouvard was an enthusiastic participant in urban theatrics as well. He created fairylandlike settings in front of the Hôtel de Ville to celebrate two occasions: the visit of the Admiral Avvelean in 1893 and the visit of the Russian sovereigns in 1896.

10. De Cuers, "J. A. Bouvard," p. 312.

11. Ergin, *İmar ve İskan*, pp. 45–47.

12. Ergin, *İmar ve İskan*, p. 47.

13. I located the following five drawings in the Istanbul University Library: "Nouveau Pont de Galata," no. 90591; "Place de l'Hippodrome," no. 90592; "Place du Sultan Bayezid," nos. 90593, 90594; "Place de la Sultane Validé," no. 90595. There should, however, exist at least two others. I could not find the "Yeniköy'de Avusturya Sefarethanesi" (the Austrian Embassy in Yeniköy), marked as no. 90596 in the catalogue. O. N. Ergin mentions another drawing that depicts a scheme for the Marmara shore with a wide boulevard parallel to the shoreline (Ergin, *İmar ve İskan*, pp. 46–47). The goal here might have been to surpass the beauty of "Nice and Italian seaside cities." Unfortunately, I could not find it either. The Istanbul University Library is currently being reorganized and, with luck, these drawing will surface in the process. The drawings are approximately 70 centimeters by 100 centimeters.

14. Begun in A.D. 203 by Septimius Severus and remodeled by Constantine in the fourth century.

15. Both brought to Constantinople in the fourth century. See

16. BBA, İrade, Dahiliye, no. 33429 for the excavation report.

16. BBA, İrade, Şehremaneti, no. 1, Muharrem 1317.

17. Designed by Fossati Brothers as the Istanbul University (Darülfunun) in 1846, this building housed various governmental departments as well (see chapter six).

18. This scheme was realized later in 1910 (Ergin, *Mecelle* 3:1006).

19. De Amicis, *Constantinople* 1:45–46.

20. De Amicis, *Constantinople* 1:46–47.

21. De Amicis, *Constantinople* 1:48.

22. Ergin, *İmar ve İskan*, p. 48.

CHAPTER SIX

1. This is not a definitive list of the turn-of-the-century styles for the Ottoman capital, but a tentative classification to organize the discussion on the pluralistic architectural language. The styles often borrow from each other and overlap.

2. It is interesting to note that neoclassicism came to the Ottoman Empire via Europe and that the many Greek and Roman sites under excavation during the time within the empire did not exert any influence.

3. De Amicis, *Constantinople* 1:88.

4. *Plan d'assurance de Constantinople* (1905). The names of some of the insurance companies were Helevetia Companie d'Assurance, Assurazioni Generali, Scottish Insurance Company, and Spanish Insurance Company. The foreign banks included Crédit Lyonnais, Wiener Bank, Deutsche Bank, and Banque de Salonique.

5. G. Goodwin, "Turkish Architecture, 1840–1949," *Art and Archaeology Research Papers* (June 1977): 8.

6. Mehmet Raif, *Mirat-ı Istanbul* (Istanbul, 1896), p. 395.

7. *Le Moniteur Oriental*, 21 May 1899.

8. *La Turquie*, 10 January 1888.

9. Goodwin, *History*, p. 419.

10. Inciciyan, *XVIII. Asırda Istanbul*, p. 150 nn2, 3.

11. Koçu, *Istanbul Ansiklopedisi*, p. 2096.

12. *The Levant Herald*, 31 December 1894.

13. Eyice, "Istanbul," *İA* 5:2:1214/54; Grosvenor, *Constantinople* 1:156.

14. De Amicis, *Constantinople* 1:93.

15. H. Sumner-Boyd and J. Freely, *Strolling through Istanbul* (Istanbul, 1973), p. 74.

16. The original French Embassy dated from 1535.

17. H. R. Hitchcock, *Architecture, Nineteenth and Twentieth Centuries* (London, 1968), p. 74.

18. Naum-Duhani, *Vieilles gens*, pp. 43–99.

19. Naum-Duhani, *Vieilles gens*, pp. 56–62.

20. Naum-Duhani, *Vieilles gens*, p. 30.

21. Naum-Duhani, *Vieilles gens*, pp. 29, 45–83.

22. *Journal de Constantinople*, 25 January 1855.

23. BBA, İrade, Meclis-i Vala, no. 23721.

24. Naum-Duhani, *Vieilles gens*, pp. 99–100.

25. *The Levant Herald*, 25 September 1893.

26. *Journal de Constantinople*, 2 July 1864.

27. Théophile Gautier was quite harsh in his judgment of these apartment buildings:

> Some ugly houses, of six and seven stories, line the road on one side, and rejoice a superb view, of which they are quite unworthy. It is true that these houses pass for the best in Constantinople, and that Pera is proud of them—judging them (rightly) as fit to figure honorably at Marseilles or Barcelona, or even Paris; for they are, in fact, of an ugliness the most civilized and modern. (T. Gautier, *Constantinople* [New York, 1873], p. 87)

28. *La Turquie*, 8 February 1875.

29. *La Turquie*, 8 February 1875.

30. *La Turquie*, 31 May 1876.

31. *Le Moniteur Oriental*, 21 March 1900.

32. These ratios are worked from the figures in Shaw, "The Population," p. 269.

33. A. Batur, A. Yücel, and N. Fersan, "Istanbul'da On-dokuzuncu Yüzyıl Sıra Evleri," *Orta Doğu Teknik Üniversitesi Mimarlık Fakültesi Dergisi* (Fall 1979): 189.

34. Batur, "Istanbul'da Ondokuzuncu Yüzyıl," p. 193.

35. Eyice, "Istanbul," *İA* 5:2:1214/126–27.

36. Eyice, "Istanbul," *İA* 5:2:1214/43.

37. BBA, İrade, Meclis-i Vala, no. 11058; Meclis-i Hususi, no. 2008.

38. BBA, İrade, Dahiliye, no. 48863.

39. Eyice, "Istanbul," *İA* 5:2:1214/118–19.

40. Eyice, "Istanbul," *İA* 5:2:1214/118–19. After housing many different functions, including a hospital (BBA, İrade, Hariciye, no. 5781) and the Ministry of Finance (BBA, İrade, Dahiliye, no. 37705), it was destroyed in a fire in 1936.

41. *Journal de Constantinople*, 20 April 1864.

42. Eyice, "Istanbul," *İA* 5:2:1214/123.

43. BBA, İrade, Dahiliye, no. 41355.

44. "Müze-i Hümayun Nizamname-i Dahiliyesi," art. 2, in *Düstur*, vol. 4, p. 344.

45. The building was enlarged first between 1899 and 1903, then in 1908, according to its original stylistic characteristics.

46. S. Ciner, *Son Osmanlı Devri Ahşap Konutlarında Cephe Bezemeleri* (Istanbul, 1982), p. 18.

47. S. Muthesius, *The High Victorian Movement in Architecture* (London, 1972), p. 99.

48. Sumner-Boyd, *Strolling through Istanbul*, p. 338.

49. The architect of this mosque is uncertain. According to Eyice, the architect was Montani (S. Eyice, *Istanbul, Petit Guide* [Istanbul, 1955], pp. 87–88) and according to Pamukciyan, it was Agop Balyan (see Goodwin, *History*, p. 425).

50. Elements of Victorian Gothic revivalism were quite common among the residential architecture of the capital. A large number of Victorian houses in wood were built in the summer resorts of the capital, such as the Bosporus villages, Yeşilköy on the Sea of Marmara, and the Princes' Islands.

51. For example, in the early nineteenth-century England, S. P. Cockerell's country house, Sezincote (1803) and John Nash's Brighton Pavilion (1815) became the pioneers of a neo-Islamic style inspired from Indian examples. In the mid nineteenth century, Owen Jones's two influential books, *Plans, Elevations, Sections, and Details of the Alhambra* (1842–45) and *Grammar of Ornament* (1856) emphasized the universal aesthetics of Islamic architecture and especially of Islamic decoration.

52. İ. Tekeli, "The Social Context of the Development of Architecture in Turkey," in *Modern Turkish Architecture*, ed. R. Holod and A. Evin (Philadelphia, 1984), p. 11.

53. Tekeli, "The Social Context," p. 12. For a thorough account of this movement and Mimar Kemalettin, see Y. Yavuz, *Mimar Kemalettin ve Birinci Ulusal Mimarlık Dönemi* (Ankara, 1981).

54. On D'Aronco, see M. Nicoletti, *L'Architettura Liberty in Italia* (Rome, 1978).

55. Goodwin, "Turkish Architecture," p. 12.

56. Montani Efendi and Boghos Efendi Chachian, *Usul-u Mimari-i Osmani* (*L'Architecture ottomane*) (Constantinople, 1873), pp. vii and 6–7. Nuruosmaniye (1755) and Laleli (1763) mosques were among the first examples of Ottoman architecture that employed baroque elements.

57. Montani Efendi, *Usul-u Mimari-i Osmani*, p. 7.

58. Montani Efendi, *Usul-u Mimari-i Osmani*, p. 7.

59. Montani Efendi, *Usul-u Mimari-i Osmani*, p. 15.

60. Montani Efendi, *Usul-u Mimari-i Osmani*, p. 17.

61. An attempt was made to put these principles into practice in the Ottoman pavilion built for the 1873 Vienna exposition. According to two articles published in *Basiret*, this building was modeled after Turkish houses and elaborately decorated by Turkish craftsmen (*Basiret*, 14 Ramazan 1289/1872 and 23 Cumadelevvel 1289/1872, quoted in M. Cezar, *Sanatta Batıya Açılış ve Osman Hamdi* [Istanbul, 1971], pp. 491–92).

62. BBA, Yıldız, Kısım 14, Evrak 2022, Zarf 126, Kutu 10.

63. BBA, Yıldız, Kısım 31, Evrak 1933, Zarf 45, Kutu 82.

64. Celal Esat, "Osmanlı Sanayi-i Nefisesi" (Ottoman Fine Arts), *İkdam*, 13 December 1906.

65. For example, "Garp Sanayi-i Nefisesi" (Western Fine Arts) was published in *İkdam* on 18 December 1906 and "İran ve Türk Sanayi-i Nefisesi" (Iranian and Turkish Fine Arts) on 24 December 1906.

66. Celal Esat, "Osmanlı Mimarisi," *İkdam*, 3 January 1907.

67. S. Turan, "Osmanlı Teşkilatında Hassa Mimarları," *Ankara Üniversitesi Tarih Araştırmaları Dergisi* 1 (1964): 157–79.

68. Cezar, *Sanatta Batıya Açılış*, pp. 452–66.

69. *The Levant Herald and Eastern Express*, 24 July 1893.

70. See, for example, J. Guadet's *Eléments et théorie de l'architecture* (Paris, 1894).

CHAPTER SEVEN

1. De Amicis, *Constantinople* 1:29–31.

2. Raif, *Mirat-ı Istanbul*, p. 395.

3. W. H. Hutton, *Constantinople* (London, 1904), pp. 225–28.

4. De Amicis, *Constantinople* 1:93–94.

5. BBA, Yıldız, Kısım 18, Evrak 94/24, Zarf 94, Kutu 4.

6. Ergin, Şehreminleri, p. 29.

7. The translation of this book by Jouaillan was published in Istanbul. Although undated, it was published after the declaration of the Republic and before the Alphabetical Reform, hence, between 1923 and 1927.

8. For a survey of plans developed for Istanbul during the republican period, see N. Duranay, E. Gürsel, and S. Ural, "Cumhuriyetten Bu Yana Istanbul Planlaması," *Mimarlık* 7 (1972): 65–109.

9. Duranay, "Cumhuriyetten Bu Yana," pp. 84–93.

Bibliography

Adshead, S. D. *Town Planning and Town Development*. London, 1923.

Amicis, E. de. *Constantinople*. 2 vols. Philadelphia, 1896.

Arel, A. *Onsekizinci Yüzyıl Istanbul Mimarisinde Batılılaşma Süreci* (Westernization Process in Eighteenth-Century Istanbul Architecture). Istanbul, 1975.

Barey, André. "Istanbul, 1453–1980." *Archives d'architecture moderne* 23 (1982).

Barkan, Ö. L. and E. H. Ayverdi. *Istanbul Vakıfları Tahrir Defteri* (Registers of Istanbul *Vakıf*s). Istanbul, 1970.

Batur, A.; A. Yücel; and N. Fersan. "Istanbul'da Ondokuzuncu Yüzyıl Sıra Evleri" (Nineteenth-Century Rowhouses in Istanbul). *Orta Doğu Teknik Üniversitesi Mimarlık Fakültesi Dergisi* (Fall 1979): 185–205.

Baysun, C. "Mustafa Reşit Paşa'nin Siyasi Yazıları (Political Writings of Mustafa Reşit Paşa). *Istanbul Üniversitesi Edebiyat Fakültesi Tarih Dergisi* 11 (September 1960): 15, 124–25.

Benevolo, L. *The Origins of Town Planning*. Cambridge, Mass., 1971.

Berkes, N. *The Development of Secularism in Turkey*. Montreal, 1964.

Beylié, L. M. E. de. *L'Habitation byzantine*. Grenoble, 1902.

——— . *L'Habitation byzantine, supplément*. Grenoble, 1903.

Bilge, Z. *Istanbul Rıhtımları Tarihçesi* (History of Istanbul's Quays). Istanbul, 1949.

Çavdar, T. *Türkiye'de Liberalizmin Doğuşu* (Birth of Liberalism in Turkey). Istanbul, 1982.

Cezar, M. *Sanatta Batıya Açılış ve Osman Hamdi* (Exposure to the West in Art and Osman Hamdi). Istanbul, 1971.

Choay, F. *The Modern City*. New York, 1969.

Ciner, S. *Son Osmanlı Devri Ahşap Konutlarında Cephe Bezemeleri* (Façade Decorations on Late Ottoman Period Timber Houses). Istanbul, 1982.

Clark, E. C. "The Ottoman Industrial Revolution." *International Journal of Middle East Studies* 5 (1975): 65–76.

Collins, G. R. "The Ciudad Lineal of Madrid." *Journal of the Society of Architectural Historians* (May 1959): 38–53.

Cuers, F. de. "J. A. Bouvard." *The Architectural Record* (July 1900–1901): 290–312.

Dagron, G. *Naissance d'une capitale*. Paris, 1974.

Duranay, N.; E. Gürsel; and S. Ural. "Cumhuriyetten Bu Yana Istanbul Planlaması" (Planning of Istanbul since the Republic). *Mimarlık* 7 (1972): 65–109.

Düstur. First Series (*Birinci Tertib*). Vol. 2 (Istanbul, 1289/-1872). Vol. 3 (Istanbul 1293/1876). Vol. 4 (Istanbul, 1299/1881). Vol. 5 (Istanbul, 1304/1888). Vol. 6 (Ankara, 1939).

Egli, E. *Sinan*. Zurich, 1954.

Ergin, O. N. *Mecelle-i Umur-u Belediye* (Book of Municipal Affairs). 5 vols. Istanbul, 1914–22.

——— . *Şehreminleri* (The Mayors). Istanbul, 1927.

——— . *Istanbul'da İmar ve İskan Hareketleri* (Building and Settlement Activities in Istanbul). Istanbul, 1938.

Erinç, O. "92 Yıl Önce Istanbul Metrosu Çalışmaları ve Yeni Liman Projesi" (Works on the Istanbul Subway and the New Harbor Project 92 Years Ago). *Belgelerle Türk Tarihi Dergisi* 4 (1968): 7, 48–52.

Esat, Celal. "Osmanlı Mimarisi." *İkdam*. 3 January 1907.

——— . *Eski Istanbul* (Old Istanbul). Istanbul, 1909.

——— . *Eski Galata ve Binaları* (Old Galata and Its Buildings). Istanbul, 1911.

Evenson, N. *Paris, A Century of Change, 1878–1978*. New Haven, 1979.

Evliya, Efendi. *Narrative of Travels in Europe, Asia, and Africa*. Translated by J. Von Hammer. 1 vol. in 2 pts. London, 1937.

Eyice, S. "Istanbul." *İslam Ansiklopedisi* (Encyclopedia of Islam). Istanbul, 1950. Vol. 5, pt. 2, sec. 1214–15, pp. 44–157.

——— . *Istanbul, Petit Guide*. Istanbul, 1955.

——— . *Galata ve Kulesi* (Galata and Its Tower). Istanbul, 1967.

Gautier, T. *Constantinople*. New York, 1873.

Gibb, H. A. R. and H. Bowen. *Islamic Society and the West.* 1 vol. in 2 pts. New York, 1950–57.

Goodwin, G. *A History of Ottoman Architecture.* Baltimore, 1971.

———. "Turkish Architecture, 1840–1940." *Art and Archaeology Research Papers* (June 1977): 6–14.

Grosvenor, E. A. *Constantinople.* 2 vols. Boston, 1895.

Haussmann, E. *Mémoires.* 3 vols. Paris, 1893.

Hautecoeur, L. *Histoire de l'architecture classique en France.* 7 vols. Paris, 1957.

Hearsey, J. E. N. *City of Constantine.* London, 1963.

Hitchcock, H. R. *Architecture, Nineteenth and Twentieth Centuries.* London, 1968.

Holod, R., and Evin, A., eds. *Modern Turkish Architecture.* Philadelphia, 1983.

Hutton, W. H. *Constantinople.* London, 1904.

İlter, İ. *Boğaz ve Haliç Geçişlerinin Tarihçcsi* (History of Bridges across the Bosporus and the Golden Horn). Istanbul, 1973.

İnalcık, H. "Istanbul." *Encyclopedia of Islam.* 2d ed. (Leiden, 1978). Vol. 4, pp. 224-48.

İnciciyan, P. G. *XVIII. Asırda Istanbul* (Istanbul in the Eighteenth Century). Istanbul, 1956.

Issawi, C., ed. *The Economic History of the Middle East, 1800–1919.* Chicago and London, 1966.

Janin, R. *Constantinople byzantine.* Paris, 1964.

Koçu, R. E. *Istanbul Ansiklopedisi* (Encyclopedia of Istanbul). Istanbul, 1968.

Konyalı, İ. H. *Koca Mimar Sinan ve Eserleri* (The Great Architect Sinan and His Works). Istanbul, 1950.

Krautheimer, R. *Three Christian Capitals.* Berkeley and Los Angeles, 1983.

Kuban, D. *Türk Barok Mimarisi Hakkında Bir Deneme* (An Essay on Turkish Baroque Architecture). Istanbul, 1954.

———. "Anadolu-Türk Şehri Tarihi Gelişmesi, Sosyal ve Fiziki Özellikleri Üzerinde Bazı Gelişmeler" (Some Developments on the Historical Development, Social, and Physical Characteristics of the Anatolian-Turkish City). *Vakıflar Dergisi* 7 (1968): 53–73.

———. "Istanbul'un Tarihi Yapısı" (Historical Structure of Istanbul). *Mimarlık* 5 (1970): 26–48.

———. "Sinan." *Macmillan Encyclopedia of Architecture.* New York, 1982. Vol. 4, pp. 62–73.

Lewis, B. *The Emergence of Modern Turkey.* London, 1961.

MacDonald, W. *Early Christian and Byzantine Architecture.* New York, 1979.

MacFarlane, C. *Turkey and Its Destiny.* 2 vols. London, 1850.

Mantran, R. *Istanbul dans le deuxième moitié XVIIè siècle.* Paris, 1962.

Montani Efendi and Boghos Efendi Chachian. *Usul-u Mimari-i Osmani* (L'Architecture Ottomane). Istanbul, 1873.

Mumford, L. *The Culture of Cities.* New York, 1970.

Muthesius, S. *The High Victorian Movement in Architecture.* London, 1972.

Mutluçağ, H. "Boğaziçi Köprüsünün Yapılması Yolunda İlk Çabalar" (The First Efforts in the Construction of the Bosporus Bridge). *Belgelerle Türk Tarihi Dergisi* 1 (1968): 32–38.

Naum-Duhani, S. *Vieilles gens, vieilles demeures, topographie sociale de Beyoğlu au XIXème siècle.* Istanbul, 1947.

Nicoletti, M. *L'Architettura Liberty in Italia.* Rome, 1978.

Oberling, P. "The Istanbul Tünel." *Archivum Ottomanicum* 4 (1972): 217–63.

Orhonlu, C. "Osmanlı Türkleri Devrinde Istanbul'da Kayıkçılık ve Kayık İşletmeciliği" (Rowboat Management in Istanbul under the Ottoman Turks). *Istanbul Üniversitesi Edebiyat Fakültesi Tarih Dergisi* 3 (1966): 109, 131.

Ortaylı, İ. *Tanzimattan Sonra Mahalli Idareler, 1840-1878* (Local Administrations after Tanzimat). Ankara, 1974.

Ökçün, G. "XIX Yüzyılın İkinci Yarısında İmalat Sanayi Alanında Verilen Ruhsat ve İmtiyazların Ana Çizgileri" (The Outlines of the Concessions and Permissions Given in the Field of Production Industry during the Second Half of the Nineteenth Century). *Ankara Üniversitesi Siyasal Bilgiler Fakültesi Dergisi* 17 (March 1972): 135–66.

Pardoe, Julia. *Beauties of the Bosphorus.* London, 1839

Pinkney, D. *Napoleon III and the Rebuilding of Paris.* Princeton, 1958.

Polk, W., and R. Chambers, eds. *Beginnings of Modernization in the Middle East.* Chicago and London, 1968.

Procopius. *Buildings.* Translated by H. B. Dewing. London, 1914.

Rahmi, H. *İffet* (Honor). 1896; Istanbul, 1973.

Raif, Mehmet. *Mirat-ı Istanbul* (The Mirror of Istanbul). Istanbul, 1896.

Réseau de tramways urbains et suburbains de Constantinople, projet présenté par la Société Générale d'Entreprises. Paris, 1910.

Rosenthal, S. *The Politics of Dependency, Urban Reform in Istanbul.* Westport, Conn., 1980.

Sait Paşa. *Sait Paşa'nın Hatıratı* (Memories of Sait Paşa). 2 vols. Istanbul, 1910.

Sauveget, J. "Esquisse d'une histoire de la ville de Damas." *Revue des études islamiques.* (1934): 425–80.

———. *Alep.* Paris, 1941.

"Sauvegarder des monuments d'art et des sites pittoresques." *Génie civil ottoman.* 4 (April 1917): 80–81.

Schneider, A. B. "XV. Yüzyılda Istanbul Nüfusu" (Population of Istanbul in the Fifteenth Century). *Belleten.* (1962): 1–39.

Schorske, C. *Fin-de-Siècle Vienna.* New York, 1981.

Shaw, S. "The Central Legislative Councils in the Nineteenth Century Ottoman Reform Movement before 1876." *International Journal of Middle East Studies* 1 (1976): 51–84.

———. "The Population of Istanbul in the Nineteenth Century." *International Journal of Middle East Studies* 10

(1979): 265–77.

Shaw, S., and E. K. Shaw. *History of the Ottoman Empire and Modern Turkey.* 2 vols. Cambridge, 1977.

Sözen, M., et al. *Türk Mimarisinin Gelişimi ve Mimar Sinan* (The Development of Turkish Architecture and the Architect Sinan). İstanbul, 1975.

Sumner-Boyd, H., and J. Freely. *Strolling through Istanbul.* Istanbul, 1973.

Sutcliffe, A., ed.. *The Rise of Modern Urban Planning.* New York, 1977.

Şirket-i Hayriye. *Chirket-i Hairié, Annuaire de la société.* Istanbul, 1914. (French summary as appendix).

Tanzimat. Istanbul, 1940.

Turan, S. "Osmanlı Teşkilatında Hassa Mimarları" (Palace Architects in the Ottoman Organization). *Ankara Üniversitesi Tarih Araştırmaları Dergisi* 1 (1964): 157–97.

Ubicini, M. A. *Letters on Turkey.* 1856; New York, 1973.

Van Millingen, A. *Byzantine Constantinople.* London, 1899.

——— . *Constantinople.* London, 1906.

Weber, E. F. *The Growth of Cities in the Nineteenth Century.* Ithaca, 1967.

Williams, F. B. *The Law of City Planning and Zoning.* New York, 1922.

Yavuz, Y. *Mimar Kemalettin ve Birinci Ulusal Mimarlık Dönemi* (The Architect Kemalettin and the First National Period in Architecture). Ankara, 1981.

Yirmisekiz, Mehmet Çelebi. *Fransız Seyahatnamesi* (Journey to France). Istanbul, 1970.

OTTOMAN ARCHIVAL SOURCES

Başbakanlık Arşivi (BBA)
Archives of the Prime Ministry, Istanbul
    İrade
        Dahiliye
        Hariciye
        Meclis-i Mahsus
        Meclis-i Vala
        Şehremaneti
        Şura-i Devlet

    Yıldız

    Cevdet
        Belediye

Istanbul University Library
Topkapı Palace Museum Archives
Topkapı Palace Museum Library

NEWSPAPERS

İkdam
Journal de Constantinople
La Turquie
Le Moniteur Oriental
The Levant Herald

Index

Numbers in italics indicate pages on which illustrations appear.

THIS MONOGRAPH WAS COMPOSED USING DONALD KNUTH'S TEX TYPE-
SETTING SYSTEM. IT IS SET IN COMPUTER MODERN TYPEFACES ON
AN ALPHATYPE CRS PHOTOTYPESETTER. TECHNICAL WORK HAS
BEEN SUPPORTED IN PART BY GRANTS TO THE UNIVER-
SITY OF WASHINGTON FROM BELL-NORTHERN
RESEARCH AND NORTHERN TELECOM, INC.
TEX IS A TRADEMARK OF THE AMERICAN
MATHEMATICAL SOCIETY.